ABOUT ISLAND PRESS

Island Press, a nonprofit organization, publishes, markets, and distributes the most advanced thinking on the conservation of our natural resources—books about soil, land, water, forests, wildlife, and hazardous and toxic wastes. These books are practical tools used by public officials, business and industry leaders, natural resource managers, and concerned citizens working to solve both local and global resource problems.

Founded in 1978, Island Press reorganized in 1984 to meet the increasing demand for substantive books on all resource-related issues. Island Press publishes and distributes under its own imprint and offers these services to other nonprofit organizations.

Support for Island Press is provided by Apple Computers, Inc., The Mary Reynolds Babcock Foundation, The Charles Engelhard Foundation, The Ford Foundation, The Glen Eagles Foundation, The George Gund Foundation, The William and Flora Hewlett Foundation, The Joyce Foundation, The John D. and Catherine T. MacArthur Foundation, The Andrew W. Mellon Foundation, The Joyce Mertz-Gilmore Foundation, The New-Land Foundation, Northwest Area Foundation, The J. N. Pew, Jr., Charitable Trust, The Rockefeller Brothers Fund, The Florence and John Schumann Foundation, The Tides Foundation, and individual donors.

For additional information about Island Press publishing services and a catalog of current and forthcoming titles, contact Island Press, Box 7, Covelo, California 95428.

ABOUT MONTANA LAND RELIANCE

Montana's only private statewide land trust, established in 1978, Montana Land Reliance is dedicated to protecting and enhancing the public benefits of Montana's private lands. The combination of open spaces, abundant wildlife, and renowned trout fisheries makes Montana a national treasure. Fish and wildlife depend on quality habitat. In recent years many farms, ranches, and other properties have been broken up into smaller tracts for recreational and residential homesites or converted to other nonagricultural uses. This trend degrades the habitat. Because ecosystems do not begin and end at fence lines, private landowners, and public land managers, make key decisions affecting the quality of life in Montana.

Montana Land Reliance works with conservation-minded landowners, especially within the greater Yellowstone ecosystem, to slow the loss of productive agricultural lands and habitat and, at the same time, preserve the livelihood and lifestyles of the people who work these lands. To learn more about this private conservation effort and what you can do to help, please write Montana Land Reliance, P.O. Box 355, Helena, MT 59624 or phone (406) 443–7027.

SPONSORS

This book has been sponsored through contributions from the following: Montana Department of Fish, Wildlife, and Parks; National Fish and Wildlife Foundation; Patagonia, Inc.; The Tides Foundation; William S. Towne; Trout Unlimited; U.S.D.A. Forest Service; and U.S. Fish and Wildlife Service (with Sport Fish Restoration Funds under U.S. Fish and Wildlife Service Grant Agreement no. 14-16-0009-89-1219).

BETTER TROUT HABITAT

A Guide to Stream Restoration and Management

CHRISTOPHER J. HUNTER

Edited by Tom Palmer
Illustrated by Ellen Meloy
Foreword by Nick Lyons

MONTANA LAND RELIANCE

ISLAND PRESS
Washington, D.C. □ *Covelo, California*

Library of Congress Cataloging-in-Publication Data

Hunter, Chris (Christopher J.)
    Better trout habitat : a guide to stream restoration and
management / Christopher J. Hunter : edited by Tom Palmer ;
illustrated by Ellen Meloy.
      p. cm.
    "Montana Land Reliance."
    Includes index.
    ISBN 0-933280-78-5 (alk. paper). — ISBN 0-933280-77-7 (pbk. :
alk. paper)
    1. Fish habitat improvement—Handbooks, manuals, etc. 2. Stream
conservation—Handbooks, manuals, etc. 3. Trout—habitat.
I. Palmer, Tom, 1952– . II. Meloy, Ellen Ditzler. III. Montana
Land Reliance (Trust) IV. Title.
SH157.8.H86 1991
639.3'755—dc20   90-47860
                                        CIP

Printed on recycled, acid-free paper

Manufactured in the United States of America

10 9 8 7 6 5 4 3 2

This book is for Pat and Jim Hunter.

Down through the mist, the young Tuolumne was seen pouring from its crystal fountains, now resting in glassy pools as if changing back again into ice, now leaping in white cascades as if turning to snow; gliding right and left between granite bosses, then sweeping on through the smooth, meadowy levels of the valley, swaying pensively from side to side with calm, stately gestures past dipping willows and sedges, and around groves of arrowy pine; and throughout its whole eventful course, whether flowing fast or slow, singing loud or low, ever filling the landscape with spiritual animation, and manifesting the grandeur of its sources in every movement and tone.

John Muir, "A Near View of the High Sierra"
in *The Mountains of California*, 1894

CONTENTS

FIGURES

FOREWORD

For those who love trout and trout rivers, the past decade has been one of volatile confrontation, dramatic challenge, and considerable confusion. There has been a steady increase in the pressure on trout streams—from developers of all kinds, road builders and dam builders, construction zealots who insist on straightening stream channels, from pump-storage projects, acid rain, increasing numbers of trout fishermen, farmers, a thirsty country, ever-present threats of personal and industrial pollution, clear-cutting, strip-mining, imprudent stocking of inferior fish, and that gradual and ineluctable cancer we call progress. The lines of battle are not always clear. The demands of vying groups are not always easy to resolve. But, in specific instances, good men have tipped the tenuous balance toward preservation and restoration. There may be more fishermen, but many more are wiser about the rivers and trout without which there can be no trout fishing—returning the fish they catch, supporting wild-trout rather than stocked-trout programs, backing sound conservation groups like the Montana Land Reliance (which backed this book), Trout Unlimited, The Nature Conservancy, Cal Trout, Theodore Gordon Fly Fishers, the Federation of Fly Fishers, and many others. As the threats to the waters have become greater and more insidious, the resistance to these threats has become more informed, more powerful, more sophisticated, and ultimately more effective. No resistance can be adequate that does not squarely address the world in which trout live—their habitat.

This wise and helpful book is one instance of the best that is being done in our time. In clear, detailed, and eminently readable prose—supported by Ellen Meloy's superb line drawings, the best I've seen of every aspect of stream life and stream improvement—*Better Trout Habitat* provides what we have long needed: a major. overview of the theory and practice of modern trout-stream protection, management, and restoration. I cannot think of a trout fisherman who would not benefit from reading this book closely, a trout club that would not find its mandate clarified.

Surely there is no single solution to the problems with which trout streams are beset. For a river—in the most vital and dynamic way—is a living resource. Its path affects those along its banks—those who live there, those whose business or farm depends upon its assets, those (like boaters, swimmers, and fishermen) who go to it for recreation. Each of those who is connected to it may contribute to its health or merely deplete its special qualities. Land use probably affects the river most, and must be scrutinized with the shrewdest eye; people, of course, are its most critical destroyers or saviors.

"Each stream," says Christopher Hunter, "is a whole greater than the sum of its geologic, climatic, hydrolic, and biologic parts." Those who would save rivers must first see each river whole, as a separate, vital, and unique group of elements and energies that constantly seeks its own dynamic equilibrium. But there are elements and principles common to each, and Hunter patiently gives each its due—from the fish themselves to the gradient and meander of a river, to the sediment rate and the soil texture and the precise land use and its "organic litter."

Salmonids are at the heart of this book, and Hunter describes the various species—landlocked and seagoing—and their life histories concisely and well. He outlines needs common to all: clean water, an adequate food supply, areas in which to rest, places where trout may be protected from predators, places where they may spawn. Since this is a book focused on habitat, the author is surely sensible to recognize that a living creature, with needs that vary according to the time of year, climate, and the time in its life cycle, living in a river each unique unto itself, will need a diverse habitat that includes pools, riffles, glides, eddies, backwaters, side channels, cover such as undercut banks, overhanging vegetation, rocks, root tangles, and much more. Everything affects everything else. All is interconnected. Only by understanding the full complex of forces that affect a river can we hope to protect or rehabilitate it.

Habitat preservation and restoration is thus a matter requiring the subtlest study and care, lest the solution to one problem create five worse problems (and there are examples in this book). Hunter notes the benefits of allowing a stream to heal itself whenever possible, and he presses always for long-term solutions, not those that will lose what they have gained because they are not consonant with prevailing land-use practices or are inadequate in a dozen kinds of shortsightedness. He stresses meticulous planning of the most specific sort—to identify the problem, design the difficult true solution, effect the project, and eventually monitor the results. No book available to the general public outlines such necessary planning in more helpful terms.

Fully half the book is devoted to detailed analyses of representative case histories—of more than a dozen rivers, from Oregon to Pennsylvania—studying streams affected by agriculture, those in forested areas, and then three that can be classified as that brand most sorely put upon, most often abandoned as hopeless—urban streams. The case histories are fascinating and instructive; they show what has—and can—be done.

For some years I have had the privilege of fishing a remarkable spring-fed river, privately controlled and firmly protected. Its source is clear, its insect hatches fecund and intact, its trout wild and of large average size. The river has shown me what trout fishing at its best can be—with an untrammeled river, in the condition it was in 50 or 100 or 500 years ago. Its marvelously fortuitous balances have provided me with one of the great fly-fishing experiences of my life, but even more than that, the river is a kind of yardstick: It is what a trout river ought to be.

There is little enough of this left.

The threats to rivers across the country will only increase, as greedy progress spreads and devours.

But you come away from *Better Trout Habitat* with a rich hopefulness that the knowledge and technology and will are now in place, that rivers closer to that spring creek are now possible. We must preserve and rehabilitate our trout rivers one by one, with all the specific knowledge that entails in each case. And we *can*. This thoughtful, authoritative book shows us how.

NICK LYONS

PREFACE

Trout fishing in Montana probably offers the greatest variety in America, from the gin-clear Armstrong Spring Creek to the riffled flows of the upper Madison River. Overall, however, trout fishing in America ain't what it used to be. More and more fishermen are chasing fewer trout on fewer rivers. Those of us who live and fish in Montana have seen the neoprene hatches proliferate on our blue-ribbon trout streams. That's because trout fishing in Montana comes close to how it used to be. Montana's Department of Fish, Wildlife and Parks pioneered wild-trout protection in its management of the Madison River. Meanwhile anglers in other states lament the demise of wild trout in local streams. But we trout bums all can take hope, now that our desire to catch fish is rivaled by our desire for better trout habitat, for all over America there is a growing interest in trout-stream management and restoration. The Montana Land Reliance hopes that this book, *Better Trout Habitat*, will help to focus greater attention on protecting and enhancing America's trout fisheries.

The reader may wonder why Montana Land Reliance, a private land-conservation organization, has produced this book. The link between the Reliance and trout is not hard to decipher: Abuse of land can have dreadful consequences to fisheries. By helping to prevent certain abusive land uses, the Reliance saves trout. The dollars spent on an ounce of prevention for habitat protection are worth a pound of cure for trout-habitat restoration.

The Reliance practices its preventive medicine against residential subdivision of Montana's open spaces. Although a home on the range along the river or stream may be one person's dream, it is a nightmare for many others. It takes very few riverbank homes to mar riparian scenery, and just a few more to destroy the riparian area itself. Rivers are topographical low points where fish, wildlife, and vegetation congregate in a dazzling array of biological diversity. Riparian areas are the richest of all biological habitats in the arid West. Unfortunately, water not only concentrates fish and wildlife. It also accumulates the waste products of civilization—sediment from timber harvesting, heavy metals and toxic minerals from mining, pesticides and herbicides from farming, and industrial and residential sewage from cities, towns, and subdivisions. When these wastes overload the natural riparian filters, the wild critters of the riparian zone are overwhelmed. Trout are among the first casualties, and, like canaries in the mines, they give us warning of fouled elements in our midst.

Wild trout are the product of a complex interaction of physical, chemical, and biological factors, and a by-product of habitat. Trout succeed as long as their habitat requirements—clean water, adequate food supply, protection from predators, and protected resting areas and spawning sites—are met. In prosperous surroundings trout prosper; when the surroundings degrade, trout cannot fight back and struggle in vain to survive.

The guiding assumption of this book and Montana Land Reliance is that land use is the key to trout-habitat quality. As this book goes to press, the Reliance has received 27 conservation easements, saving over 72,000 acres and 145 miles of stream and riverbanks from subdivision. Landowners donate these conservation easements to the Reliance. In doing so, they freely relinquish their non-agricultural rights in perpetuity, thereby ensuring a constant stream of public benefits.

Our initial interest in producing this book was to provide landowners with a basic appreciation of trout-habitat requirements, not only to help preserve existing habitat, but also to encourage restoration of trout habitat. Recognizing that millions of Americans who love to fish are finding diminished opportunity for quality fishing, we realized that a trout-stream management and restoration handbook would be useful in every state with a cold-water fishery. When we explored the feasibility of producing this book, we discovered that there is a wealth of technical information entombed in technical and esoteric monographs, and that much of the restoration experience has not been widely shared. This book synthesizes that information and experience, rendering them intelligible to the lay reader, as well as valuable to the professional practitioner. It will be a dear friend to anyone concerned about streams with cold-water fisheries.

A pledge by The Tides Foundation of San Francisco toward book-production costs spurred the Reliance to seek other sponsors. The response to sponsorship was convincingly overwhelming. *Better Trout Habitat* strengthens the nascent field of restoration ecology. Make no mistake about it, Montana Land Reliance supports habitat restoration, but, more importantly, it supports habitat protection. Habitat restoration should complement, but not be traded for, habitat protection. Wounded habitat must be nursed back to health; in 1990 we can no longer afford to degrade remaining fish and wildlife habitat. Healthy habitat deserves our adulation. *Better Trout Habitat* deserves your attention. The Reliance hopes that this book will enhance the lives of millions of trout and trout fishermen.

JAN KONIGSBERG
Montana Land Reliance

ACKNOWLEDGMENTS

I had a great time working on this book. It gave me the opportunity to travel around the United States, meeting people, learning from them, and exchanging ideas with those who have dedicated their professional lives to trout and trout-habitat management. It has been a wonderful learning experience and I want to thank everyone who made it so rewarding and fun.

First to be thanked are Bill Dunham, Jan Konigsberg, and Bill Long of Montana Land Reliance, who conceived the idea for the book, piqued the interest of Island Press, and gave me the opportunity to work on the project.

Bill Platts and Wayne Elmore encouraged me from the beginning. Without their encouragement, I doubt I would have undertaken the project. Having the opportunity to meet and work with Bob Beschta, Robert Hunt, and Bill Jackson during the course of this project was a real treat. Their enthusiasm and support were greatly appreciated and their critical reviews, particularly of the first half of the book, added tremendously to the quality of the finished product. Many of the ideas, concepts, and principles found here were conveyed to me by these five individuals.

The second half of the book could not have been written without the help of several stream-restoration practitioners. These people took time from their busy field seasons to show me their projects, provide written materials describing their work, and review my descriptions of their efforts. They also helped with travel arrangements and even invited me into their homes. Their generosity was exceeded only by their enthusiasm for their work. They include Monte Seehorn, Larry Neuhs, Jim Kidd, Peter Zurbuch, Ray Menendez, Karl Lutz, David Houser, Ron Glover, Ken Siebel, Joe Armstrong, Wayne Poppich, Robert Hunt, Ed Avery, Max Johnson, Wayne Elmore, Bob Franklin, Terry Roelofs, Mike Parton, Errol Claire, Jeff Neal, Dave Odell, Gerry Dinkins, and Ray White.

I also want to thank Fred Everest, Jeff Kershner, Jennifer Nielsen, and Ray White for reviewing portions of the text and for providing valuable insights.

Bill Helm allowed the use of the Western Division of the American Fisheries Society (WDAFS) publication *Aquatic Habitat Inventory Glossary and Standard Methods* as the basis for the glossary of this book. The WDAFS glossary is an invaluable reference for anyone interested in aquatic biology.

K. V. Koski provided the exceptional photo of the chum salmon redd taken from beneath an artificial stream channel. Others who provided photos include Monte Seehorn, Robert Hunt, Ron Glover, and Wayne Elmore.

The generosity of the several agencies, private entities, and individuals whose financial contributions made the publication of this book possible is gratefully acknowledged.

Tom Palmer's editing and Ellen Meloy's illustrations have rendered my attempts at scientific obfuscation ineffective. Tom's interest in the subject matter and commitment to the project made this truly a joint effort. The three of us wish to thank Woody, Nick, and Milt for keeping morale high during a tough winter in Helena.

Kathi Brown, Diana Halverson, and Harold Chambers of the Montana State Library made the vast literature regarding salmonid ecology, stream geomorphology, and stream restoration accessible.

Lois Delger of Montana Land Reliance cheerfully and patiently did all the word processing.

Barbara Dean of Island Press was helpful throughout the process. Barbara's suggestions greatly enhanced the readability of the book. I would also like to thank Barbara Youngblood, Beth Beisel, and Robin Barker from Island Press. Elizabeth Gehman, who copyedited the final manuscript, also deserves my thanks.

The love, patience, and support of my wife, Carol, and our kids, Kyle and McKenzie, make all things possible.

Thank you all very much for your help.

INTRODUCTION

This book was written in response to an explosion of interest in habitat restoration in general, and trout-stream habitat restoration in particular. The intent was to synthesize state-of-the-art technical information and present it in such a way that it would be readable and informative for both the lay and professional reader. Thus, the writing style, which is fairly informal and very accessible compared to most scientific publications, belies the technical nature of the book.

Throughout the book the pronoun *you* is used to draw the reader into the subject matter. It does not imply that single individuals, whether they be baker, biologist, or engineer, should undertake a stream restoration project alone. Each stream is a whole greater than the sum of its geologic, climatic, hydrologic, and biologic parts. The design of a successful restoration project requires the efforts of a team of specialists who can analyze the parts and synthesize them into an understanding of how the stream and its valley function to create trout habitat.

Despite the groundswell of interest in the subject, there is not a detailed, readable, up-to-date book that describes the science and art of trout-stream restoration. This book attempts to fill that void and give the reader an understanding of the physical, chemical, and biological needs of trout. This includes understanding the importance of the interactions among climate, geology, vegetation, flowing water, and land use that create trout habitat. With this base of information, it is hoped the reader will learn how to evaluate existing habitat conditions and trout populations to help determine specific habitat restoration objectives.

Chapters 1 through 6 provide the historical context and technical background necessary to understanding the theory behind trout-stream restoration and management. Chapters 7 through 9 examine 14 case histories showing how theory has, and has not, been put into practice. Chapter 10 provides some concluding thoughts on stream restoration management and protection.

We will consider this book a success if the next time you are thinking about your favorite trout stream, your thoughts drift away from the emerging insects to how land use in the drainage has affected riparian vegetation. Or if, as you stalk a lunker in your favorite pool, you begin to think about the processes that created the pool. Maybe the next time you go fishing you will become so absorbed in observing and trying to understand the interactions between land use, streamside vegetation, and trout habitat your rod never makes it out of the case.

BETTER TROUT HABITAT

Chapter 1

STREAM RESTORATION: CURRENT INTEREST AND HISTORICAL PERSPECTIVE

THE sport of trout fishing is growing and it is growing fast. By the year 2000, there will be 10 million trout anglers in North America. Many of them will simply take up rod and reel to escape the pressures of their daily lives and seek the solitude they expect trout fishing to offer.

Thoreau said that many a man went fishing all of his life without ever realizing that it was not fish he was after. Modern surveys of trout anglers are showing that Thoreau was at least half right. Trout anglers are on an outdoor quest to lose themselves in the scenery and catch a wild trout in the process. Unfortunately, the number of streams capable of supporting wild trout—trout that are actually products of a natural stream system—is dwindling.

Sadly, we are all to blame. In too many places the cost of economic prosperity has been the destruction of trout habitat. With that destruction go the natural environments trout anglers find such fine complements to their fishing trips.

Our domestic and industrial wastes have polluted streams and eliminated wild-trout populations. The evidence can be found in West Virginia's Cranberry River, Oregon's Camp Creek, Pennsylvania's West Valley Creek, and other streams described in this book. Even the seemingly innocent removal of streamside vegetation by livestock, farming, logging, mining, and urban development has led to wide, shallow, and warm troutless streams.

Straightening stream channels, a surprisingly common flood-control practice, has caused water to gouge wide, shallow channels, resulting in related changes in the streamside vegetation. Perhaps such streams in now-barren landscapes could still be stocked with hatchery trout, but, in the end, it would not take a lifetime to discover that wasn't what one was after.

The growing population and increased interest in trout fishing, coupled with decreasing trout habitat, have heaped new pressures on fish and game agencies to provide quality trout-fishing opportunities. All of the fish and game agencies of trout-producing states have, at some time, developed programs of planting hatchery-reared trout to meet the increasing demand for trout fishing.

In 1983 approximately 54 million catchable-sized trout were stocked in 43 states at a cost of $36 million. At the same time, our stream resources were dwindling, and by 1988 the U.S. General Accounting Office's study of streamside management on public rangelands showed that in some states as much as 90 percent of federally managed streams were in a degraded condition.

The easily managed stocked fishery allows many anglers to catch and keep trout that are genetically programmed to die quickly in the wild from waters that need not be capable of supporting naturally reproducing wild-trout populations. But for many anglers, hatchery-reared trout are a poor substitute for wild trout. A hatchery trout doesn't look or fight as well as a wild trout, and, for growing numbers of anglers, much of the mystery and beauty of trout fishing is lost when the quarry is just another mass-produced product.

RESTORATION—AN ALTERNATIVE SOLUTION

One could look at it as a simple problem of supply and demand, but at the heart of the movement to restore degraded trout streams is a desire to set things right. As you shall see, stream restoration is not a simple process. It is often difficult and costly, but the benefits—such as gaining a deeper understanding and appreciation of the complex relationships among the trout, the stream, and the valley through which it flows—go far beyond improved trout fishing. There is also a sense of satisfaction in returning to the land some of its former productivity.

Stream restorationists invariably confront a wide range of trout-habitat problems linked to poor land use within the drainage. For instance, soon after an eastern Pennsylvania chapter of Trout Unlimited (TU) looked into restoring a local stream's trout habitat, the members realized that new housing and industrial developments posed a larger problem to the stream than did the one channelized section that originally sparked their interest.

The new construction introduced large sediment loads, removed riparian vegetation, and led to increased water temperatures in the stream and its trout-spawning and trout-rearing tributaries. That, in turn, began to instill a new concern within the TU chapter about the potential of chemical spills in light-industrial areas and the possibility of toxic substances in urban storm-water runoff, which find their way into the stream.

With that experience behind its membership, today TU's Valley Forge chapter is devoted to working with city councils, land developers, and the state Department of Transportation to ensure that as land use changes, the character of the stream and its tributaries remains relatively unaltered.

A more extensive example of the effect land use has on trout habitat can be found along the John Day River, a famous central Oregon tributary to the Columbia River, which provides important spawning and rearing habitat for steelhead trout and chinook salmon.

Prior to 1964 the John Day River gracefully meandered down its valley, and bridges spanned the river along its course. Adding to the picturesque scene were hay meadows scattered along the river's rich floodplain, and willows and cottonwoods that hugged the stable stream banks. Because the shallow, streamside groundwater aquifer was near the surface, the hay meadows required little or no irrigation. All that changed in 1964 when a major flood occurred.

The flood's extremely high, fast flows eroded stream banks, threatening a number of hay meadows. To assure that it wouldn't happen again, the U.S. Army Corps of Engineers undertook a significant stream-rehabilitation project.

As an erosion- and flood-control measure, the Army Corps straightened a section of the John Day River to allow the water to move through the valley more quickly during high flows. But, by any measure, the result was a disaster. The increased water velocities in the straightened reach actually increased the erosive power of the stream, and the John Day River began to cut away at both bed and bank, severely degrading the stream's steelhead and chinook habitats.

As the channel became wider and shallower, the streamside groundwater level dropped, and the ranchers in the area had to step up the irrigation of their hay meadows. At first, that didn't seem to be such a bad trade-off because with the straightened channel the ranchers had developed larger, contiguous hay meadows.

When the highway was rebuilt, it was constructed in a straight line down the valley, nearly parallel to the straightened river. Traffic moved faster, the river moved faster, and tractors moved faster in the fields. However, somewhere in these fast lanes someone realized that to keep everything moving along, the river had to remain in its straightened channel or the new hay meadows and the new highway would be ruined. That realization cost some landowners $10,000 to $15,000 per year for riprap and channel maintenance. From the comforting distance of one generation, the damages and costs associated with the 1964 flood pale in comparison to those that resulted from the stream-rehabilitation project. Spawning populations of steelhead and chinook have been greatly reduced.

These two examples illustrate how important streamside, or riparian, vegetation is to the health of the stream. Riparian vegetation is a critical aspect of trout habitat. The vegetation influences stream-channel shape, reduces erosion, and contributes to trout habitat when tree branches and logs are washed into the channel. The vegetation also is an important source of organic material, such as leaves, twigs, and berries, that eventually becomes food for the stream's many life forms.

HISTORICAL PERSPECTIVE

For most of this century, the desire to provide sport-fishing opportunities through habitat restoration has experienced a series of fits and starts. In the United States, the first real commitment to trout-habitat restoration emerged in the early 1930s, a decade marked by a renewed enthusiasm for wildlife conservation and preservation.

In 1934 the U.S. Bureau of Sport Fisheries (USBF) was about to undertake the first nationwide program of stream surveys and habitat improvements. H.S. Davis, chief of USBF, addressed the 1934 annual meeting of the American Fisheries Society and actually attempted to douse the swell of enthusiasm by saying that he felt the small dams and other devices used to create shelter for trout were being overdone. "In some instances," Davis told the crowd, "hardly a foot of stream has been left in its original condition. . . . Of what benefit to a stream is it to construct cover for many times the number of fish the stream [food resources] can support?"

Even in the face of Davis's reservations, in 1934 USBF moved to enhance a number of national forest streams. By activating the tremendous labor resources available during an era of national economic depression, an incredible number of in-stream habitat structures were built between 1933 through 1937. For example, from 1933 through 1935, a total of 31,084 stream structures were constructed on 406 mountain streams. Many of the dams, which created pools, and deflectors, which forced streams to follow a more meandering flow, are still in place.

Unfortunately, durability is not the best measure of a successful habitat restoration program. Both pre- and post-construction surveys of trout, aquatic insects, and physical habitat components, which are necessary to evaluate the success of any habitat management program, were sorely limited. But it should be remembered that the fishery biologists of the thirties were forging new ground and had little more than their own enthusiasm to guide them.

In 1952, the U.S.D.A. Forest Service published its second *Fish Stream Improvement Handbook*. The opening paragraphs indicate that important lessons were learned from mistakes made in the 1930s:

> Many mistakes were made in the earlier stages of the work, but much has been learned as a result. At first, considerable emphasis was placed on a large variety of stream improvement structures. Stream improvement was looked upon by some as a cure-all for the environmental ills of a trout stream. Experience showed that only a relatively few types of simply designed structures were necessary and that stream improvement fell far short of making a desirable stream habitat if destructive forces were at work in the watershed.
>
> Unless stream improvements are carefully planned much damage may result. One of the first things learned in the earlier stream improvement work was that it could be easily overdone.

In addition to a description of structural devices, the handbook notes that streamside conservation is one of the best, and least expensive, methods of stream improvement. The handbook is an extremely enlightened and important divergence from earlier volumes, particularly in its description of how streamside vegetation reduces erosion, provides cover for trout, is a source of terrestrial insects, and helps to reduce water temperatures by providing shade.

The Trout-Stream Habitat Revolution

A great deal of interest in trout-stream improvement was piqued by the 1967 publication of Ray J. White and O.M. Brynildson's *Guidelines for Management of Trout Stream Habitat in Wisconsin*. The bulletin quickly became the manifesto of the trout-habitat improvement revolution.

White and Brynildson's contribution to the literature was a quantum leap for trout-stream management. They began by stating that trout-stream habitat improvement in Wisconsin was largely a task of restoration and went on to sternly warn against overmanagement of unspoiled waters. It was White and Brynildson's radical idea that the remaining unspoiled waters in Wisconsin were highly valuable aesthetically and that management efforts should be directed toward preserving these streams and their surroundings.

When the discussion addressed provision of more cover and increased living space for trout, White and Brynildson began by describing techniques to protect and manage bank vegetation *before* they described more traditional structural techniques, such as dams, wall-like stream-flow deflectors, and riprap.

This 1967 publication made several significant contributions to the literature, but perhaps its most important contribution is its emphasis on preproject planning. White and Brynildson's work has greatly broadened the scope of stream habitat improvement because they made it obvious that professional fishery biologists need to confer with professionals of other disciplines, such as vegetation specialists and stream geomorphologists, to properly plan and execute a habitat improvement project.

TWENTY YEARS LATER: INTEREST AGAIN ABOUNDS

In 1987 TU and U.S.D.A. Forest Service entered an agreement to help anglers catch more trout and salmon by improving salmonid habitat in the national forests. The agreement is a reflection of the burgeoning interest in stream restoration shared not only by many conservation organizations, state fish and game, and federal land-management agencies but also by private landowners who want to protect and enhance their trout fisheries.

Although the role of private landowners in trout-stream restoration is becoming increasingly important, it is often overlooked, because it is difficult to estimate the number and cost of privately funded restoration projects. There are, however, some indicators of private-landowner interest. The proliferation of habitat-enhancement consultants advertising in popular trout-fishing journals, as well as the explosion of articles describing habitat restoration projects and techniques in the same journals, show that trout-habitat restoration is no longer solely in the realm of state and federal agencies. There is a growing market for such restoration among private landowners.

Despite the increasing public interest in stream management, however, federal land-management agencies suffered significant staffing and funding cuts in this area in the early 1980s. In 1988 a General Accounting Office report stated, "Staff positions and funding for activities that relate to riparian improvements have, because of budgetary restrictions, been substantially reduced over the past eight years." Recent and proposed changes in several federal agency programs may correct this deficiency. It is likely that with increased involvement of federal agencies the drive to restore stream and riparian habitat will continue to gain momentum.

One can only hope that the current interest in trout-habitat restoration and preservation has enough momentum to reverse the sad and ever more rapid destruction of the nation's dwindling trout-stream habitat.

SOURCES

Davis, H. S. 1934. The Purpose and Value of Stream Improvement. *Trans. Am. Fish. Soc.* 64:63–68.

_____. 1936. Stream Improvement in National Forests. *Trans. 1st N. Amer. Wild. Conf.* 1:447–53.

Duff, D. 1982. *Historical Perspective of Stream Habitat Improvement in the Rocky Mountain Area.* Jackson, WY: Rocky Mountain Stream Habitat Management Workshop.

Feast, C. N. 1938. Stream Improvement and Fish Planting Plans in the National Forests of the Central Rocky Mountain Region. *Trans. Am. Wild. Conf.* 3:428–32.

General Accounting Office. 1988. *Public Rangelands: Some Riparian Areas Restored but Widespread Improvements Will Be Slow.* Washington, DC GAO/RCED-88-105.

Harzler, J. 1988. Catchable Trout Fisheries: The Need for Assessment. *Fisheries* 13(2):2–8.

Needham, P. R. 1934. Quantitative Studies of Stream Bottom Foods, *Trans. Am. Fish. Soc.* 64:238–47.

Silcox, F. A. 1936. *Fish Stream Improvement Handbook.* Washington, DC: U.S.D.A. Forest Service.

Tarzwell, C. 1936. Experimental Evidence on the Value of Trout Stream Improvement in Michigan. *Trans. Am. Fish. Soc.* 66:177–87.

————. 1938. An Evaluation of the Methods and Results of Stream Improvements in the Southwest. *Trans. Am. Wildl.* 3:339–54.

U.S. Bureau of Fisheries. 1935. Methods for Improvement of Trout Streams. Memorandum I-133.

U.S.D.A. Forest Service. 1952. *Fish Stream Improvement Handbook.* Washington, DC.

White, R. J., and Brynildson, O. M. 1967. *Guidelines for Management of Trout Stream Habitat in Wisconsin.* Wisconsin Dept. Nat. Resources Tech. Bull. no. 39. Madison, WI.

Wydoski, R., and Duff, D. 1982. *A Review of Stream Habitat Improvements as a Fishery Tool and its Application to the Intermountain West.* Jackson, WY. Rocky Mountain Stream Habitat Management Workshop.

Chapter 2

THE TROUT AND THE STREAM

A LL salmonids—trout, salmon, char, and other members of the family Salmonidae—are by-products of their environment. The native brook trout that live in a clear Pennsylvania spring creek, and the chinook salmon that return from the sea to spawn in a cold river in Alaska—each evolved over thousands of years and each is specially adapted for life in those very different environments.

North America's trout have adapted to environments shaped primarily by the geological activity of the Pleistocene epoch, which began about two million years ago. During the Pleistocene's major episodes of continental glaciation, expansive ice sheets scoured and recast the northern landscape, changing the courses of rivers and the ranges of many trout species in the process.

As trout evolved in different areas—each dominated by unique vegetation and geologic characteristics—species adapted to their individual surroundings. The climate, geology, and elevation of the region; the shape of the stream bank; the mix of sediment, rock, and gravel on the streambed; the water temperature and characteristics; the insects that live in and near the stream, and the associated terrestrial and aquatic vegetation are some of the factors that have defined the evolutionary adaptations of trout to their environments.

To help a stream produce more trout, you must understand what the species needs to survive. You also must understand how trout are influenced by their immediate environment and the land-use activity in the drainage. Since it is important to visualize the *big picture*—the ecosystem within which trout live and reproduce—before delving into a stream rehabilitation project, this chapter will provide you with a summary of the factors known to influence the growth and survival of trout populations. In addition, at the end of this chapter you will be introduced to a series of diagrams that fisheries biologists call habitat suitability curves. These curves chart the habitat preferences of different trout species at different ages and at different times of the year.

The big picture is a panorama of the ecological relationships that bind trout to their environment. Like all living things, trout have developed such fastidious relationships with their environment that the abuse of one environmental component can affect many other components needed to sustain healthy, productive trout populations. Although difficult to comprehend, broad, geographic environmental conditions, such as a region's geology, climate, soils, and vegetation, can play as compelling a role in trout production as a timber harvest in the distant forested hills, farming operations that ceased 50 years ago, or the immediate availability of food and space in a stream. Trout are dynamic creatures that depend on very specific aspects of stream habitat for their own survival and for the survival of their offspring.

SALMONID LIFE CYCLES AND LIFE HISTORIES

The life cycle of an animal consists of distinctive stages of growth and development—from conception to death—that transpire over the course of its life. The life history of an animal describes how or where each stage of the life cycle occurs.

The life cycle of salmonids consists of four stages:

1. Spawning—the period of migration that lasts until the female (hen) constructs a redd (gravel nest) and lays its eggs.
2. Incubation—the period of time extending from the laying of eggs until the hatched fry emerge from the spawning gravel into open water.
3. Juvenile rearing—the period between the emergence from the spawning gravel as fry and adulthood or sexual maturity.
4. Adult—the time of sexual maturity that generally begins when the trout grow to be eight inches or longer and, depending on a variety of environmental factors and the species, when they reach one to three years of age.

For spawning and egg incubation, all salmonids seek similar types of habitats and use nearly identical redd-building techniques. They prefer to build redds in cold, well-oxygenated, gravel-bottomed streams because their incubating eggs require a constant water flow through the gravels to deliver oxygen to the eggs and remove waste products.

The trout redd is usually constructed in gravel substrate at the head of a riffle or the downstream edge of a pool. It begins as a pocket from which the female has removed the fine sediments with her tail by turning on her side and vigorously flexing her body. The water current carries the finest sediment downstream as the disturbed gravel forms a pile—the tailspill—downstream of the pocket (figure 2.1).

As the female continues to dig, she eventually reaches substrate particles that are too large for her to move. These form the bottom of the first egg pocket. The female deposits the first group of eggs into this pocket as the male simultaneously fertilizes them. The female

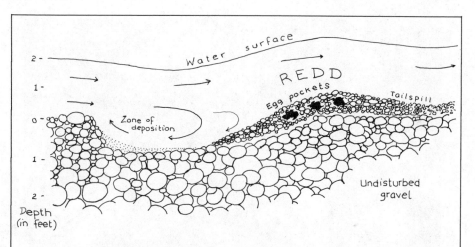

2.1 Salmonid redd (nest) in cross section. *Lengthwise cross section of salmonid redd showing the downstream tailspill where the egg pockets are located and the upstream area where excavation stopped. The upstream basin becomes an area of fine sediment deposition. Water accelerates as it approaches the riffle formed by the tailspill. This forces oxygen-rich water through the gravels and to the eggs. This constant flow of fresh water not only supplies oxygen to but removes waste products from the developing eggs.*

then quickly begins digging upstream from the first pocket. The current again carries the finer materials downstream below the redd, and the newly excavated gravels fall on top of the first egg pocket or travel downstream to the tailspill. When the final most upstream egg pocket has been prepared, the upstream digging covers the last egg pocket and forms a depression or basin upstream of the tailspill.

The redd, shown in a lengthwise section in figure 2.1, consists of an upstream basin and a series of egg pockets located in the tailspill. The egg pockets themselves consist of several large substrate particles that form the floor and smaller gravels that surround the eggs and fill the remainder of the pocket. The chum salmon redd in figure 2.2, which was taken through the glass bottom of an artificial spawning channel, shows the large substrate material of the egg pocket moments after the eggs were deposited. Redds can be seen in streams as bright, clean gravel areas.

Many of the similarities in the different species that mark their

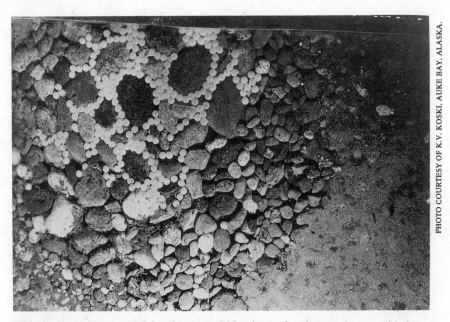

PHOTO COURTESY OF K.V. KOSKI, AUKE BAY, ALASKA.

2.2 Chum salmon redd. *This incredible photo of a chum salmon redd shows the eggs and the distribution of sediments. It was taken just minutes after spawning from below the redd through a glass plate on the bottom of the stream.*

early existence end when the tiny fry emerge from their redds. Once they abandon the gravel and enter the stream, different species and races of salmonids follow the different life-history blueprints that their ancestors have followed for thousands of generations.

The life-history strategies of salmonids fall into three distinct categories (figure 2.3):

1. Salmonids that migrate from the stream to larger bodies of water almost immediately after emergence from the spawning gravels. Fish that migrate to the sea (e.g., pink salmon and chum salmon)

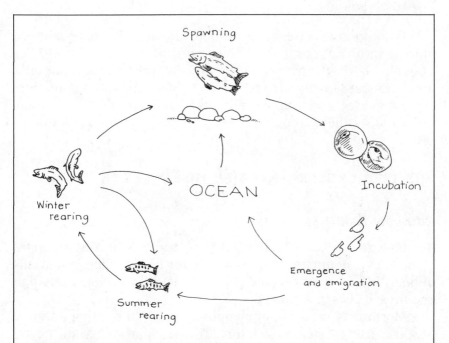

2.3 Life cycle of salmonids. *All salmonids spawn in fresh water with the eggs incubating in gravel redds. The fry of some species begin their journey to the ocean shortly after emergence. Others spend one to several summer and winter seasons rearing in fresh water before immigrating to the sea. Resident fish remain in fresh water their entire lives, although some species move between lakes and streams and big rivers and streams. All species return to their natal stream to spawn.*

are anadromous. Fish that migrate to lakes (e.g., kokanee salmon) are adfluvial.
2. Salmonids that spend one, two, three, or more years in fresh
   water and then migrate to the sea to complete their growth. These
   include coho salmon, chinook salmon, masu salmon, and Atlantic salmon, as well as anadromous races or strains of rainbow
   trout, brown trout, cutthroat trout, brook trout, and Dolly Var-
   den. This category also includes the numerous adfluvial races of
   trout that spawn in streams but feed and grow to maturity in
   lakes.
3. Stream-dwelling trout races that spend their entire lives in
   streams. (With very few exceptions, freshwater salmon spend
   part of their lives in lakes.)

   Within most species of trout there are races that have adopted
more than one of the three life-history strategies listed above. For
example, although most races of rainbow, brown, cutthroat, and
brook trout are strictly stream dwelling, there are anadromous races
of these species. Anadromous rainbow trout, for instance, are widely
known as steelhead trout.

THE LIFE CYCLES AND LIFE HISTORIES OF TROUT

Rainbow Trout

Rainbow trout (*Oncorhynchus mykiss*) are native to the western slopes
of the Rocky Mountains. They spawn at the head of riffles or the tails
of pools in gravel and rubble particles that vary between one-half
and three inches in diameter.

   Most rainbow-trout populations spawn in the spring during a
period of rising water temperature. The period of embryonic development is short in comparison to that of fall-spawning brown and
brook trout. Rainbow are considered to be fry from the time they
emerge from the gravel—late May to mid-June—until they lose
their yolk sacs, a fry's self-contained food source. Until survivors
reach approximately eight inches, they are generally considered to be
juveniles.

   Rainbows that migrate to the ocean, called steelhead trout, or to
a lake generally live one to three years in their natal stream before

migration and commonly spend one to three years in the ocean or lake before returning to spawn. Although many age combinations occur, the majority of female rainbow trout are four years old at first spawning; males often spawn for the first time when they are three years old. Mature fish in very productive streams can weigh between 6 to 17 pounds.

Brown Trout

Brown trout (*Salmo trutta* Linnaeus) are native to Europe, North Africa, and western Asia. They have been naturalized in North America since the late 1800s. Brown trout spawn in the fall when temperatures and daylight hours begin to decrease. Spawning can occur as early as late September and as late as December.

Brown trout appear to be highly selective when choosing spawning sites. Females prefer spawning locations near cover and often adjacent to a spring or up-welling discharge area. Frequently, brown trout will spawn only in one area of a riffle year after year. The average size of brown-trout redds is usually 12 inches wide and 36 inches long. The elongated redd shape can be easily distinguished from the rest of the riffle bottom because the disturbed gravel has a bright washed look. The gravel darkens over a period of one month.

Brown-trout eggs incubate in the gravel over the winter. Depending upon water temperatures, the eggs usually hatch in late February to mid-March, but the fry remain in the gravel for another three to six weeks until they fully absorb their yolk sacs. Although anadromous races occur, brown trout usually remain stream residents for their entire lives. However, the larger, older trout may move downstream into deeper water as they increase in size and weight.

Female brown trout generally reach sexual maturity at three years of age and are approximately 11 to 12 inches long. The majority of a brown-trout spawning population is composed of three- to six-year-old fish.

Brook Trout

Brook trout (*Salvelinus fontinalis* Mitchill) are the only native stream-dwelling trout in eastern North America. Brook trout are members of the char genus, as are lake trout and arctic char. Brook trout require cooler water temperatures than either rainbow or brown trout, and they cannot survive in the deteriorated environmental conditions that the other two species can sometimes withstand. Today, brook trout are generally considered trout of the small brook or creek, but historically they were found in larger streams and rivers before their watersheds were altered and the water quality in the larger rivers began to deteriorate.

Brook trout spawn in the fall, usually between late October and early December, but in the far northern climes they are known to spawn as early as late August or early September. Spawning preparation is usually initiated by decreasing daylight and dropping temperatures. Because of their small size, brook trout prefer smaller-sized pea gravel for spawning. In most streams wider than three feet, this gravel is found on the inside bend of curves or in side channels of the main river. In slow-flowing streams not prone to flooding, this fine gravel may be found throughout the stream.

Brook trout, to a greater degree than any other species, build their redds adjacent to or on top of up-welling springs or in areas where groundwater can flow upward through the redd. Their redds are usually saucer shaped rather than the elongated shape of redds built by rainbow and brown trout.

Brook-trout eggs incubate in the gravel until late February or early March, and the young fry remain there until their yolk sacs are absorbed. Brook trout have a relatively short life cycle. Most two-year-old females are sexually mature and all are sexually mature by the age of three.

THE INFLUENCE OF GEOGRAPHY ON SALMONID LIFE HISTORIES

The life-history strategies of salmonids have evolved in response to disparate environmental conditions. An example is the life histories adopted by salmonids inhabiting the Pacific and Atlantic drainages. Today, because of widespread stocking programs, each area supports rainbow, brook, and brown trout, with both freshwater and anadromous races, but there is little similarity between the native anadromous species of the Pacific and the Atlantic.

West of the Continental Divide, the native sea-running salmon and trout belong to the genus *Oncorhynchus*, of which several species descend to the sea or to lakes immediately after they emerge from the spawning gravels. A few Pacific salmonids—steelhead, coho, and chinook, for instance—spend a bit more time (but usually less than one year) in their natal streams before the inevitable descent to the sea or lake.

In the Atlantic drainage, which is east of the Continental Divide, the only native anadromous salmon species is the Atlantic salmon. Atlantic salmon spend at least one year in fresh water, but are more likely to spend two or three years in the river (and occasionally up to seven years) before descending to the sea.

The story of why West Coast salmon hightail it to the sea and East Coast salmon have adapted a more leisurely pace can be read in each area's geography. The lands bordering the Pacific Ocean are mountainous, summers are generally short, and the inland winters can be so severe that free-flowing streams often become clogged to a standstill with ice and snow. With few exceptions streams born in these mountains are short, steep, and often characterized by fluctuations in flows that range from torrents to trickles. In the arduous game of survival, the opportunity to live a long, productive life in such streams has proven to be less inviting than the sea, where the fish live among slow ocean currents and abundant sources of food.

In contrast, the lands bordering the Atlantic Ocean are characterized by rivers that drain gentler slopes, so they run quieter and deeper. Since the mountains are of a lower relief and flows do not fluctuate as widely, the winters have less dramatic effects on stream flows and are generally more hospitable to young trout than those of the Pacific drainage.

Sea-running salmonids are not the only fish that have been affected by the area's geography and environment. Stream-dwelling brown and brook trout probably prefer slow-moving waters, close to the shrubs and brush that provide riverbank cover, because they evolved in the flat, meandering streams of Europe and the eastern United States, respectively.

Rainbow and cutthroat trout, on the other hand, evolved in the mountainous western United States, where steep, rapid-flowing streams are the norm. So, as most experienced anglers know, rainbow and cutthroat can often be found feeding in riffle habitats and resting near cover provided by boulders or logs, branches, and other woody debris.

If you want to restore a trout stream in the image of a western river, however, simply dumping boulders and logs on the riverbed is not the answer. The number of trout that can survive in a stream, any stream, will not only be affected by in-stream habitat. The number is also dependent on how the land bordering the stream is used and by the state of the general environmental conditions in and beyond the immediate drainage.

Trout are particularly sensitive to environmental changes. If you see no or few trout in a stream that once produced abundant numbers, the source of the problem may be the recent land-use activities (e.g., timber harvesting, grazing, mining, road building, and urban development). Such developments bolster the local economy but result in accelerated erosion, which fills pools with sediment, smothers incubating eggs, and warms the water. Channelized watercourses, the removal of streamside vegetation, drained wetlands, pollution, pesticides, and fertilizers can all have devastating effects on trout populations.

If you are beginning to recognize that trout-habitat protection might be an easier and more cost-effective management technique than trout-habitat rehabilitation, you have already discovered an environmental maxim that continues to elude some of the nation's land and wildlife management agencies, as well as many private landowners.

NATURAL REGULATORS OF SALMONID POPULATIONS IN STREAMS

The first year of life is extremely difficult for trout. In the struggle for survival, if they manage to outmaneuver predators and fight off disease, trout still face stiff competition for food and herculean battles against a sometimes inhospitable environment. In most cases fry that have recently emerged from their gravel birthplaces are present in abundant numbers, yet typically fewer than 1 percent of the newly hatched fry will survive a full year.

Although a trout's fight for survival does not diminish after its first year of life, its chances for continued survival increase dramatically. Researchers have shown, for example, that brook-trout mortality is far greater during the first year of life than it is in subsequent years.

Most fishery biologists will agree that the survivors that pass the one-year milestone are simply better equipped genetically to meet the challenges of life than those that perished. The discussion, however, does not end on that agreeable note. There are many factors that not only influence but actually control the stream production of salmonids.

Some of the most important physical factors limiting trout survival are water temperature, water velocity, availability of escape cover, and a stream's annual discharge or flow pattern. Pool volume—the number, depth, and size of those deep fishing holes anglers long to cast to—is a factor that controls trout populations in some streams.

The long list of limiting factors includes fluctuations in discharge that have been shown to affect the total weight of brook trout, Atlantic salmon, and brown trout. The lack of cover, which provides protection from predation in the form of in-stream boulders, logs, undercut banks, root wads, and overhead vegetation, can limit trout populations. Direct relationships have been found between trout populations and the abundance of aquatic insects, branches, logs, and other forms of large organic debris.

It is a safe bet that no single factor severely limits fish populations. Rather, it is a series of environmental variables that operate together to influence population size. How and where the fish react to those variables follows.

MICROHABITAT AND TERRITORIALITY

If you narrowed the focus of the ecosystem's natural regulators to the physical, chemical, and biological variables that limit production in a specific reach of a particular stream, you would be looking at the trout's microhabitat. Microhabitat is the space—or the place—where trout live. It consists of the specific combinations of habitat elements—in specific locations and during specific seasons—trout need to survive.

The microhabitat provides trout with the food, cover, water depth, velocity, discharge, and temperature they need to survive. The microhabitat's riverbed conforms to very specific needs, just as a well-appointed house conforms to your own needs.

The behavioral response of trout to microhabitat is an area of intense interest to those concerned with trout-habitat rehabilitation. If a trout-stream rehabilitation project, an often long and expensive proposition, is to be successful, one must be able to anticipate how trout, at various life stages, will respond to changes that are going to be made in the stream.

If you have ever attempted to observe trout in a stream, or if you have ever finally spooked a feeding lunker after a silent quarter-hour stalk, you probably know how difficult trout watching can be. Fishery biologists, too, have had difficulty watching their subjects. To observe and document trout behavior, some researchers have used large aquariums. Others have created aquariums in the wild by replacing a small portion of a riverbank with plate-glass picture windows. Some have constructed streamside towers to peer down through the water with Polarized telescopes by day and infrared telescopes by night. Still others have donned scuba gear to join the trout in their natural environs, and at least one researcher has introduced albino trout to a river system to thwart the trout's natural concealment characteristics!

But no matter what strange or ingenious method one might employ, time and again researchers have shown that the most important behavioral trait of trout and salmon is territoriality. The salmonid's territorial urge is so strong that the fry of Atlantic salmon and brown trout, for instance, move to establish territories within one to four days after emergence from the streambed gravel.

The features trout seek when establishing territory include a good food source, cover for protection from predation, and visual isolation from other trout in the stream. Once established, trout routinely defend the spaces they use for feeding, resting, and escape from predation. Within each trout's territory are one or more dominant stations, called focal points, where an individual spends the majority of its time. These focal points are usually feeding stations or nearby resting stations.

M. Gary Wickham, the researcher who planted yearling hatchery-raised albino brook trout in a Colorado mountain stream, showed that the albinos spent 94 percent of their time at their focal points. Although each focal point was surprisingly small—averaging less than 3 percent of the study section—the use of several focal points by a single trout effectively increased the average area used by the trout to 15 percent of the study section.

Additional studies of young rainbow and brown trout in streams on the east slope of the Sierra Nevada, juvenile chinook salmon and steelhead trout in Idaho, and brook trout, brown trout, cutthroat trout, and Atlantic salmon in a variety of locations throughout the United States, Canada, and Europe tend to confirm that all young salmonids are fiercely territorial, but that individual trout don't cut a wide swath in a stream. Movement from a focal point for cover or to defend a feeding station occurs, but in nearly all cases the fish quickly return to a specific station.

Salmonids tend to establish territories in direct relation to their size, so as they grow, their territories become larger. A corollary emerges: For the territory of one trout to grow, (1) the number of trout in a given area must decrease, or (2) the territories of other trout must become smaller. As territories are taken over by larger and more aggressive trout, the displaced trout must go somewhere. Many researchers believe that displaced trout tend to go downstream to fill empty territories. If there are no empty territories to fill, however, displaced trout probably die from either predation or starvation.

A recently completed three-year study of brown-trout behavior in a short reach of Spruce Creek in Pennsylvania reconfirms many of the earlier studies noted above. The study revealed that: (1) many brown trout reside in the same location day after day, year after year; (2) brown trout establish a loose social hierarchy based on territoriality; (3) brown trout spend nearly 93 percent of their time during daylight hours at their favorite feeding station; and (4) although cover is an essential component of a brown trout's territory, it is generally used during the day only when the trout is frightened.

Food and Space—How Much Are Needed?

You have already discovered that as a trout grows, so does its appetite, and as its appetite grows, so does its territory. When considering your own trout-habitat rehabilitation project, you may wonder just how much food and space one trout needs.

Unfortunately, the question is not easily answered. Trout are, for the most part, opportunistic drift feeders. That is, they prey primarily on insects and other passively drifting food organisms that may originate in the stream or on land carried through or near their territory by the natural flow of the stream.

Since a trout must have a territory that allows enough food to drift through to keep it well fed, it is reasonable to assume that if food alone controlled its size, a territory would reflect its relationship to food abundance. Therefore, in areas where food is plentiful, territories would be small and the number of trout would be great. In areas where food is scarce, the territories would be large and the trout populations would be sparse.

A study of two identical stream-channel aquariums, seeded with an equal number of fry, appears to agree with that conclusion. The trout in the aquarium that received more food created smaller territories, and the end result was more trout in the stream channel. The results were exactly opposite in the aquarium that received much less food: The most aggressive trout established larger territories, the weaker ones were displaced downstream, and the aquarium supported fewer trout.

Nevertheless, both in controlled environments and in the wild most research shows that the availability of space and the availability of food work together, not independently, to determine territory size. When you consider the case of the dominant coho salmon that would not tolerate a subordinate coho feeding in its territory—even though the dominant salmon was well fed and had no apparent interest in feeding—it appears that even where food is abundant salmonids still have minimum spatial needs.

Be it cover from predation, or a genetically programmed defense against the spread of parasites and other infections that commonly occur throughout a population, it is safe only to say that the territory must be large enough to include adequate space, food, and areas for resting and hiding. Each individual trout will ultimately determine the size of territory it needs.

TERRITORY AND ENERGY EFFICIENCY

Time and energy spent maintaining and defending a position in a territory whipped by a swift current are not time and energy well spent for a growing trout. If food and space are the basics a salmonid seeks when establishing a territory, then energy efficiency is the top-of-the-line amenity. To grow, a trout must have a territory that provides an abundance of food in an area that demands a minimum of time and energy to defend from other trout. So, given a choice, all trout prefer to live in relatively calm waters close to a swift current's steady supply of drifting insects.

From such a feeding station, a trout can dart out into the current, intercept a food item, and return to its feeding station with a minimum expenditure of energy. Because the potential for weight gain, and stream dominance, is determined by the amount of energy obtained from its diet minus the loss of energy expended to obtain its food, the most successful contenders for energy-efficient territories are always among the largest trout in the stream.

Research has shown that competition for a stream's most energy-efficient territory is intense. For instance, in several successive experiments, five trout (rainbow or brown) were placed in an isolated section of an experimental stream. Within a short time the trout established territories, and, like chickens in a barnyard, they also established an in-stream pecking order. Each trout controlled the most energy-efficient territory it was capable of defending. Each time the dominant trout was removed, the next trout in the pecking order moved into the vacancy.

Studies of the behavior of brook and brown trout in a rather calm, insect-rich Michigan stream produced similar results. The study showed that members of each species established resting and feeding focal points, and, as expected, the usually dominant brown-trout resting focal points were more energy efficient than those of the brook trout. When the brown trout were experimentally removed from the stream, brook trout moved directly to the brown trouts' more-favorable resting positions but maintained their original, and apparently adequate, feeding focal points.

The point is simply this: Stream-dwelling salmonids are strongly territorial and that territoriality is a trait that can control the number of trout in any particular area of a stream. Still, it is the quality and quantity of the microhabitat that ultimately limits the number of trout that can live in a stream. Where suitable habitat and trout are abundant, the streambed is probably covered by a mosaic of territories. The size of those territories is influenced by the habitat attributes discussed in the following pages.

PHYSICAL COMPONENTS OF SALMONID MICROHABITAT

Even under the best conditions, a stream can only accommodate a limited number of territories, so the surplus trout, usually among the smallest trout in the population, are displaced downstream. The physical components of microhabitat—the variables that are most often manipulated in stream-habitat enhancement or restoration projects—will be discussed in more detail to show how habitat needs vary as trout grow and seasons change.

Depth and Velocity

All salmonids begin their lives in relatively shallow, slow-moving water and gradually move to deeper, faster water as they mature. The shift to deeper, faster-flowing water is largely related to the amount of food that is regularly carried past a station by the higher-velocity waters. However, as discussed earlier, maintaining a station in a swift current is not the best use of a trout's time and energy.

Accordingly, when studying the water velocity's relation to trout habitat, researchers have found that feeding focal points occur in two distinct water types.

1. In shear zones, where a swift water mass flows next to a slower water mass. Such focal points allow trout to be close to food-carrying currents without constantly subjecting them to energy-sapping currents.
2. In eddies or slow current areas, where water moves counter to the main water flow. Since an eddy is associated with swift currents, it, too, contains abundant food organisms and at the same time, affords a trout the luxury of expending a minimum amount of energy to maintain its stream position.

Cover

Although some anglers seem intuitively to understand the important relationship between cover and trout, fishery biologists have had difficulty defining exactly what constitutes cover. The best definition might be by Tom Wesche, who wrote: "Trout cover can generally be described as object-oriented (i.e., rubble, boulders, undercut banks, logs, vegetation), having a water depth of at least 0.5 feet and a water velocity at the point of cover occupation of less than 0.5 feet per second."

Biologists agree that a trout's movement to deeper and faster waters may not be related to food alone. Such movement could also be explained as cover related simply because large rubble and boulders, both excellent sources of cover for some trout species, are most likely to be found in areas of high water velocity.

A Wisconsin researcher, for instance, has indicated that brook trout in Lawrence Creek spend much of their time hiding, even as considerable quantities of food drift by in more open, unshaded waters. The observation of similar behavior—behavior characterized by a preference for the safety of shade and shadow cast by overhead cover—has led many researchers to suspect that the value of cover is related to an inborn need to feel safe.

The type of cover sought for security seems to vary with age and among the species. A study of cutthroat and brook trout that were less than one year old has shown that the young trout occupy areas closer to overhead cover than do older ones. The oldest cutthroat, a species known to be an easy catch among anglers, lived twice as far from cover as did the oldest brook trout. In the same study, Jack Griffith points out that the largest cutthroat, which often live at the heads of pools under a blanket of turbulent water, may be relatively unaware of a fisherman's approach. However, the brook trout, which seek calmer water and stream bank-related cover, may actually be set on a defensive alert by the vibration of the angler's footfalls.

In any case, for trout, cover, like food, is where the fish finds it. For the brown trout and brook trout studied in various Wyoming streams, cover was a mix of undercut banks and overhanging vegetation. The same study showed Colorado River cutthroats with a preference for areas of rubble and boulders. In the Colorado study of albino brook trout discussed earlier, the albinos spent about 94 percent of their time in cover provided by large boulders, logs, and turbulent surface waters.

Studies have also shown that the availability and diversity of cover contribute significantly to the population density—the number of trout in a stream. In an attempt to provide more hiding places for brook trout, a series of dams, deflectors, and artificial cover structures were installed in a 450-yard section of a small stream in Nova Scotia. Within a year the stream's standing crop of fingerlings slightly increased, but the number of yearling and older trout doubled. In natural, unaltered sections of Prickly Pear Creek in Montana, overhanging brush, undercut banks, stumps, rocks, and log jams provided 81 percent more cover for trout than in corresponding channelized stretches. As one might expect, the number and weight of the brown and rainbow trout inhabiting the unaltered sections of Prickly Pear Creek were about 78 percent greater than in the channelized sections.

Visual Isolation

Trout seem to feel most secure when they can neither see nor be seen by other fish. So, in some respects, boulders, logs, rubble, other debris, and topographic anomalies that can screen trout from each other's view also divide a stream into territorial stations that trout occupy.

The visual isolation provided by the topography of the stream bottom and other in-stream material can influence the size and number of territories an area can support. This relationship was proven by a researcher who placed larger stones on top of smaller ones lying on the bottom of an experimental aquarium. When a broken topography was created on the bottom of the tank, the trout established more and smaller territories than they did in less rough areas.

In another experiment, the same researcher, Harry Kalleberg, increased the velocity of the water in the aquarium, which compelled the trout to establish even smaller territories. Kalleberg surmised that as the water velocity increased, the trout moved closer to the bottom to avoid a constant struggle against the current. Once close to the rugged bottom, they were then able to establish new territories, in even closer quarters, because the rock clumps effectively isolated them from the other trout in the tank. As the established trout moved down and created smaller territories as their visual isolation increased, previously displaced fry were free to establish territories without harassment.

Kalleberg's research suggests that for trout feeding largely on drift, there is generally more visual isolation provided in riffles and rubble than is provided in pools. Thus, many researchers have come to suspect that in typical riffle areas, smaller territories provide more food for more trout than in pool habitats.

Although additional work in this area is needed, it is not too early to caution would-be trout-habitat rehabilitators against back-hoeing a series of deep holes from a long stretch of riffles to make their stream more inviting to trout. It probably won't produce the desired results. Hillman, Griffith, and Platts point out: "Development of satisfactory techniques designed to rehabilitate fish habitat depends on a thorough understanding of natural systems and of factors limiting production." To enhance a trout's microhabitat, you must consider several habitat attributes, including water depth and velocity, cover, and visual isolation, as well as the species and life stage of the targeted trout.

MICROHABITAT CHANGES DURING EVENING AND WINTER

If you consider each of the factors presented thus far, you will be on your way to understanding the stream habitat trout seek during the daylight hours of spring and summer. The same trout's needs at night and in winter, however, are quite different.

Evening

Salmonids are generally inactive at night, and in a nighttime study of juvenile chinook salmon and steelhead trout, researchers discovered that trout species move inshore from their daytime focal points to quieter, shallower stations. Juvenile steelhead took up positions on the bottom, beneath rocks or in crevices in the substrate, at least 10 feet from their daytime stations. One steelhead moved more than 60 feet from its daytime station. Since the night stations were often quite different from daytime locations, several researchers speculate that nighttime cover needs may be an important part not only of the selection of microhabitat and territory but also of the density of trout in the stream as well.

Winter

In winter, even though trout are cold-blooded animals, their survival needs change dramatically. The cold, and the trouble it often creates, make winter a very demanding time for stream-dwelling salmonids. As water temperatures decline, so do the metabolism and activity of trout. A trout's once-hearty appetite diminishes, and its behavior has less to do with obtaining food than with securing a safe refuge from the strain of winter.

In winter, injury or death can result from a number of catastrophic events. Collapsing snow or buildup of anchor ice—stream bottom ice that grows toward the surface of the stream—can divert water out of channels and leave trout high and dry. Variations in flows can scour the streambed and force the trout into unfamiliar territories, where they become easy prey and have difficulty finding the little food they need to survive.

Although limited, research that focuses on the winter habitat of salmonids indicates that temperatures from 44 to 50 degrees Fahrenheit spur fish to establish their winter stations. At these temperatures trout tend to find a station on the stream bottom, in a deep pool, or, in some cases, in an off-stream marsh, where they remain sluggish until the temperature rises in the spring.

Summaries of some of the best work on winter-habitat requirements are provided below:

STREAMBED HOLLOWS

In a study of the fall-habitat shift of Atlantic salmon in a small New Brunswick stream, researchers found that at temperatures from 48 to 50 degrees Fahrenheit the salmon retreated to solitary, natural streambed chambers beneath rubble and boulders. The chambers were closed on all sides, except for at least one distinct opening large enough for a juvenile salmon to pass through. Loose debris and sediment accumulated in the chambers, but the salmon were neither wedged nor buried in their winter homes.

A CLEAR PASSAGE

Working under the notion that sediment could affect the winter survival of juvenile chinook salmon if it clogged the chambers and crevices they seek as a winter refuge, researchers set out to test the theory in a heavily sedimented stream in Idaho. They first established a control section of stream, conducted a population census of the area, and then began to study the sediment/trout interactions.

In the experimental stream section, the researchers piled cobble—grapefruit-sized rocks—in ten-inch mounds in several square-yard patches in exposed riffles and glide areas of undercut banks. Winter-rearing densities in the glide increased eightfold over the previous winter and ninefold over the control area. Although a similar winter increase was noted in the riffle area, by spring some of the cobble in the riffles had been moved by ice scour, and most of it was severely embedded in silt, rendering it unsuitable for future use as winter cover.

A TANGLE OF ROOTS

A study of the winter ecology of juvenile coho salmon and steelhead trout in streams on Vancouver Island, British Columbia, showed that as water temperatures fell below 47 degrees Fahrenheit the fish moved into deeper water than they inhabited during the summer. The steelhead trout held stations closer to the streambed than did the coho salmon, but each species preferred winter habitats characterized by low water velocities.

As the water temperature dropped from 48 to 35 degrees Fahrenheit, the coho and steelhead—especially the older ones—moved to winter cover provided by upturned tree roots, logs, and associated deep pools. Overhanging banks, distinguished by a mass of dense roots, were also used as cover. When the temperature dropped to 44 degrees Fahrenheit, the youngest juvenile coho and steelhead sought cover either very close to or under rocks as small as billiard balls.

Logs, overhanging brush, root masses, cutbanks, and debris provided the most important winter cover for juvenile coho and steelhead in side pools, back channels, and main channels. Therefore, the researchers have inferred that streamside logging, road building, overzealous stream clearing, or channelizing could severely alter winter habitat and result in reduced winter survival for these trout and salmon.

A NEED FOR SHELTER

In a study of coho and coastal cutthroat trout, the availability of winter habitat in an artificial stream was found to be more important to survival than the availability of food. Low water temperatures and, in this case, high stream flows created distressing conditions that caused the trout to spend more time in shelter and rest areas than in search for food. Such behavior may serve to reduce downstream displacement—and predation losses—during periods of high flows.

The study suggests that because the number of fish that salmon- and trout-producing streams can harbor in winter may be limited by the cover available, enhancement projects should consider: (1) manipulating in-stream boulders and overhead vegetation in areas of shallow, fast water to benefit winter survival of juveniles under one year; and (2) manipulating the natural cover, such as root masses and log jams, in the main stream and side channels to benefit winter survival of yearling and older salmon and trout.

WINTER SOLACE

Robert Hunt, of the Wisconsin Department of Natural Resources, has probably conducted more research to evaluate effects of stream-enhancement work than any other biologist. On Lawrence Creek, where one of Wisconsin's major habitat development projects was evaluated, Hunt wanted to determine why habitat development leads to better trout populations. The Lawrence Creek case history is presented in chapter 7.

A series of bank-cover/current-deflector structures were installed in the mile-long study reach to enhance its trout-carrying capacity. Physical changes from the intensive refabrication of the channel shape included a 51 percent reduction in surface area and a 65 percent increase in average water depth. Pool area increased nearly 300 percent and underbank hiding cover increased more than 400 percent.

An unaltered downstream area served as a reference, or control, zone. In the study zones trout-population inventories were carried out for three years before the enhancement project was initiated and for six years after it was completed. During the first three years after improvements were made, the average number of brook trout over eight inches increased 156 percent. During the next three-year period, brook trout were 244 percent more abundant in the spring than they were prior to the habitat restoration effort. These dramatic improvements occurred despite a 200 percent increase in angler harvests.

Hunt concluded that the dramatic improvements in the trout population were the result of increased winter survival. For that reason alone, the importance of winter habitat must be considered for trout-habitat enhancement projects.

HABITAT SUITABILITY CRITERIA AND CURVES

The U.S. Fish and Wildlife Service's Instream Flow Incremental method is a mathematical system used to develop recommendations for in-stream flows for trout. An important aspect of this mathematical model has been the development of habitat suitability curves. (A discussion of the model is beyond the scope of this book. Nevertheless, you can discover more about the model, and how it is used, by reading: Ken Bovee and Tom Cochnauer, *Development and Evaluation of Weighted Criteria, Probability-of-Use Curves for Instream Flow Assessments* [1977] and K. Bovee, *A Guide to Stream Habitat Analysis Using the Instream Flow Incremental Methodology* [1982]).

These curves are used in the context of developing recommendations for in-stream flows for trout. Trout habitat is dependent upon adequate water flows. What appears to be a dry side channel at low flow may provide excellent juvenile-rearing habitat at higher flows.

The habitat suitability curves themselves are central to the following discussion and serve as increasingly important components needed to plan effective trout-habitat rehabilitation projects.

Some of the curves are built based on information available from the scientific literature, such as that reviewed in the earlier portion of this chapter, combined with the professional judgment of biologists familiar with the species. Other graphs are based on the measured condition of a trout population (growth, survival, or total weight). Then, the measurements are converted into an index of suitability for the species ranging from 0.0 to 1.0. An index of 0.0 means the conditions are poor or unsuitable; an index of 1.0 reflects excellent conditions.

The vertical line of the graphs (figures 2.4 and 2.5) represent the suitability index. The horizontal line—percentage of stream consist-

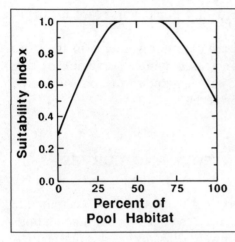

2.4 Relationship between rainbow-trout abundance and pool habitat. *Habitat suitability curve showing the relationship between adult rainbow trout and the percent of pool habitat available in the fall.* (SOURCE: RALEIGH ET AL. 1984 AND 1986.)

ing of pool habitat—shows the range of values for the habitat variable—depth or velocity, for instance—being considered. The lines on the graph are the researchers' best estimate of the suitability of a range of values for a particular trout-habitat attribute.

Figure 2.4 describes the autumn relationship between adult rainbow trout and the amount of pool-type habitat available at the end of the trout's growing season when the water in the stream is generally low. The graph shows that if 25 percent of the stream habitat is pool habitat during late-season low flows, suitability for rainbow trout is 0.8, a near-excellent index value. If 100 percent of the stream consisted of pool habitat at this time of year, the suitability for rainbow would be 0.5. A suitability index of 0.5 is considered fair. The ideal suitability exists when the amount of pool habitat available at this time of year is between 35 and 65 percent of the stream habitat.

The curve presented in figure 2.5 looks similar to figure 2.4, but it was developed in a different manner. The curve in figure 2.5 is based on actual observations of rainbow trout in the stream by biologists who swim slowly upstream and carefully mark the location where adult, juvenile, or fry trout are observed. After marking these locations, the water depth, velocity, substrate composition, cover, and other habitat variables are measured in the same locations.

The information is then graphed as described above. In this case

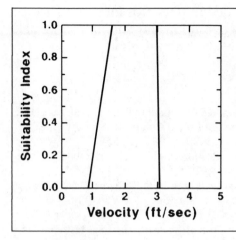

2.5 Relationship between rainbow trout spawning and water velocity. *Habitat suitability curve depicting suitability of various water velocities for spawning rainbow trout.* (SOURCE: RALEIGH ET AL. 1984 AND 1986.)

the suitability of 1.0 is given to the value of the habitat variable that was used by most of the fish observed. For example, figure 2.5 presents information on suitability of various water velocities for spawning rainbow trout. The graph shows that, although rainbow were observed spawning in velocities ranging from 0.8 to 3.2 feet per second, the preferred range was 1.6 to 3.0 feet per second.

Because it is based on direct observations rather than professional judgment, this curve may initially seem to provide better information than the curve in figure 2.4. However, curves based on direct observations have limitations because the majority of the criteria have been developed in the Pacific Northwest. Experts warn that it would be a mistake to apply criteria established for Pacific Northwest streams to northeastern streams, where hydraulic characteristics and trout size can differ greatly.

Therefore, these graphs can serve only as guidelines for fishing-housing specifications for habitat enhancement projects. You should also be aware that researchers continue to collect habitat suitability data. (These data are compiled by the National Ecology Research Center [NERC], 2627 Redwing Road, Creekside Building #1, Fort Collins, CO 80526-2899. NERC may be able to provide you with habitat suitability curves developed in the area you are working or, at the very least, offer a series of curves most appropriate for the problem you want to solve.)

Learning to read these curves may require some effort. Nevertheless, their value in providing design standards for stream-habitat enhancement work, and for determining the amount of suitable habitat available in a stream, is well worth the effort.

SOURCES

Allen, K. 1969. Limitations on Production in Salmonid Populations in Streams. H.R. McMillan Lectures in Fisheries, Univ. of British Columbia, Vancouver, BC.

Bachman, R. 1989. Trout Watching. *Trout,* Winter 1989, pp. 62–71.

Binns, N., and Eiserman, F. 1979. Quantification of Fluvial Trout Habitat in Wyoming. *Trans. Am. Fish. Soc.* 108(3):215–28.

Bovee, K. 1982. *A Guide to Stream Habitat Analysis Using the Instream Flow Incremental Methodology.* Instream Flow Information Paper no. 12. FWS/OBS-82/26.

Bovee, K., and Cochnauer, T. 1977. *Development and Evaluation of Weighted Criteria, Probability-of-Use Curves for Instream Flow Assessments: Fisheries.* Instream Flow Information Paper no. 3. FWS/OBS-77/63.

Bustard, D., and Narver, D. 1975. Aspects of the Winter Ecology of Juvenile Coho Salmon (*Oncorhynchus kisutch*) and Steelhead Trout (*Salmo gairdneri*). *J. Fish. Res. Bd. Can.* 32:667–80.

Chapman, D. 1966. Food and Space as Regulators of Salmonid Populations in Streams. *The Am. Naturalist* 100 (913):345–57.

Chapman, D., and Bjornn, T. 1969. Distribution of Salmonids in Streams, with Special Reference to Food and Feeding. H.R. McMillan Lectures in Fisheries, Univ. of British Columbia, Vancouver, BC.

Dolloff, C. 1983. "The Relationship of Wood Debris to Juvenile Salmonid Production and Microhabitat Selection in Small Southeast Alaska Streams." Ph.D. diss., Montana State Univ., Bozeman, MT.

Edmundson, E.; Everest, F.; and Chapman, D. 1968. Permanence of Station in Juvenile Chinook Salmon and Steelhead Trout. *J. Fish. Res. Bd. Canada* 25 (7): 1453–64.

Elser, A. 1968. Fish Populations of a Trout Stream in Relation to Major Habitat Zones and Channel Alterations, *Trans. Am. Fish. Soc.* 97:389–97.

Everest, F. 1987. Salmonids of Western Forested Watersheds. In *Streamside Management: Forestry and Fishery Interactions,* eds. E. Salo and T. Cundy, pp. 3–8. Univ. of Washington Institute of Forest Resources Contribution no. 57.

Everest, F., and Chapman, D. 1972. Habitat Selection and Spatial Interaction by Juvenile Chinook Salmon and Steelhead Trout in Idaho Streams. *J. Fish. Res. Bd. Can.* 29:91–100.

Fausch, K. 1984. Profitable Stream Positions for Salmonids: Relating Specified Growth Rate to Net Energy Gain. *Can. J. Zoology.* 62:441–51.

Fausch, K., and White, R. 1981. Competition Between Brook Trout (*Salvelinus fontinalis*) and Brown Trout (*Salmo trutta*) for Positions in a Michigan Stream. *Can. J. Fish. Aquat. Sci.* 38:1220–27.

Fraser, F. 1969. Population Density Effects on Survival and Growth of Juvenile Coho Salmon and Steelhead Trout in Experimental Stream-Channels. H. R. McMillan Lectures in Fisheries, Univ. of British Columbia, Vancouver, BC.

Gerking, S. 1953. Evidence for the Concepts of Home Range and Territoriality in Stream Fishes. *Ecology* 34 (2):347–65.

Glova, G., and Mason, J. *Interactions for Food and Space Between Sympatric Populations of Juvenile Coho Salmon and Coastal Cutthroat Trout in a Stream Similar During Winter and Spring.* Fisheries and Marine Service Manuscript Report no. 1429. Nanaimo, BC.

Griffith, J. S. 1972. Comparative Behavior and Habitat Utilization of Brook Trout (*Salvelinus fontinalis*) and Cutthroat Trout (*Salmo clarki*) in Small Streams in Northern Idaho. *J. Fish. Res. Bd. Can.* 29 (1972):265–73.

Harvey, K., and Davis, R. 1970. Factors Influencing Standing Crops and Survival of Juvenile Salmon at Barrows Stream, Maine. *Trans. Am. Fish. Soc.* 99:297–311.

Hillman, T.; Griffith, J.; and Platts, W. 1987. Summer and Winter Habitat Selection by Juvenile Chinook Salmon in a Highly Sedimented Idaho Stream. *Trans. Am. Fish. Soc.* 116:185–95.

Hunt, R. 1969. Overwinter Survival of Wild Fingerling Brook Trout in Lawrence Creek, Wisconsin. *J. Fish. Res. Bd. Can.* 26:1473–83.

_____. 1974. *Annual Production of Brook Trout in Lawrence Creek During Eleven Successive Years*, Dept. of Nat. Res. Tech. Bull. no. 82. Madison, WI.

_____. 1976. A Long-Term Evaluation of Trout Habitat Development and Its Relation to Improving Management-Related Research. *Trans. Am. Fish. Soc.* 195 (3):361–64.

Hynes, H.B.N. 1972. *The Ecology of Running Waters.* Liverpool, England: Liverpool Univ. Press.

Jenkins, T. 1969. Social Structure, Position Choice and Microdistribution of Two Trout Species (*Salmo trutta* and *Salmo gairdneri*) Resident in Mountain Streams. *An. Beh. Mon.* 2(2):57–123.

Kalleberg, H. 1958. Observations in a Stream Tank of Territoriality and Competition in Juvenile Salmon and Trout (*Salmo salar* and *Salmo trutta*). *Inst. of Freshwater Res.* 39:55–99. Drottingholm, Sweden.

Kennleyside, M., and Yamamoto, F. 1962. Territorial Behavior of Juvenile Atlantic Salmon. *Behavior 19* (1/2):139–69.

Latta, W. 1965. Relationship of Young-of-the-Year Trout to Mature Trout and Groundwater. *Trans. Am. Fish. Soc.* 94:32–39.

_____. 1969. Some Factors Affecting Survival of Young-of-the-Year Brook Trout, *Salvelinus fontinalis*, (Mitchell) in Streams. H.R. McMillan Lectures in Fisheries, Univ. of British Columbia, Vancouver, BC.

Lewis, S. 1969. Physical Factors Influencing Fish Populations in Pools of a Trout Stream. *Trans. Am. Fish. Soc.* 98:14–17.

Miller, R. 1957. Permanence and Size of Home Territory in Stream Dwelling Cutthroat Trout. *J. Fish. Res. Rd. Canada* 14(5):687–91.

Murphy, M. 1979. "Predator Assemblages in Old-growth and Logged Sections of Small Cascade Streams" Master's thesis, Oregon State Univ., Corvallis, OR.

Needham, P., and Jones, A. 1959. Flow, Temperature, Solar Radiation and Ice in Relation to Activities of Fishes in Sagehen Creek, CA. *Ecology* 40(3):465–74.

Platts, W., and McHenry, M. 1988. *Density and Biomass of Trout and Char in Western Streams.* Gen. Tech. Rept. no. INT-241. U.S.D.A. Forest Service Intermountain Research Station, Ogden, UT.

Raleigh, R. 1982. *Habitat Suitability Index Models: Brook Trout.* USFWS Biological Services Program. FWS/OBS-82/10-24.

Raleigh, R.; Hickman, T.; Soloman, R.; and Nelson, P. 1984. *Habitat Suitability Information: Rainbow Trout.* U.S. Fish and Wildlife Serv. FWS/OBS-82/10-60.

Raleigh, R.; Zuckerman, L.; and Nelson, P. 1986. *Habitat Suitability Index Models and Instream Flow Suitability Curves: Brown Trout.* Rev., U.S. Fish and Wildlife Service Biol. Rpt. no. 82 (10-124).

Reiser, D., and Bjornn, T. 1969. *Influence of Forest and Rangeland Management on Anadromous Fish Habitat in Western North America: Habitat Requirements of Anadromous Salmonids.* U.S.D.A.-Forest Service Pacific Northwest Forest and Range Expt. St. Gen. Tech. Rpt. no. PNW-96.

Reiser, D., and Wesche, T. 1977. *Determination of Physical and Hydraulic Preferences of Brown and Brook Trout in the Selection of Spawning Locations.* Univ. of Wyoming Water Resources Research Institute no. 64.

Rimmer, D.; Paim, U.; and Saunders, R. 1983. Autumnal Habitat Shift of Juvenile Atlantic Salmon (*Salmo salar*) in a Small River. *Can. J. Fish. Aquat. Sci.* 40:671–80.

Rinne, J. 1982. Movement, Home Range, and Growth of a Rare Southwestern Trout in Improved and Unimproved Habitats. *N. Am. Jrnl. of Fish. Management* 2:150–57.

Saunders, J., and Smith, M. 1962. Physical Alteration of Stream Habitat to Improve Brook Trout Production. *Trans. Am. Fish. Soc.* 91(2):185–88.

Sedell, J.; Bisson, P.; June, J.; and Speaker, R. 1982. Ecology and Habitat Requirements of Fish Populations in South Fork Hoh River, Olympic National Park. In *Ecological Research in National Parks of the Pacific Northwest*, ed. E.E. Starkey, J. Franklin and J. Mathews, pp. 47–63. Corvallis, OR: Forest Research Laboratory, Oregon State Univ.

Wesche, T. 1980. *The WRRI Trout Cover Rating Method Development and Application*, Water Resources Series, no. 78. Laramie, WY: Univ. of Wyoming, Water Resources Research Institute.

White, R. 1975. Trout Population Responses to Streamflow Fluctuation and Habitat Management in Big Roche-a-Cri Creek, WI. *Verh. Internat. Verein. Limnol.* 19:2469–77.

Wickham, M. 1967. "Physical Microhabitat of Trout." Master's thesis, Colorado State Univ., Fort Collins, CO.

Chapter 3

HOW THE STREAM AND ITS VALLEY MAKE TROUT HABITAT

To say a river is a living thing is neither a new nor a radical notion. Anglers fall in love with rivers. Poets have written odes to them. The ancient Greeks used rivers as metaphors in philosophical arguments to help explain some of the earliest theories of an ever-changing universe. Heraclitus wrote: "You cannot step into the same river twice/for other waters are ever flowing." But rivers are more dynamic than even the ancients might have imagined. From moment to moment, day to day, year to year, a river changes and is transformed by the landscape through which it flows.

As a river torrent storms down a steep canyon, it is easy to see that gravity provides the water with energy and power to carve its way through the rock to form its channel. The energy a river possesses, however, goes beyond the mechanical force of gravity.

Less obvious than the stream's mechanical energy is the biological energy the stream possesses. Below the water's surface, the dynamic of a river includes the infusion of biological energy—energy from the sun—that is incorporated by algae and aquatic plants, as well as streamside grasses, shrubs, leaves, pine cones, bark, and trees that are washed into the river. Once trapped in the stream, these organic energy sources offer the stream much of what it needs to support the healthy production of aquatic life from insects to trout.

The goal of nearly every trout-stream rehabilitation project is to restore, create, or improve trout habitat. Oftentimes, the best way to meet that goal is to allow the stream, and its associated riparian vegetation, an opportunity to heal itself. Your success as a trout-stream rehabilitator, then, may well come down to how much patience you have and how well you understand what must be done to naturally restore trout habitat in your stream and in your region.

Because all streams are not created equal, each rehabilitation project must be singular and designed to improve one particular stream, in one specific drainage, that is affected by the specific geologic and climatic conditions that dominate that region. For example, there have been many attempts to rehabilitate Rocky Mountain streams using habitat enhancement techniques developed for midwestern streams. In-stream structures developed for meandering streams in agricultural settings have been placed in steep, sinuous forested streams with well-armored beds. Most of these structures were washed out, as were the banks they were built into, during the first spring freshet, because the stream rehabilitators did not understand the natural forces that create trout habitat.

Don't make the same expensive mistake. Remember, the natural habitat-forming processes are exactly what you want to simulate.

THE INFLUENCE OF CLIMATE AND GEOLOGY

A river can only be as healthy and productive as its surroundings. As you consider a trout stream for protection or rehabilitation, you must look beyond the stream bank and consider the ecological health of the countryside. And since the life of a river—the amount of water it carries, its flow patterns, and its shape—is largely determined by the climate and the geology that dominate its watershed, you should also attempt to understand the natural systems at work in the entire drainage basin (figure 3.1).

In a nutshell, climate dictates the amount and distribution of precipitation in a watershed, which ultimately affects the runoff collected by a river. The way precipitation shapes a landscape is determined by the geologic characteristics that dominate the drainage. The richness and texture of the soil—functions of climate and geology interacting with vegetation—influence both the amount of sediment that is washed off the landscape and into a stream when winter fades into spring and the amount of water delivered to a stream when summer turns hot and dry. Vegetation, leaf litter, and roots influence the infiltration of water into the soil and runoff into the stream.

For instance, in humid climes, the relentless pressure of running water—from raindrops to rills, gullies, brooks, streams, and rivers—weathers rock into soil much faster than in an arid region (figure 3.1). Where water and soil are abundant, myriad plant life thrives, dies, and decays to create productive and well-textured soils. There is generally limited overland runoff in these areas because the precipitation absorbed by the soils flows slowly beneath the ground surface. As a result, even though there is abundant precipitation, the streams do not experience extreme swings in discharge, and because of the lack of overland flow, the landscapes generally appear soft and round. The stream drainage systems that have evolved, however, are as tangled and complex as the root systems that feed and bolster a stand of quaking aspen.

In arid and semi-arid regions, where there is less water falling on the landscape, soils are not as rich or as well textured, and the vegetation is more sparse than lush. Here rainfall, although more limited than in humid climates, is not as readily absorbed by the soil. As a result, overland runoff during high-intensity storms carves a rugged landscape, and stream flows respond dramatically to these short-term precipitation events. The stream drainage systems in arid and semi-arid regions are not as extensive as those in humid climes, simply because there is less water to transport from the watersheds.

No matter what the climate may be, soils and vegetation play key roles in every watershed. The texture of the soil—from the deep, dark, moist organic soils of the humid midwestern grasslands to the shallow, gray, thirsty soils of the semi-arid western rangelands—determines how rapidly water runs off the land and how susceptible the land is to erosion. The vegetation that is supported by the soil serves to slow the runoff, especially during storms, by absorbing raindrop energy and by producing porous soils that soak up water, which then can be slowly released to groundwater and streams.

GRAVITY, FRICTION, AND STREAM-CHANNEL FORMATION

Climate, geology, and vegetation set the stage on which the shaping of a stream channel takes place. Gravity and friction play the lead roles in a complicated and not entirely well-understood play. Grav-

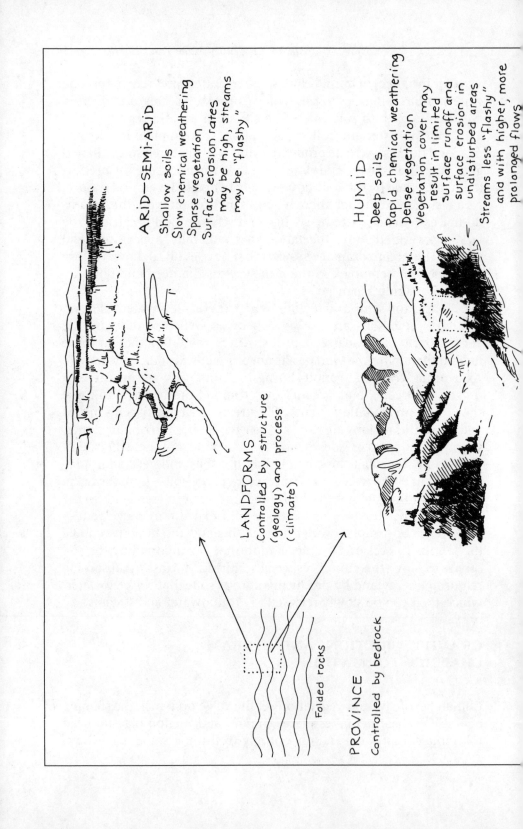

ARID—SEMI-ARID

Shallow soils
Slow chemical weathering
Sparse vegetation
Surface erosion rates
may be high, streams
may be "flashy"

HUMID
Deep soils
Rapid chemical weathering
Dense vegetation
Vegetation cover may
result in limited
surface runoff and
surface erosion in
undisturbed areas
Streams less "flashy"
and with higher, more
prolonged flows

LANDFORMS
Controlled by structure
(geology) and process
(climate)

Folded rocks

PROVINCE
Controlled by bedrock

WATERSHED

Soil and vegetation patterns may be different on opposing slopes.

cooler slope

south-facing slope (warmer)

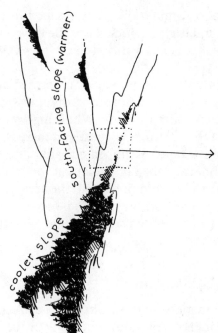

STREAM HABITAT

3.1 Geology and climate influence drainage characteristics. *The interplay of geology and climate shapes the basic character of the drainage. This influence is felt both regionally and on opposite sides—south- and north-facing slopes—of the stream.*

ity, which forces water downstream, also causes a river to carve at bed and banks, while friction between the water and the stream's bed and banks resists the river's ambition to flow undeterred downstream.

The velocity of the flowing water depends on the slope of the channel, the resistance offered by the stream's bed, vegetated banks, and its depth of flow. A deep river with the same gradient, or slope, as a shallow stream will have a much greater velocity. The resistance to the flow, however, will always be influenced by the stream's roughness, which includes the: (1) size of the materials that make up the stream's bed and banks; (2) amount and type of vegetation along the stream banks and within the wetted portion of the channel; (3) channel's degree of curvature; and (4) rock outcrops, logjams, and other flow obstructions.

The shearing action of water running over a streambed results from the interaction of gravity and friction, and causes the erosion of streambed and banks. As the water velocity increases, shear stresses tend to increase.

Many stream habitat attributes, or components, are formed during high flows, when running water encounters a roughness element, such as a log, boulder, or clump of roots. When high-water flows encounter roughness: (1) the obstruction causes an increase in turbulence and directs flows toward the streambed or banks and (2) the shear stress intensifies on the streambed or bank near the roughness element and scours the streambed and/or bank in the area of the roughness element. After the channel-forming flow has receded, the angler sees a pool near a logjam, boulder, or brushy stream bank that may be inviting habitat for lunker trout.

Channel Shape—Dynamic Equilibrium

The transport of water and sediment from the drainage basin results in the formation of stream channels. In the course of being formed, a stream may flood, change channels, scour pools, and otherwise seem unruly. Over time, if the amount of water and sediment that leaves a particular stream reach equals the amount that has entered it, the stream is said to be in dynamic equilibrium. Generally speaking, dynamic equilibrium is a condition that streams are constantly striving to maintain.

To reach and maintain dynamic equilibrium as the stream transports water and sediment, the stream and its channel will change in response to changing conditions in the watershed. For instance, if something in the watershed puts the system out of whack, such as a dramatic increase in sediment from soil and debris washed off a hillside from either natural or man-caused events, the stream's velocity, depth, and/or slope will begin to naturally adjust to maintain dynamic equilibrium.

To establish and maintain dynamic equilibrium, streams may erode the streambed to create a deeper channel, focus their energy on stream banks to create a wider channel, or deposit large loads of sediment that eventually become islands in the stream. The shape of the channel offers clues as to the health of the stream and its watershed. These clues are as important to stream rehabilitators trying to restore trout habitat as fingerprints are to detectives trying to solve a crime.

Channel Shape: Sinuous and Meandering Channels—A Matter of Degree

Because water does not flow naturally in a straight line, reaches of straight stream channels are hard to find. Even in what appears to be a straight stream channel—be it natural or artificial—the thalweg, or line of maximum water depth, shifts back and forth between the banks, creating an alternating series of gravel or mud bars from one side of the channel to the other in its wake (figure 3.2A).

This meandering flow pattern, like a switchback trail, increases the length of the channel, which effectively dissipates the force of the stream's energy over longer distances than a straight channel (figure 3.2B). The result is a more stable stream.

Nearly all stream channels have a meandering or sinuous channel pattern when viewed from above. The difference between these channel patterns is the amount of curvature of the stream channel. Measuring the distance along the center line of a channel (channel length) and dividing it by the distance measured in a straight line across the stream bends (valley length) yields a measure of stream sinuosity. Streams with a channel length versus valley length ratio less than 1.5 are considered sinuous. Those 1.5 or greater are considered meandering.

3.2 Meandering stream channels.

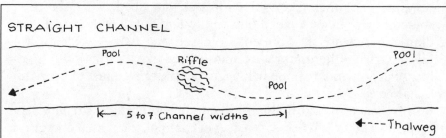

A. Even in a straight channel, the thalweg meanders within the channel creating pools, riffles, and bars.

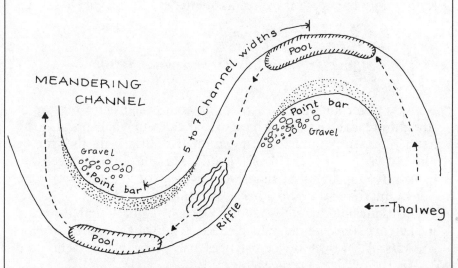

B. The meandering flow pattern increases the length of the channel between two points. This increased length effectively dissipates the force of the stream's energy over a longer distance than in a straight channel.

GRADIENT

Figure 3.3 shows that when viewed from the side, in longitudinal profile, some streams lose a great deal of elevation over short distances; others lose very little elevation over relatively long distances. The former are said to have high gradient, the latter, a low gradient. Sinuous channels generally have a high—greater than 1 percent—gradient and are associated with steep mountain headwaters and canyons. Meandering streams have a lower gradient—less than 1 percent—and are found in broad, flat valleys (figure 3.3).

Despite the fact that streams have different channel patterns and gradients, they have similar habitat types—pools, riffles, or glides. These similar habitat types are formed in different ways in different channels. A high-gradient step/pool stream reach resembles a staircase in longitudinal profile. There are abrupt drops over logs and boulders into small pools, and as the water leaves the pool, it again crashes over coarse substrate deposits into the next pool. Riffle/pool channel reaches are less steep than step/pool sections and, as the name suggests, consist of alternating riffles and pools. Meandering-channel courses have even lower gradients, but they, too, contain alternating pool and riffle habitats.

In many rivers and streams—from their headwaters to their mouths—pools, riffles, glides, eddies, backwaters, and side channels are found in both sinuous and meandering channels. The great diversity of habitats—created in part by an array of water depths and velocities—is essential to meet the needs of trout during their different life stages. This diversity of habitats is created in response to the interaction of the water's erosive power, the moderating effects of streambed and bank roughness, and the influence of streamside vegetation.

RIPARIAN VEGETATION

In the following sections you will be introduced to how very similar habitat types are created in very different ways in sinuous and meandering channels. The importance of a healthy, functioning riparian vegetation zone to the creation of trout habitat will also be continually emphasized because riparian vegetation contributes to the

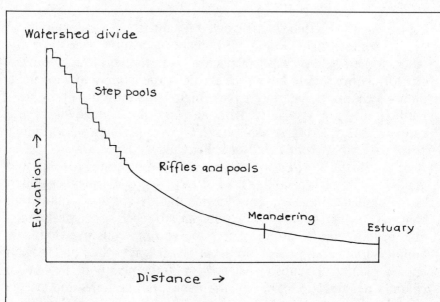

3.3 Profile of a river drainage. *The left half of the figure shows the longitudinal profile of a drainage. In the headwaters a great deal of elevation is lost over short distances. The streams in this area are relatively straight and have a stair-step or step-pool appearance. Farther downstream the gradient is less, and the stream assumes a pool and riffle configuration. As the gradient continues to flatten, the river becomes more meandering and creates a wide and fertile floodplain.*

The right half of the figure shows the location of these stream types in the landscape.

WATERSHED DIVIDE

STEP POOLS
Gradient more than 4%
Boulder, cobble
Cutthroat, brook trout

RIFFLES AND POOLS
Gradient 1—4%
Boulder, cobble, gravel
Coho, steelhead, cutthroat

MEANDERING
Gradient less than 1%
Gravel silt
Brown trout, rainbow trout

healthy functioning of a stream channel and helps to create trout habitat in the following ways:

1. Roots of trees, shrubs, sedges, and grasses bind the stream bank soil particles and provide resistance to the erosive forces of flowing water. This leads to a narrower, deeper channel with complex and diverse banks.
2. Stems and leaves of stream-bank vegetation provide shade that prevents high water temperatures.
3. Leaves, stems, cones, fruit, and other plant parts that fall into the stream provide food for microbes, insects, and, ultimately, trout.
4. Large woody debris that falls into the stream from a healthy riparian forest provides cover, as well as channel roughness elements that lead to the formation of pools and other habitat types.
5. Stems of healthy floodplain riparian vegetation reduce water velocity during floods, leading to sediment deposition and storage in the floodplain.
6. Healthy floodplains store water during floods and release it to the stream during summer, which helps to maintain base flows even during hot, dry months.

Sinuous Channels

The streambed of sinuous channels is often composed of relatively large substrate materials, such as gravel, cobble, and boulders. These are resistant to the tremendous shear stress caused by the high-velocity flows that occur in moderate- to high-gradient streams. This layer of erosion-resistant substrate particles is called armor. Channel erosion in sinuous channels is also reduced by a series of washboardlike gravel bars and pool-forming log steps, which are created by fallen trees and other large woody debris recruited to the stream from the riparian forest.

As flowing water approaches these natural obstructions, it forms ponds behind the gravel bars and log dams. In turn, water velocities slow, allowing the fine sediment the water is transporting to be deposited, particularly near channel banks. Over time, as these deposits accumulate, a gentler channel slope will be established. As water flows over roughness elements during high flows, its turbulent energy attacks the bed and eventually scours a pool.

LARGE WOODY DEBRIS

As suggested above, woody debris is the product of an old-growth riparian forest ecosystem. It is important in the creation of a variety of habitat types in sinuous streams and contributes to habitat diversity. Debris dams create roughness in the channel, which leads to an increase in turbulence and a corresponding decrease in the water's mechanical energy as the water scours pools.

In addition to creating pools, woody debris serves to stabilize sinuous streams, as it actually increases the complexity and diversity of stream habitats. In figure 3.4 you will notice that even where large logs do not span the channel, smaller logs and root-wad accumulations along the banks cause cutoffs, which create backwater pools and eddies. Sometimes woody debris can even help to develop side channels that provide excellent rearing and wintering habitats for trout.

The root systems of the riparian vegetation provide stream-bank stability in the face of high stream flows. Important escape cover is often provided by undercut banks and the exposed root systems that hold the bank together.

The riparian forest and the woody debris it contributes to the stream are also major factors in determining the bioenergetics of the stream. Debris dams and jams trap waterborne grasses, twigs, cones, and leaves that in time decay behind the dam. This decaying organic matter becomes the food for aquatic insects, which, in turn, are the principal food item for trout.

Sediment Storage. Large woody debris creates important storage areas for inorganic sediment, such as sand and silt. In small headwater streams, debris can prevent large quantities of fine sediment from being suddenly and catastrophically deposited on important spawning areas. If the woody debris were not in place to buffer against rapid changes in sediment loading, rearing pools could be filled, spawning gravels could be degraded, and aquatic insects, commonly associated with riffle habitats, could be reduced or eliminated.

Bioenergetics. The retention of organic litter—leaves, needles, twigs, branches, bark, nuts, and fruits—in pools formed by woody debris is

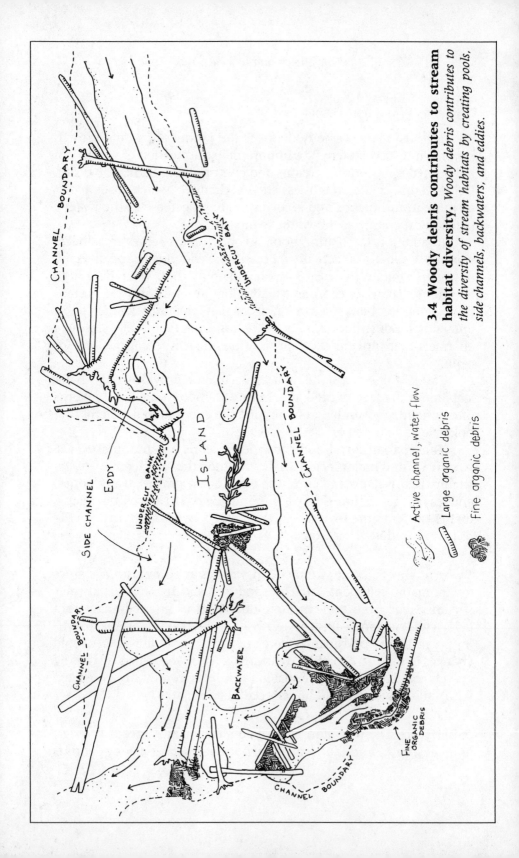

3.4 Woody debris contributes to stream habitat diversity. *Woody debris contributes to the diversity of stream habitats by creating pools, side channels, backwaters, and eddies.*

Active channel, water flow

Large organic debris

Fine organic debris

CHANNEL BOUNDARY

UNDERCUT BAN

ISLAND

EDDY

SIDE CHANNEL

UNDERCUT BANK

CHANNEL BOUNDARY

CHANNEL BOUNDARY

BACKWATER

FINE ORGANIC DEBRIS

CHANNEL BOUNDARY

a fundamental component of healthy trout habitat because it forms the base of the food chain in most headwater streams.

Organic litter is especially important in small streams where the sunlight has difficulty penetrating dense riparian forests and canyon walls to activate photosynthesis by algae and other in-stream plant life. By slowing the downstream flow of organic litter, ample time is provided for the material to decompose and become the prime food source of microbes. The microbes become the prime food source of aquatic insects, which are, of course, the principal food of the trout that inhabit the stream.

How important is woody debris to the bioenergetics of a stream? In a study of a very small stream in a deciduous forest in New Hampshire, researchers found 99 percent of the stream's biological energy came from the bits, pieces, and chunks of terrestrial vegetation that fell into the stream, and not from in-stream algae as one might suspect.

The moral is trout-stream rehabilitators can adequately fashion an artificial series of log structures, but without a healthy riparian forest to regulate the energy base of the aquatic system, they will have created riffles and pools that are not very productive. Conversely, if the riparian forest is eliminated, the sun can reach the in-stream algae and increase the production of in-stream food sources, but there will be no woody debris to contribute to habitat diversity, store sediment, and otherwise contribute to the functioning of the stream's ecosystem.

Meandering Channels

The same forces that shape sinuous channels—gravity and the balancing counterforce of frictional resistance—are at work in meandering channels. However, since meandering streams usually flow across broad, gentle floodplains rather than down narrow, steep canyons, the forces combine to create a much different river system.

Meandering channels generally form in easily eroded alluvium, or water-deposited, sediments. Over time, as the channel migrates back and forth across the valley floodplain, the water works its way through old territory. Shallow aquifers, which provide natural off-stream, underground water storage within the alluvium, are refilled during floods with water that can later be tapped by riparian vegetation. As stream flows recede, the aquifer also can repay old debts to the river as its water seeps into the stream to help maintain late-summer base flows. All the while, the river locally erodes, transports, and deposits sediments that were once part of its streambed.

Migration of the meander, over a period of many years, results in a river channel that has occupied several positions between the valley walls, as it has formed a broad, flat, and generally, very fertile floodplain.

In meandering channels, pools usually form at outside bends, where turbulence increases because of the curvature of the channel. Riffles normally form where the thalweg crosses over from a pool on one bank to a pool on the opposite side.

An idealized flow pattern of a typical meander is shown in figure 3.5. The left side of the illustration shows how the depth of the channel changes as water shapes the meander bend. The deepest portion, which occurs at the apex of the curve (cross section C), is the pool where undercut banks and overhanging brush test the mettle of anglers. Opposite the pool, a gravel bar forms where the sediment load that has been eroded from upstream banks is deposited (figures 3.5 and 3.6).

The riffle, or shallowest point—where trout often feed—is where the thalweg crosses the channel as it leaves one bank and moves toward the opposite bank (cross section E; figure 3.5). The streamlines that illustrate the surface flow are shown in the right-hand portion of the figure. In brief, the water slowly bounces from bank to bank as the thalweg sways from side to side in the channel. The result is the alternative occurrence of pools and riffles as the stream flows through the channel.

Riparian Vegetation and Woody Debris

The natural process of bank erosion that creates pools with undercut banks on the outside bends of a meandering channel also leads to the creation of eddies, backwaters, sloughs, and oxbows, all of which provide important trout habitat. A common mistake in stream reha-bilitation efforts is to try to stabilize the eroding banks on the outside of meander bends. This eroding process is natural and creates prime habitat. However, the benefits of erosion are directly related to the rate of erosion, which is a function of the condition of the stream

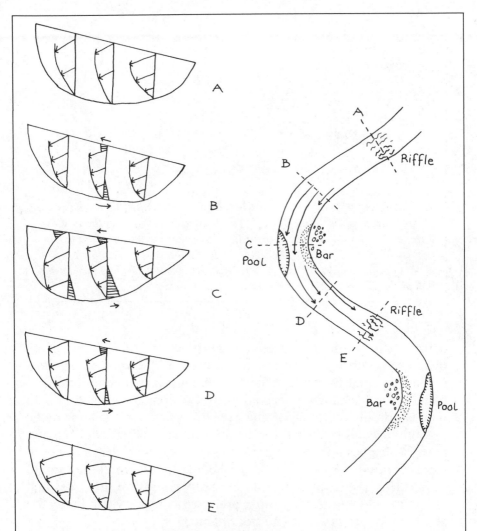

3.5 Water velocity and depth through a meander. *The left side of this illustration shows how water depth and velocity change through a meander. Relative velocity is indicated by the length of the arrows. In the riffle at cross section A, the water is deepest and fastest along the left downstream bank. As water flows through the meander (cross section C), the water is much deeper and faster on the right downstream concave bank than elsewhere along the channel cross section.*

The right side of the figure shows pool formation on the concave bank and gravel deposition on the convex bank, where velocity is much lower.

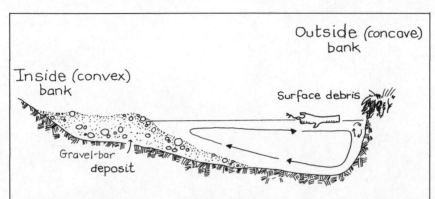

3.6 Cross section of a meander bed. *This figure shows the cross-sectional detail of pool and gravel-bar formation of the apex of the meander bend. The arrows show that as the water flows downstream, it is also moving in a circular motion within the channel. This is because of the differences in water velocities along the cross section. This circular motion causes pool formation at the concave bank and deposition on the convex bank.*

bank. If healthy riparian vegetation is present, the root systems of the plants will allow the erosion to proceed and, at the same time, manage to hold the banks together. The result will be an undercut bank with overhanging vegetation. If the riparian vegetation is in poor condition, the erosion can be greatly accelerated, leading to the loss of land and to dished out banks—those with an angle greater than 90 degrees—that do not provide cover. Often the response to this situation is to provide structural bank protection in the form of riprap. However, riprap retards the natural erosion processes and attempts to lock a stream into a preferred course, which limits the ability of the stream to create trout habitat.

Riparian vegetation plays an essential protective role by supplying the floodplain with a blanket of vegetation that slows the eroding power of swift floodwaters. During flood flows, the streamside vegetation lies flat against the banks and protects them from accelerated erosion. As the floodwaters rise, leave the channel, and flow out over the floodplain, the riparian vegetation slows the water and allows it to percolate into the alluvial groundwater aquifer. The vegetation also filters out the sediment, which is then incorporated into the floodplain. This is the process by which fertile floodplains are formed.

Riparian vegetation contributes large amounts of leaf litter to the valley streams, just as it does in headwater streams. However, since meandering streams are generally wider than headwater streams, sunlight can reach the stream and supply energy for in-stream algae and other aquatic plant growth.

Braided Channels

Although similar to a meandering channel, a braided channel is an easily distinguished pattern of river bars or islands that are woven together by a net of numerous small, interconnected watercourses (figure 3.7). The principal difference between meandering and braided channels is that braided channels generally have poorly defined, unstable banks and are characterized by steeper and shallower watercourses. Because braided channels are shallow and relatively broad, their overall greater roughness reduces flow velocities. Thus, the sediment loads that are deposited form the bars or islands characteristic of this channel pattern.

Where sediment loads of coarse material are relatively high,

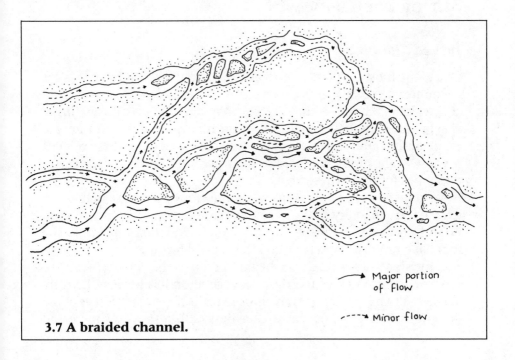

→ Major portion of flow

---→ Minor flow

3.7 A braided channel.

braiding appears to result from the inability of the stream to transport this eroded material. When the rocks drop from the slowing water flow, other debris and finer sediments in the load become trapped in the coarse rock deposits. These deposits gradually grow to form midstream bars. The midstream bars then divert the flow toward other channel deposits and banks, which results in the formation of yet another bar or island downstream (figure 3.8).

The factor essential to formation of a braided channel is a sediment supply that greatly exceeds the river's ability to transport it, which is why many braided rivers occur in active glacial areas. The easily eroded character of the banks stems from the fact that they consist of recently deposited alluvium. These streams are so dynamic that the riparian vegetation needed to stabilize the banks does not have time to become established. Therefore, there is a constant and abundant source of material to form the bars and islands. Accordingly, braiding does not usually occur where banks are densely vegetated and sediment transport is low.

ALTERED STATES—STREAM CHANNELS OUT OF EQUILIBRIUM

Incised Channels

One of the most frequent stream ailments trout-habitat rehabilitators encounter, especially in the western U.S. and Canada, is down-cut and widened channels that are virtually devoid of bank-stabilizing vegetation. Incised channels can occur in any climate, but they are particularly common in arid and semi-arid deserts and rangelands because of the easily eroded, fine-textured soils and dry-site vegetation types found in these areas.

An incised channel results when the erosive forces of high flows exceed the capability of the streambed to resist erosion. Incision can occur in response to events in the stream or surrounding landscape that have radically upset the channel's equilibrium.

Incision of the channel begins because the stream's erosive power has escalated or the riparian vegetation has been sufficiently abused so that it no longer functions to resist the erosive forces of the flowing water. Perhaps the swifter flows are a result of increased

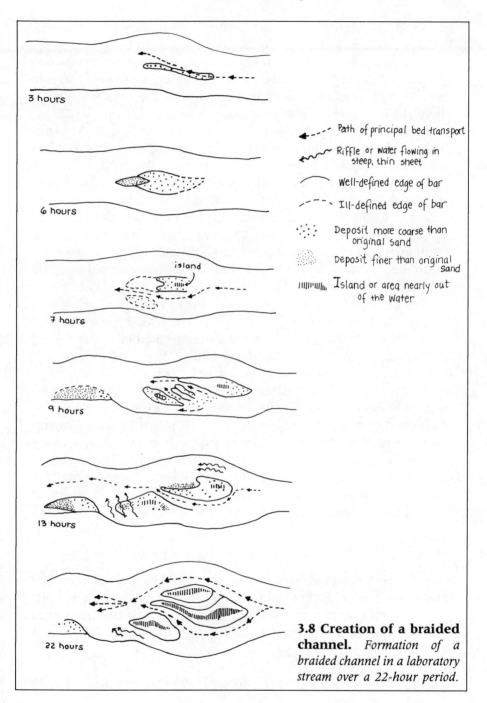

3.8 Creation of a braided channel. *Formation of a braided channel in a laboratory stream over a 22-hour period.*

runoff, channelization, or debris removal (including beaver dams). Perhaps streamside vegetation has been removed by grazing, logging, farming, or urbanization. The nick point migrating upstream as an erosive head cut may initiate incision (described in detail later in this chapter). For any of a variety of reasons, the channel initiates down cutting and begins to establish a new equilibrium.

Once incision has been initiated, the stream channel will continue to enlarge until a new equilibrium is established. The problem is that after incision begins, channel-forming flood flows become confined within the channel, because the stream channel has been cut below the floodplain. Confined flood flows can be incredibly erosive, and the erosional response of stream channels to incision can be dramatic. For instance, 15 years after it was channelized, width increases of up to 800 percent were measured in Mississippi's Oaklimiter Creek. The stream also had depth increases of up to 400 percent and cross-sectional increases of up to 1,000 percent.

On the other hand, extreme decreases in sediment input to a stream result in water with such excessive erosive power that it erodes the bed and begins to incise the stream channel. Water energy is dissipated, in part, by picking up and transporting sediment. If upstream sediment supplies are cut off, the stream may initiate long-term erosion of the bed and banks. This is seldom, if ever, a management problem for trout streams. However, a classic example of this phenomenon is the Colorado River downstream of Glen Canyon Dam. Because the dam traps sediment, water leaving the dam has an increased erosive capability. As a result, downstream of the dam, the Colorado River has been eroding beaches (gravel bars) along the riverbanks. Today, people floating the Colorado River are finding it increasingly difficult to locate beaches for camping.

EVOLUTION OF AN INCISED CHANNEL

Figure 3.9 offers an idealized look at an incised stream channel. The illustration shows the evolution of an incised channel at a specific point over time and how the stream degradation or incision migrates from its point of inception upstream as the stream cuts down to a new base level.

Condition 1. The channel is not incised and supports a productive riparian vegetation resource.

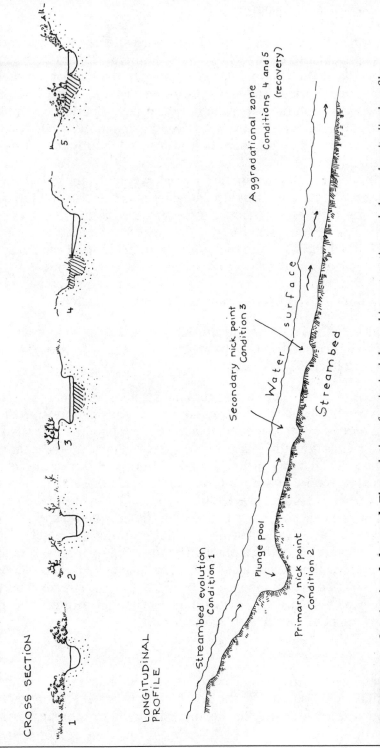

CROSS SECTION

LONGITUDINAL PROFILE

Streambed evolution
Condition 1

Plunge Pool

Primary nick point
Condition 2

Secondary nick point
Condition 3

Water surface

Streambed

Aggradational zone
Conditions 4 and 5
(recovery)

3.9 Evolution of an incised channel. *The evolution of an incised channel in cross section and along a longitudinal profile.*

Condition 2. Riparian vegetation is degraded and no longer provides protection against erosive flood flows (and/or stream-hydrology changes), and the channel becomes incised. The local water table, which is tied to the stream-water surface elevation, also is lowered, and over a period of years much of the typical riparian vegetation dies. The riparian vegetation is replaced by dryland vegetation with thin, weak root systems that are less effective at providing stream-bank stability.

This is the nick point in the longitudinal profile, the point where the stream is actively cutting through the bed. Directly below the nick point, where the stream is already incised, is a plunge pool or waterfall. The cutting will continue at the nick point until a new base level is reached. Then the nick point will continue to migrate upstream. The upstream adjustment in base level will continue until the stream and its tributaries have been degraded to a new base level or until a nonerosive material, such as bedrock, is reached.

Condition 3. The banks become too steep for the weak root systems of the dry-site vegetation to hold and begin to slough off, creating a very wide, unstable, shallow channel.

Conditions 4 and 5. The stream channel begins to gradually reestablish its original form in the aggradation zone, as riparian vegetation begins to reestablish a new floodplain. The new floodplain, located at a lower elevation than the original, was created as the channel widened. Flood flows are no longer confined as during the early stages of incision. Thus, flood flows may spread out, slow down, and deposit their sediment load. This fertile soil can be invaded by riparian-plant species, since the level of the new floodplain is once again near the elevation of the alluvial groundwater aquifer that provides water for riparian plants. The invading riparian vegetation traps more sediment and leads to further development of the floodplain. Riparian vegetation also helps to stabilize the stream channel as the water begins to carve a narrow channel through the reestablishment of a more stable floodplain.

Incised-channel Restoration

Activities leading to channel incisement can have far-reaching effects in a drainage basin and to the pocketbook of anyone interested in stream restoration. The key to incised-channel restoration is reestablishment of an effective floodplain and its associated riparian vegetation. The major management effort should be directed at maintaining and enhancing riparian vegetation typically adapted to the conditions in the floodplain.

Effective options for restoration of an incised channel that rely on in-stream structures are limited. Conditions 2 and 3 are extremely difficult and expensive to treat structurally because the stream is actively cutting at bed and banks. The best option is probably to wait until the channel evolves into conditions 4 and 5. The most cost-effective management strategy for conditions 4 and 5 is simply to allow for vigorous reestablishment of stream-bank and riparian vegetation and to permit for the natural development of effective floodplains.

Aggrading Stream Channels

An aggrading stream channel is one that is rising relative to the surrounding landscape because its pools, backwaters, and channel edges are being filled with sediment. Aggradation is caused by the decreased ability of a stream to transport its sediment load. Sediment that is not transported fills pools and covers riffles as it is deposited.

To learn more about the effect increased sediment loads have on riffles, researchers added sand to water at the head of a large flume fashioned to resemble a streambed with sand and gravel riffles. Following the test, the researchers surprisingly found only a small increase in the amount of sand in the riffles. An even greater surprise was that the volume of gravel in the riffles decreased. Increased amounts of sand sediment apparently reduced gravel stability and resulted in sand deposits in pools, backwaters, and channel edges as flows receded. It was not until these areas became full of sediment that the sand was deposited on the riffles. The end result was that the channel lost its pool/riffle expression and became hydraulically smoother.

It is interesting that both an event that leads to degradation of a stream channel—like channelization—and one that leads to aggradation—like increased sediment loads—can result in a wide, shallow stream. In each case, however, the physical processes set in motion to restore dynamic equilibrium are spurred on for opposite reasons: Previously deposited bed materials are sluiced out of the degrading stream channel. On the other hand, the aggrading streambed is burdened by an inability to transport its sediment load. Unlike incised channels, channels undergoing pronounced aggradation are relatively rare and short in length.

Laterally Unstable Channels

A laterally unstable channel often occurs when changes in riparian vegetation—whether from poor livestock-grazing practices, timber harvests, road construction, urbanization, farming, or other land-use activities—affect stream-flow patterns in well-armored channels. This channel type is common, and several examples of trout-habitat rehabilitation work that address this problem are discussed in chapter 7. Without the roughness and soil-binding properties provided by the roots of riparian vegetation, and the bank protection provided by overhanging vegetation during flood flows, the stream banks become increasingly susceptible to erosion. The outcome can be a wide, shallow stream channel (figure 3.10A).

In most cases the prescription for this type of stream-channel problem is a healthy dose of riparian vegetation to restore stability to the stream banks. As the recovery of the vegetation progresses, it will trap the sediments at high flows. These will be used to build new, healthy stream banks (figures 3.10B and 3.10C).

More aggressive management, however, may be required if the soil has been removed or if the stream system has become too unstable to permit successful revegetation. Bank-erosion controls, such as the strategic placement of conifer trunks and limbs to retard erosion and trap sediment that can be colonized by riparian plants, are among the many techniques that may improve revegetation. In extreme cases channels may have to be totally reconstructed—a very expensive endeavor—to create the conditions needed to reestablish a riparian community.

Restoration Requires Changes in Land Use

Attempts to create trout habitat that ignore the land-use problems that led to the stream's altered condition will meet with minimal success. A U.S.D.A. Forest Service study of two reaches of Utah's Big Creek illustrates this point. Because the pastures along Big Creek were heavily grazed for nearly 100 years, the surrounding riparian vegetation was degraded, and, as a result, the channel was laterally unstable.

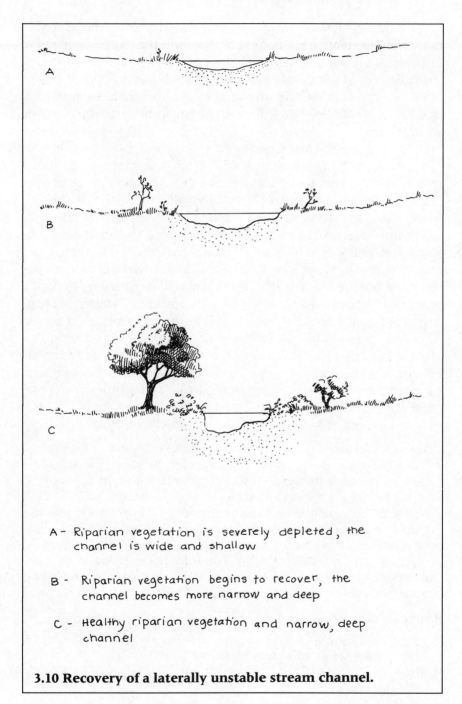

A – Riparian vegetation is severely depleted, the channel is wide and shallow

B – Riparian vegetation begins to recover, the channel becomes more narrow and deep

C – Healthy riparian vegetation and narrow, deep channel

3.10 Recovery of a laterally unstable stream channel.

Cattle were fenced out of one area, and structures were placed in the stream to create trout habitat both within the fenced area and in an upstream reach that was still being grazed by cattle. The upstream structures could not be maintained and soon failed. Cattle inadvertently destroyed many of the structures, and their trampling of the bank eventually caused most of the other structures to be washed out.

The structures within the fenced area proved to be more durable and appeared to improve the reach's trout habitat, but they didn't result in an increase in the number of trout. Although the structures improved the pool/riffle habitat and overall pool quality within the fenced area, the structures also trapped large amounts of fine sediments from the upstream cattle-caused erosion. The sediment deposition apparently counteracted the trout-habitat improvements.

With that in mind, all trout-stream habitat-rehabilitation project leaders should remember: (1) the stream and its riparian vegetation work together to create trout habitat; (2) a protected stream left to its own devices will tend to heal itself; (3) a stream restoration project must consider not only the stream channel and riparian corridor but also the land uses throughout the drainage that may be affecting the condition of the stream channel; and (4) trout-habitat rehabilitation may eventually involve the entire drainage and all the factors that contribute to the shaping of the stream channel.

As biologist H.B.N. Hynes so eloquently wrote:

> We may conclude . . . that in every respect the valley rules the stream. Its rock determines . . . its soil, its clay, even its slope. The soil and climate determine the vegetation, and the vegetation rules the supply of organic matter. The organic matter reacts with the soil to control the release of ions, and the ions control the decay of litter, and hence lie right at the root of the food cycle. One could go on and on, building up an edifice of complexity, all linked and cross linked . . . [that] will take much unravelling. [These relationships] do, however, make it clear that every stream is likely to be an individual [and that] changes in the valley wrought by man have large effects.

SOURCES

Beschta, R., and Platts, W. 1986. Morphological Features of Small Streams: Significance and Function. *Water Resources Bulletin* 22 (3):369–79.

Bilby, R., and Likens, G. 1980. Importance of Organic Debris Dams in the Structure and Function of Stream Ecosystems. *Ecology* 61 (5):1107–113.

Bisson, P.; Bilby, R.; Bryant, M.; Dolloff, C.; Grette, G.; House, R.; Murphy, M.; Koski, K.; and Sedell, J. 1987. Large Woody Debris in Forested Streams in the Pacific Northwest: Past, Present and Future. In *Streamside Management: Forestry and Fishery Interactions*, ed. Salo and Cundy, pp. 143–90. Seattle: Univ. of Washington Institute of Forest Resources Contrb no. 57.

Cummins, K. 1974. Structure and Function of Stream Ecosystems. *BioScience* 24 (11):631–41.

Elmore, W., and Beschta, R. 1987. Riparian Areas: Perceptions in Management. *Rangelands* 9 (6):260–65.

Harvey, M., and Watson, C. 1986. Fluvial Processes and Morphological Thresholds in Incised Channel Restoration. *Water Res. Bull.* 22(3):359–68.

Heede, B. 1980. *Stream Dynamics: An Overview for Land Managers*. U.S.D.A. Forest Service Gen. Tech. Rpt. no. RM-72. Fort Collins, CO: Rocky Mountain Forest and Range Expt. Station.

————. 1986. Designing for Dynamic Equilibrium in Streams. *Water Res. Bull.* 22(3):351–58.

Hynes, H. B. N. 1975. The Stream and Its Valley. Edgardo Baldi Memorial Lecture: Vern. Internat. Verein. Limnol 19.

Jackson, W., and Beschta, R., 1984. Influences of Increased Sand Delivery on the Morphology of Sand and Gravel Channels. *Water Res. Bull.* 20(4):527–33.

Leopold, L., and Langbein, W. 1966. River Meanders. *Sci. Am.* 214(6):60–70.

Leopold, L.; Wolman, M.; and Miller, T. *Fluvial Processes in Geomorphology*. San Francisco, CA: W.H. Freeman and Company.

Lotspeich, F. 1980. Watershed as the Basic Ecosystem: This Conceptual Framework Provides a Basis for a Natural Classification System. *Water Resources Bulletin* 16(4):581–86.

Meehan, W.; Swanson, F.; and Sedell, J. 1977. Influences of Riparian Vegetation on Aquatic Ecosystems with Particular Reference to Salmonid Fishes and Their Food Supply. Symposium on the Importance, Preservation and Management of the Riparian Habitat.

Ministry of Environment, 1980. *Stream Enhancement Guide*. Province of British Columbia, Vancouver, BC.

Platts, W., and Rinne, J. 1982. *Riparian-Stream Protection and Enhancement Research in the Rocky Mountains*. Jackson, WY: Proceedings of the Rocky Mountain Stream Habitat Management Workshop.

Schumm, S.; Harvey, M.; and Watson, C. *Incised Channels: Morphology, Dynamics and Control*. Littleton, CO: Water Resources Publications.

Sullivan, K.; Lisle, T.; Dolloff, C.; Grant, G.; and Reid, L. 1987. Stream Channels: The Link Between Forests and Fishes, In *Streamside Management: Forestry and Fishery Interactions*, eds. E. Salo, and T. Cundy, pp. 39–98. Seattle: Univ. of Washington Institute of Forest Resources Contrib. no. 57.

Van Haveran, B., and Jackson, W. Concepts in Stream Riparian Rehabilitation. *Trans. 51st N. A. Wildl. and Nat. Res. Conf.*

Vannote, R.; Minshall, G.; Cummins, K.; Sedell, J.; and Cushing, C. 1980. The River Continuum Concept. *Can. J. Fish. Aquat. Sci.* 37:130–37.

Chapter 4

INVENTORY, MONITORING, AND EVALUATION

TROUT-STREAM rehabilitation—especially when it employs deflectors and other artificial in-stream constructions—too often appears to resemble something akin to wizardry. If its methods appear to use more magic than science, it is, at least in part, because it is such a young scientific discipline. In the United States and Canada, there are but a handful of trout-habitat rehabilitation experts. Even though they have come by their expertise the hard way—through decades of painstaking experience—none will claim full mastery of the trout-habitat rehabilitation process.

A STREAM TO REHABILITATE

The business of trout-habitat rehabilitation can get technical, so it is imperative to prepare early to seek help, especially when it comes time to collect, analyze, and interpret the data. In many states and provinces, fish and game agencies are often eager to provide assistance for fish and wildlife habitat rehabilitation projects. (See the table 4.5 at the end of this chapter.)

At the outset, you must acquire a general understanding of historic and current land uses in the stream drainage. By now, this should be a familiar theme, and you should accept the notion that even minor changes in land use can often result in major changes in in-stream trout habitat.

To gain an essential critical eye, you'll need to develop or employ skills to observe and interpret the elements that affect the stream's world. An ancillary requirement is the ability to state the observations in a numerical form, so they can be measured to make meaningful comparisons. This chapter offers a detailed course to help you develop such observation skills and make the measurements essential to a trout-habitat rehabilitation project. Without a doubt, it is a difficult and often very technical exercise, but if it is dutifully followed, you will emerge with a clearer understanding of the problems that plague your stream.

For the purposes of this book, there are eight major phases to every trout-habitat rehabilitation project:

1. Select your stream.
2. Gather a group of experts to guide you through the interdisciplinary inventories and planning processes.
3. Take inventory of the physical and biologic features of the drainage basin.
4. Identify the problems that limit trout production.
5. Design the project.
6. Finalize planning and preparation.
7. Estimate project maintenance.
8. Monitor and evaluate the project.

The goal of this chapter is to successfully guide you through the first three phases of the process, and to introduce you to the importance of monitoring the project once your initial work has ended.

LAND-USE MAPPING

The reasons trout are not as abundant as they once were in a particular stream probably are related to adjacent and distant land uses. It is, therefore, important to take a thorough inventory of physical and biologic features of the drainage basin. Some of the work that must be performed may already be available but much will have to be done by yourself, state or federal agencies, or by professional consultants. Check with the state fish and game agency, federal land-management agencies, and the local college or university.

In the most basic sense, land-use mapping is an exercise that forces you to look very closely at the drainage and how land-use patterns affect the stream. When you physically map the land use, you will be actively observing an ongoing activity or the evidence of past use and abuse that may have forced the stream out of its dynamic equilibrium and diminished trout habitat in the process.

An aerial photograph of the area, especially a series taken over a period of several years, can be the best investment made in this phase of the restoration project. Black-and-white photographs will show the location of trees, shrubs, streams, highways, urban, industrial, and agricultural areas. Color infrared photos, which are not as widely available and slightly more expensive than black-and-white photos, often provide more information, especially with regard to vegetation types and species. However, they are not absolutely necessary for this general mapping strategy.

Aerial photos can be obtained for a minimal cost from the local U.S. Department of Agriculture Soil Conservation Service-Agricultural Stabilization and Conservation Service (SCS-ASCS), the U.S. Forest Service (USFS), the Bureau of Land Management (BLM), or the U.S. Geological Survey (USGS). If you have difficulty obtaining aerial photos, obtain the brochure: *How to Order Aerial Photographs* from the following sources: *United States* at the National Cartographic Information Center, U.S. Geological Survey, 507 National Center, Reston, VA 22092 (703-860-6045); *Canada* at the National Air Photo Library, 615 Booth Street, Ottawa, Canada KIA OE9 (613-995-4510).

If you are still unable to find aerial photographs, consider having some taken by a local flying service. If the pilot does not have to travel far and takes only black-and-white photos, the cost may not be prohibitive.

A great supplement to aerial photos are USGS 7.5 minute-series topographic maps. Because these detailed maps are at a 2.64 inches-per-mile scale, it may require several maps to cover your area, but the cost of the maps is minimal. Likely sources of topo maps include the USGS, USFS, BLM, sporting good stores, bookstores, or the local college. If you have difficulty obtaining a topo map of your area, contact the National Cartographic Information Center in the United States or in *Canada* at the Map Distribution Office, 615 Booth Street, Ottawa, Canada KIA OE9 (613-995-4510).

If aerial photos and topographic maps are absolutely unavailable, try to obtain any map that is scaled so that you can identify small (20-acre) parcels of land. A county road map may suit your purposes.

MAPPING LAND-USE PATTERNS

With map and aerial photos in hand, take a tour of your drainage by car, bike, foot, or small airplane, and draw in the current land uses. Whether working with a map or an aerial photo, it is a good idea to tape several sheets of clear mylar on the map or photo. That way you can draw each different land use on a separate sheet to clearly identify it without marring the originals.

On forested land, note the extent of logging, the harvest practices used, and whether roads are failing or otherwise contributing sediment to the stream.

On agricultural land, determine the crops planted, the livestock grazed, and, if possible, the grazing techniques employed (rest rotation, season long, Savory method, etc.). Also note if the land is farmed adjacent to the stream banks or if there is a strip of riparian vegetation between fields and the stream. Draw in fence lines, noting differences in vegetation on both sides of the fence.

On land developed for housing and industry, note where sewage treatment plants discharge to the stream and which industries use or manufacture potentially toxic chemicals, pesticides, or herbicides.

When you map the riparian zone, note where vegetation exists and where it has been removed by logging, livestock grazing, or housing developments. Make note of the width of the riparian zone and its composition. Is the vegetation composed of grasses, sedges, willows, trees, or a mix of these components?

Finally, pay particular attention to the stream channel. Try to determine if it has been straightened or channelized. Look for places on the aerial photographs to see if old meander channels of the stream have been cut off. A long-practiced water-management technique is to short-circuit the meander pattern with a straight reach, which shortens the stream length and leads to increased velocities and, most likely, an incised channel. Old photos or local historical records may document conditions of a channel prior to major land-use activity and may be helpful in understanding how the channel has evolved.

STREAM CHANNEL AND IN-STREAM HABITAT INVENTORIES

At the conclusion of your broad reconnaissance of the drainage, it is not unusual for a fit of depression to set in. The realization that the surrounding landscape—not just the stream—has been drastically altered can be disheartening. The enormous land-use complications can seem to dwarf a comparatively insignificant stream rehabilitation project. But, don't despair. The extent of the problems within the stream will not be apparent until you begin to measure and rate the trout-habitat attributes. Once you understand how important cover, pools, and streamside vegetation are to trout, you will begin to recognize how land-use practices are related to the specific problems that may be limiting the stream's trout production.

Trout-stream inventories take time and effort but, in the end, are worth every minute. The ultimate objective of an inventory is to determine the present condition of a stream in relation to its potential or desired condition. Through this inventory you will eventually discover the condition of the existing habitat, document what is lacking, and finally decide where improvements must be made to produce more trout. The basics for a thorough habitat inventory begin with a transect system, habitat maps, and a series of photo points.

Transect Systems

A transect is a sample area established to determine and monitor the environmental condition of a stream reach. It's a simple procedure to establish a number of transects, or straight lines, across the stream channel perpendicular to the flow. The transects become reference points and the stream inventory's sampling points (figure 4.1).

To establish a transect, on a point well above the high-water mark on each bank, drive steel reinforcing bars at least three feet deep into the ground to prevent them from moving should the soil freeze or a flood occur.

How far upstream you place the next transect depends on what you want to accomplish. For an intensive study of stream ecology, the transects will be closely spaced, perhaps no more than ten feet apart. Generally, however, to obtain the reconnaissance information you will need to select a project reach, a regular 100- to 200-foot spacing between transects is adequate. Later, when you gather infor-

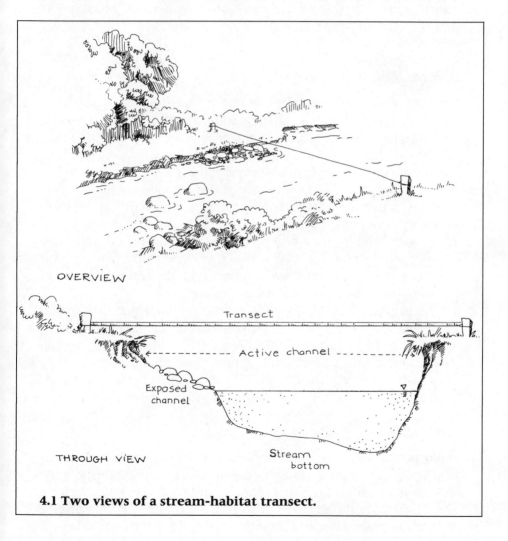

OVERVIEW

Transect

Active channel

Exposed channel

THROUGH VIEW

Stream bottom

4.1 Two views of a stream-habitat transect.

mation to determine the habitat conditions that will ultimately drive your rehabilitation project, transects should be established every 10 to 50 feet within the project area.

Once you have established the transect points, and are prepared to gather information about the reach, stretch a fiberglass measuring tape between the stakes on both banks. Along these transects you will inventory and measure the following: riparian vegetation, stream-bank stability, substrate composition and condition, water depth and velocity, in-stream cover, and pool/riffle habitats. You need to think about how these conditions have been altered and how they compare to potential or desirable conditions for any particular stream.

Habitat Mapping

The most important companion to a transect system is a habitat map. Preparing a habitat map is somewhat more demanding than collecting data along habitat transects, but maps can vary from freehand sketches of a stream reach (figure 4.2) to very accurate, professionally surveyed and plotted representations.

As in the use of aerial photos and USGS topographic maps, the best habitat inventory will combine transects and mapping. You will discover that some habitat attributes are more amenable to mapping than others. The location of woody debris, pools, riffles, water and channel width, eroding banks, and cover are easily mapped. Yet other important attributes, such as water depths and velocities and substrate compositions, are not mapped so easily.

By using a regularly spaced transect system in combination with a land-use map, even your first stream inventory will identify areas that require restoration. Within the reaches you identify needing rehabilitation, you can establish a more intensive transect system. With transects established from 10 to 50 feet, you can draw freehand a fairly accurate map of in-stream habitat attributes.

Photo Points

Photo points are easily identified spots near the project area from which you can take a series of photographs to document the progress of the rehabilitation project. A photo point could be a boulder or a tree, or you could paint a fence post to mark the spot that gives a clear, photographic view of the project area. In any case, it is best to

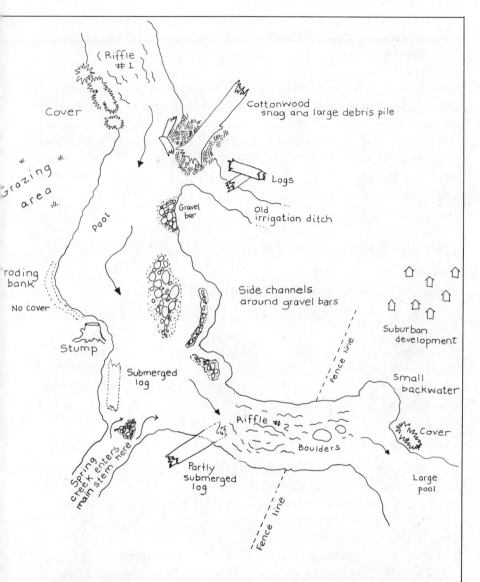

4.2 A stream-habitat map. *An example of a hand-sketched stream-habitat map.*

select several photo points, because habitat improvement is a gradual process. When you have been working on a project for ten years, it is easy to forget how things looked at the outset before work commenced.

Soon after you establish a transect system, it is a good idea to also establish permanent photo points to help you monitor habitat changes over time. Nothing is more dramatic than photos, taken several years apart, to document the habitat changes. A series of photographs taken at these photo points every two to three years is an easy and inexpensive monitoring technique that is too often overlooked.

STREAM HABITAT INVENTORY MEASUREMENTS

Riparian Vegetation—What to Measure and How

The contribution of riparian vegetation to trout habitat is enormous. Riparian vegetation is the source of large woody debris and provides stream-bank stability, shade, overhanging cover, and leaf litter for insect production. The extent to which the riparian vegetation contributes to the structure of the stream depends upon the type, amount, and health of vegetation present.

VEGETATION TYPE

Riparian vegetation can be described by the species present or by a more general classification that simply lists the vegetation as grass, sod, brush, conifer, or deciduous trees. For most trout-stream rehabilitation projects, a general classification system that helps you to understand how riparian vegetation affects stream-bank stability, and how it contributes to cover and shade, will suffice.

To help standardize the way these attributes are measured, a habitat-rating system for the intermountain West was developed in 1983 by a group of researchers led by William Platts. The system is best used to evaluate the most abundant—dominant—and second most abundant—subdominant—materials that make up a streamside environment. Because combinations of plant and soil usually comprise riparian environments, both are included in the rating system.

Because the system was designed with the assumption that streamside environments composed of fine sand, with little or no vegetation, have limited value to trout, they are given the lowest rating. The brush/sod environments—those that produce a tangle of roots and vegetation—receive the highest rating.

Although developed for the intermountain West, this rating system is sufficiently general that it may be applicable to all parts of the country. If it is used over a period of years, it will help to detect changes in vegetation, such as a streamside environment that changes from brush/sod to sand/grass under an improper grazing strategy, that ultimately affect the quality of trout habitat.

VEGETATION OVERHANG

Measurements of terrestrial vegetation hanging over a stream bank, combined with measurements of stream-bank undercuts and water depth where it meets the shore, provide valuable information on the amount of streamside cover available for trout. Measurements of vegetation overhang are most accurate if measured along a transect extending from the bank to the end of vegetation overhang (figure 4.3). The vegetation must be within 12 inches of the water surface to provide effective cover.

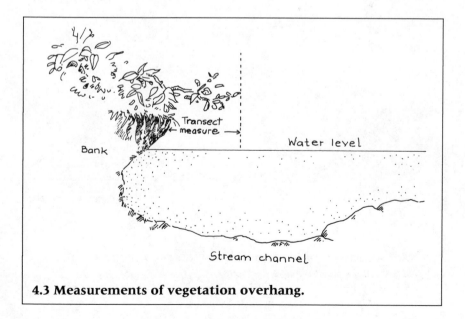

4.3 Measurements of vegetation overhang.

SHADE

Shade provided by riparian vegetation can be critical for maintaining the cool water temperatures trout need. The degree of shade provided can be measured in several ways, depending upon the degree of precision required. The easiest method is to visually estimate the amount of shading that covers the stream at noon (figure 4.4).

For trout a stream reach that is 40 to 60 percent shaded is generally considered to be excellent. More detailed approaches for measuring shade, such as using a small mirror called a spherical densiometer or a device called a solar pathfinder, might be more quantitative if you suspect that water temperature may be a limiting factor.

Stream-bank Condition

Stream-bank measurements can help to evaluate a stream bank's stability, its susceptibility to erosion, and the amount of cover its undercut banks provide. In most cases your first glance at a stream bank will offer plenty of information. When you see a stream bank

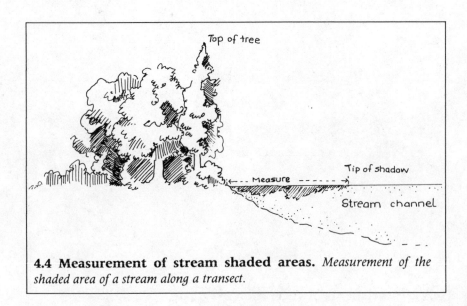

4.4 Measurement of stream shaded areas. *Measurement of the shaded area of a stream along a transect.*

fortified by a rich mix of riparian vegetation—regardless of bank undercutting—your mind's eye should also see excellent cover for trout and very stable banks.

On the other hand, if a vertical stream bank has little or no vegetative cover, the reach will be of little use to trout because the bank is being undercut so rapidly that it continues to slough into the stream.

Stream banks should be evaluated on the basis of how far they have moved away from their optimum condition. Compare the bank conditions in figures 4.5 and 4.6. Ideally, the bank should be well vegetated and stable. And, ideally, it would be best for the person making these evaluations to have acquired the training and experience needed to interpret the data.

Bank alteration is best rated at the point where a transect intercepts the stream bank (refer to figure 4.1). A visual evaluation that yields a stream-bank alteration rating of 80 percent stable and only slightly altered is considered to be excellent. A rating of less than 25 percent stable is usually a sign of a severely altered stream bank that will not provide trout with basic habitat requirements.

BANK ANGLE

To measure bank angle, place a clinometer, a device that measures angles of elevation and inclination, on a measuring rod or staff. Position the base of the rod on the streambed or bank, so that the rod rests parallel to the angle of the sloping stream bank (figure 4.5). In lieu of the clinometer, simply eyeball the bank to determine if the angle is greater or less than 90 degrees.

Vertical 90-degree bank angles and streams with dished out bank angles that measure greater than 90 degrees provide little or no stream-bank cover for trout and may be unstable. Undercut banks tend to have bank angles less than 90 degrees, which provide good cover and valuable rearing habitat for trout.

BANK HEIGHT

Bank-height measurements are taken from the stream water surface to the top of the bank (figure 4.6). Generally, a bank height that averages less than one foot can meet the best habitat requirements

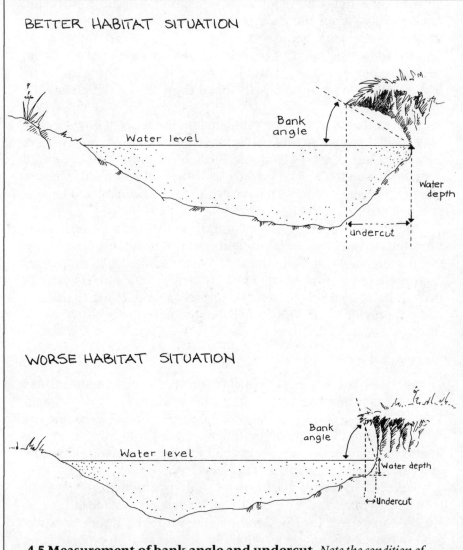

BETTER HABITAT SITUATION

Water level

Bank angle

Water depth

undercut

WORSE HABITAT SITUATION

Water level

Bank angle

Water depth

Undercut

4.5 Measurement of bank angle and undercut. *Note the condition of the bank.*

for trout, but a bank as high as three feet can still provide good-to-fair habitat. A vertical bank higher than three feet is an indication of an unstable, incised channel.

Stream-bank Undercut

Stream-bank undercuts often provide excellent cover for trout and should indicate how well the stream bank is protected by streamside vegetation.

If an undercut exists, use a rod or staff in the same manner described to measure vegetation overhang to measure the extent of the undercut where the transect intercepts the bank. A measurement of greater than six inches on 50 percent of the transects indicates excellent cover for trout. The same measurement on less than 20 percent of the transects will not bode well for trout. This measurement, combined with the measurement of overhanging vegetation, will help you to evaluate total overhead stream-bank cover.

Stream-channel Shape

Shape of the stream channel is controlled by the bank, channel gradient, the streambed substrate, and the volume of water it carries. Because the water's constant three-dimensional movement patterns often combine with unpredictable flows, the following attributes can be difficult to measure and describe. The measurements, however, will provide information on stream-channel shape and will aid in classifying the stream type. Classifying or grouping streams according to their channel characteristics allows you to make comparisons between streams that have similar channels. This important concept is discussed in detail in chapter 5. To help obtain the most meaningful information, each of the following measurements should be taken at approximately the same flow, so that comparisons will not be undermined by wide water-flow fluctuations.

Active Channel Width

The relationship between active channel width and water width is important. If the channel width is much greater than the water width, any vegetation overhang or undercut banks that may exist are useless to trout because the water does not reach the stream bank. This condition usually indicates a laterally unstable channel, which is eroding at high flows (figure 4.6).

Active channel width is easily measured along a transect tape. The stream channel extends from bank to bank where its borders are marked by encroaching vegetation or where the high-water mark is distinguished by a break in the general slope in the land or by the simple lack of vegetation.

WATER WIDTH

The relationship between water width and water depth is also important (figure 4.6). A wide, shallow stream usually does not contain adequate pool habitat or cover and often resembles continuous riffle habitat. A narrow, deep channel, on the other hand, usually provides a variety of habitats characterized by undercut banks and overhanging vegetation.

Water width is measured along the transect. Subsequent measurements should be measured at the same time of year as your initial measurements. Water width is a measurement of limited value unless it is related to channel width and, more importantly, to water depth.

WATER DEPTH AND VELOCITY

Water-depth and velocity measurements are taken with a water-current meter that is attached to a measuring rod marked in one-tenth-foot increments. The rod is used to measure the depth of the stream.

Water travels faster at the stream surface than it does along the streambed. The average velocity is generally found at six-tenths of the water depth. In streams deeper than two and a half feet, it is necessary to take measurements at two-tenths and eight-tenths of the total depth and average the two current meter measurements.

Depth and velocity measurements should be taken at several points along the stream transect. Generally, the measurements can be taken: (1) at one-fourth, one-half, and three-fourths water-width intervals along the transect—for example, if the water width is ten feet, the depth and velocity measurements would be taken at two

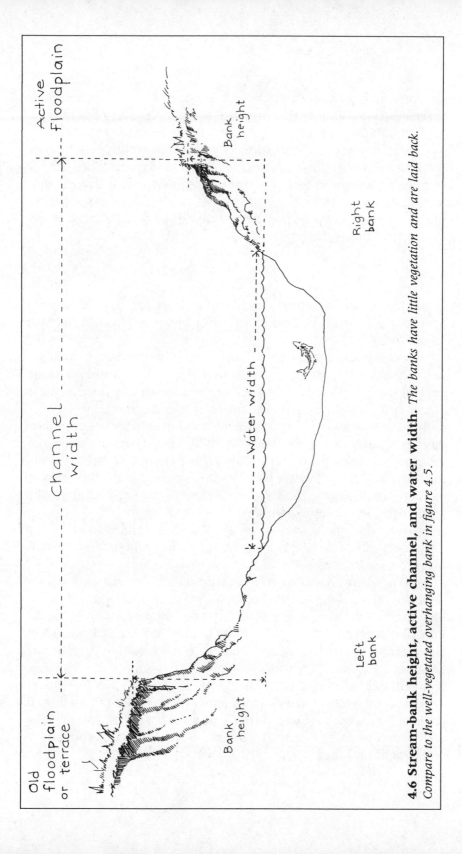

4.6 Stream-bank height, active channel, and water width. *The banks have little vegetation and are laid back. Compare to the well-vegetated overhanging bank in figure 4.5.*

and one-half, five, and seven and one-half feet; (2) at regularly spaced intervals along the transect—for example, every two, five, or ten feet; and (3) at breaks in the topography of the streambed.

Measurements taken at breaks in the topography will provide the most accurate flow information but may require more time to complete. Use of the first two techniques could inadvertently miss measuring a pool along the transect, which would not happen using the topography technique. Water depths also should be taken where the transect meets the bank.

DISCHARGE

Discharge, or the amount of water that flows past a specific point during a specific allotted time, is usually measured in cubic feet per second (cfs).

Discharge is an important consideration in the design and construction of restoration projects, as well as to the life history of trout. Several aspects of the annual discharge regime are key ingredients in a restoration program. Average flows by month, annual low flows, and the frequency and magnitude of flood events are all important design considerations, especially when in-stream structures are contemplated as part of the restoration effort. These statistics are computed from data provided by a stream-gauge record. The annual variation in discharge is also an important biological consideration, particularly in the semi-arid West.

By far the easiest way to obtain discharge data is to acquire it from the USGS, USFS, BLM, or the state's fish and game or water-resources departments.

In the event that discharge measurements for your stream have not been taken, there are several statistical techniques that allow the discharge of an ungauged stream to be approximated from the known discharge regime of a nearby gauged stream. Ask the agencies listed above about this possibility. If this is not an option, you may need to hire a consultant to measure the stream's discharge regimen and to install a permanent stream gauge.

In many western streams the factor limiting trout populations is an insufficient water supply that can greatly reduce habitat. The water supply can be affected by diversions for industrial, municipal, and agricultural uses.

Sinuosity

By dividing the distance measured along the channel by the distance measured in a straight line parallel to the general valley orientation, you can determine a stream's sinuosity. The answer can vary from one—for a straight channel—to four or more for a strongly meandering one. The value is useful for comparing aquatic habitat conditions between stream reaches.

The channel length and straight-line distance between two points on the stream can be measured on your topo map or aerial photo. First, measure the straight distance. Second, place a piece of string along the stream channel and then pull the string taut to measure its length. Divide the stream-channel distance by the straight-line distance to determine your stream's sinuosity.

Gradient

The gradient is an extremely important attribute of the stream channel because it plays a major role in determining water velocity, which is a critical component of trout habitat and the channel-forming process.

Gradient is determined by measuring the drop in water-surface elevation over a set distance. One researcher suggests the best method is to measure the difference in water-surface elevation between points located 100 feet upstream and 100 feet downstream of each cross-section transect.

The distance to these points can be easily measured with a fiberglass or steel tape laid along the bank. Although water-surface elevation measurements are best made with professional surveying equipment, a hand level or clinometer will provide an estimate of gradient (plus or minus 1 percent) in lieu of an engineer's level.

Substrate

The composition of the substrate provides information on the stream's suitability for spawning, insect production, and in-stream cover. As with the other attributes described, there is a range of techniques for measuring substrate composition and condition, but under most circumstances effective measurements can be made by visual observation.

COMPOSITION

The easiest way to evaluate substrate composition is to make a visual estimate at the same regular one-fourth, one-half, and three-fourths water-width intervals along the transect line that water-depth measurements are taken. The measurements can also be taken at topographic breaks in the bed, as for depth and velocity measurements.

When estimating the composition, use the transect tape measure to project a one-foot or one-yard-square area on the streambed. Then, observe the substrate within the imaginary square and estimate the percentage of the area that is composed of boulder, rubble, gravel, sand, and coarse and fine sediments (figure 4.7).

The classification of substrate size is based upon table 4.1. Because there are so many different substrate classification systems in use today, the use of this table is suggested to provide you with one rating system that you can use throughout your habitat rehabilitation projects.

EMBEDDEDNESS

Embeddedness is the extent to which the larger substrate particles, such as boulder, cobble, or gravel, are surrounded or covered by fine

TABLE 4.1
SUBSTRATE PARTICLE SIZE

| | Size Range | |
Name of Particle	Millimeters	Inches
Large boulder	Bigger than 1,024	40–160
Small boulder	256–1,024	10–40
Large cobble (rubble)	128–256	5–10
Small cobble (rubble)	64–128	2.5–5
Gravel	2–64	0.08–2.5
Sand	0.062–2	
Silt	0.004–0.062	
Clay	Less than 0.004	

SOURCE: Helm, W., ed. *Aquatic Habitat Inventory Glossary and Standard Methods* (Logan, UT: Habitat Inventory Committee, Western Division AFS, n.d.).

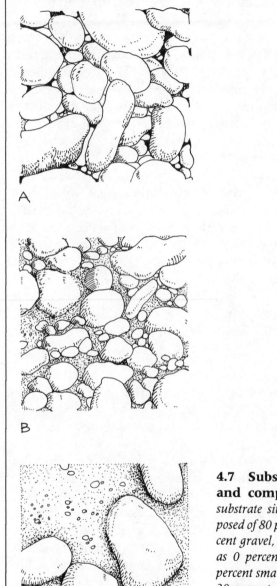

4.7 Substrate embeddedness and composition. *Three different substrate situations. Frame A is composed of 80 percent small cobble, 20 percent gravel, and embeddedness is rated as 0 percent. Frame B consists of 40 percent small cobble, 30 percent gravel, 30 percent sand, and embeddedness is rated at 30 percent. Frame C is 40 percent large cobble, 10 percent gravel, 50 percent sand, and embeddedness is rated at 50 percent.*

sediment (figure 4.7). The effect of embeddedness on trout production is often lamentable.

Because land use in the drainage can increase the delivery of fine sediment to the stream, everything from clear-cuts to parking lots can increase substrate embeddedness. Current research indicates that when the substrate becomes more than 30 to 40 percent embedded, there is an accompanying loss of spawning habitat. In addition, reductions in rearing and winter habitat also occur when pools are filled with sediment. Even aquatic-insect habitats are lost when fine sediments fill small voids in the substrate.

Again, the easiest method for evaluating embeddedness is visual observation and ranking at the same locations that your depth, velocity, and substrate composition measurements are taken. The measurement site, however, can reflect your own particular habitat-rehabilitation goals. For example, if spawning habitat for brown trout is of particular interest, choose a site that meets the depth and velocity preference criteria for spawning brown trout.

A more quantitative approach would be to select random riffle areas by throwing a metal hoop into the riffle and measuring the embeddedness of the individual rocks and gravel within the hoop.

In-stream Habitat

Physical components of in-stream trout habitat include pools, riffles, cover provided by the substrate, aquatic vegetation, woody debris, undercut banks, overhanging vegetation, water temperature, and discharge.

Most of the habitat attributes discussed to this point are most amenable to measurement along a transect system. In-stream habitat can be inventoried using either the transect or habitat-mapping technique. The use of the transect method, with transects spaced every 100 to 200 feet, could be used to inventory a large amount of stream channel. Transects spaced every 10 to 50 feet, combined with the habitat-mapping method, could be applied to the reach selected for restoration work.

THE POOL TO RIFFLE RATIO

The ratio of pools to riffles in a stream reach has traditionally been used to predict the stream's ability to provide resting and security areas (pools) near associated food-producing areas and suitable spawning areas (riffles). The pool to riffle ratio is calculated by measuring the length or percent of riffle along the transect lines, or within a mapped stream reach, and dividing the measurement into the length or percent of pool. For years a pool to riffle ratio of 1 to 1 has been the standard of presumed excellence. However, research has shown that there is a wide variety of factors related to pools and riffles, as well as to species and life stages of trout, that contributes to the definition of prime trout habitat.

For example, in Idaho's Salmon River drainage researchers learned that highest concentrations of trout in the South Fork were found in reaches with a seemingly low 0.4 to 1 pool to riffle ratio. Yet many streams with pool to riffle ratios as high as 1.5 to 1 are still good trout producers.

IN-STREAM COVER

In addition to cover provided by undercut banks, overhanging vegetation, cobble and boulders, and water depth, trout find important in-stream sanctuary in masses of aquatic vegetation and strewn jumbles of woody debris.

Aquatic Vegetation. Aquatic vegetation can be regarded as cover only when it is at least the size of large cobble and dense enough to hide a trout. Aquatic vegetation can be noted as you measure and rate the substrate along a transect. It can also be mapped, like pools, riffles, undercut banks, and woody debris.

Woody Debris. Locations of woody debris can be incorporated into a map showing other habitat features, such as pools, riffles, gravel bars, boulders, and undercut banks. A freehand map (see figure 4.2) can identify the relative locations of the debris and provide a useful data base to evaluate effects of debris on the stream channel.

WATER TEMPERATURE

Trout are quite sensitive to warm water temperatures. Water temperature of about 62 degrees Fahrenheit is considered ideal for growth of trout. Temperatures above approximately 78 degrees

Fahrenheit are potentially lethal. Water temperature should be measured for at least one minute in a shaded pool during the hottest part of the day—between 2:00 and 3:00 P.M.—to obtain maximum water temperatures. You should also record the date, time, and location of the measurement.

MEASURING BIOLOGICAL ATTRIBUTES

If it seems strange that the last item to be inventoried is the one that got you interested in a stream restoration project in the first place, remember that everything else must fall into place before trout can stake a claim in a stream. Because trout effectively integrate the effects of their physical and chemical environments, you will find them only where suitable habitat is available for their continued survival.

Aquatic Insects

Because insects are extraordinary indicators of water quality, substrate conditions, and water temperatures, the collection and analysis of aquatic insect data can help reveal a great deal about the suitability of the stream for trout.

For most research projects it is important to obtain a very large, statistically significant estimate of the numbers, per unit area of the stream bottom, of the insect species present. But for the purpose of learning about water and substrate quality, statistically significant population samples are not essential. A clear recognition of the insects present and their relative abundance will suffice.

Table 4.2 shows the great range in number of aquatic insects collected from a square meter of several streams. The stream having the fewest number, Yellowstone National Park's Firehole River, is also an internationally renowned trout fishery. Researchers do not know enough about the number of insects required to grow fish to become too concerned about collecting statistically significant samples.

It is more important to obtain an insect-population sample that contains all of the species present and yields information on relative abundance. You can obtain such a sample by placing a kick screen or a long-handled net (available from biological supply stores) at arm's length downstream of the area you want to sample. If a long-handled net is unavailable, you can make a kick screen quite easily. It can be made from a three-by-five-foot piece of fiberglass window screen. Tack the ends of the screen onto one end of five-foot-long one-inch wooden dowels or broom handles. By kicking at the substrate and streambed upstream of the net for 30 seconds, you should be able to collect representative samples of the insect population from a variety of stream habitats (figure 4.8). The insects should be immediately preserved for later identification.

Once you have collected the sample, you will probably need to have the insects identified by a professional aquatic entomologist at the college, state agency, or consulting firm nearest you. Often students studying entomology are willing to identify the insects at little or no cost.

The data analysis should be directed at determining if water quality, substrate conditions, and water temperature are suitable for trout. The presence, or absence, of typical trout food items will provide this information. If a balanced community of stone flies (*Plecoptera*), mayflies (*Ephemeroptera*), caddis flies (*Trichoptera*), and true flies (*Diptera*) is present in the stream, you can be assured that the stream should be inviting to trout.

TABLE 4.2

MEAN STANDING CROPS OF AQUATIC INSECTS IN SOME
ROCKY MOUNTAIN STREAMS

Stream	Location	Avg. Number per Square Meter
Firehole	Wyoming	940
Unnamed spring brook	Colorado	
Station 5		1,700
Station 4		4,100
Mill Creek	Idaho	6,900
Strawberry River	Utah	8,800
Mink Creek	Idaho	21,000

SOURCE: Platts, W.; Megahan, W.; and Minshall, G., *Methods for Evaluating Stream, Riparian, and Biotic Conditions.* USDA-FS Intermountain Forest and Ranger Expt. Station General Technical Report no. INT-138 (Logan, UT: 1983).

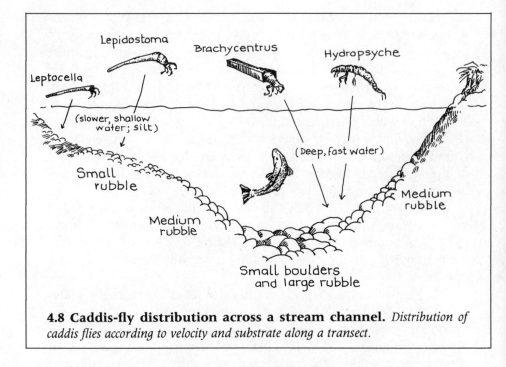

4.8 Caddis-fly distribution across a stream channel. *Distribution of caddis flies according to velocity and substrate along a transect.*

If, for example, the sample shows that the stream has no stone flies, abundant dragonflies (*Odonata*), and that the mayflies are dominated by burrowing forms, a professional biologist may, with the aid of additional data collected on temperature and substrate, conclude that the stream is too warm and silty for trout.

The biotic condition index (BCI) was developed by two researchers to compare the insect population of a stream to an ideal population for the stream. The ideal population is based on stream productivity (alkalinity), water quality (sulfate), habitat suitability (substrate), and stream maintenance (gradient) components. This index provides a standardized method to evaluate aquatic-insect communities and is a good trout-stream rehabilitation tool.

Periphyton

Periphyton, the slippery brown and green algae and other microscopic organisms that cling to rocks and other submerged objects, is as sensitive to water quality as are insects, but it is much easier to sample. To collect a representative sample of periphyton, simply scrape the algae from a variety of substrates, such as rocks, twigs, leaves, and branches, found throughout the reach of the stream. As with insects, the identification of the algae and the analysis of the data must be done by someone with specialized training.

Analyses of periphyton composition can reveal a great deal about a stream's water quality, and the process is generally less costly than interpretations of aquatic-insect data. Nevertheless, the combination of information from both insect and periphyton collections is a relatively inexpensive way to obtain information regarding water quality, substrate condition, temperature, and, in a general way, the productivity of a stream.

Trout Populations

THE MAGNET THEORY

The reasons behind an initial inventory of the trout population are more important than establishing data to judge the project's success. A number of researchers suspect that restoration and enhancement projects do not create more trout but rather redistribute them. In other words, a rehabilitation project may act like a magnet to attract fish from other parts of the stream without actually increasing the total population.

The common rebuttal to this theory recognizes that newly created habitat may indeed cause a redistribution of trout populations in the project area at the expense of other stream reaches but notes that the other stream reaches are still available for trout. As the population in the project area increases, the recently abandoned areas will eventually be reoccupied and result in a corresponding increase in the population throughout the stream.

Because this is such a critical consideration, all projects should include an inventory of the trout population in the project reach and in a control reach—a section of stream where no restoration or enhancement efforts will be undertaken. Both reaches should be inventoried and monitored before and after the project work. The data collected will help indicate the success, if any, of the enhancement program.

POPULATION SURVEYS

The two basic ways to conduct a trout-population survey are extremely technical. The traditional approach is to collect information on species present and their abundance by size and age class within a stream reach. Two common techniques are underwater observation using a wetsuit, mask, and snorkel, and electrofishing, which momentarily stuns trout and brings them floating to the surface. New evidence, however, indicates that electrofishing may cause injuries that can kill trout.

An alternative technique—and the one most efficient for a trout-stream rehabilitation project—first divides the stream reach into microhabitats, so that trout-population information can be collected from specific individual microhabitats. With this technique, in addition to data on the species present and their abundance by size and age class, researchers can acquire important habitat-preference information, which will determine a habitat's relative contribution to the total trout population.

This method has been used to evaluate a habitat improvement project on the Little Truckee River in California. The results of the electrofishing survey are presented in table 4.3.

The results show that lateral scour pools—the least abundant habitat type—were the preferred adult trout habitat and that fry were abundant and available to fill adult habitat. It follows that the lack of lateral scour pools may be the factor that is limiting the adult trout population in this reach of the Truckee River. Similarly, the lack of riffle/run habitat may be limiting the number of juvenile trout.

TABLE 4.3
NUMBERS OF RAINBOW PER YEAR CLASS BY HABITAT TYPE

Habitat Type	Fry	Juv.	Adult 1	Adult 2	Adult 3
Riffle	72				
Riffle/run	20	24			
Step/run	48				
Channel pool	8				
Lateral scour pool	3	5	7	9	15
Glide	16				

SOURCE: Kershner, J., "Planning Habitat Improvement Projects Using a Combination of Habitat Typing and Channel Typing," *N. Am. June. Fish Man.* (in press)

As you can see, the habitat preference data can be extremely useful—especially when combined with habitat suitability curves described in chapter 2—in the planning phase of the project.

A refinement of this method utilizing visual observation by divers of trout numbers and their habitats has been developed in Oregon. A small stream was divided into upper, middle, and lower reaches of approximately the same length. The habitats within each reach were classified as pool, riffle, glide, or side channel. Following the habitat classification, researchers put on their snorkeling gear to visually establish trout-population estimates for each of the habitat types within the three reaches. They found that about twice as many trout were in pools in the lower reach than in the middle and upper reaches.

They discovered that trout densities—the total amount of trout in one place—were from 4 to 15 times higher in pools than in riffles. They also found that when coho salmon were in pools, they preferred to stay near the surface. In contrast, steelhead trout preferred to stay close to the bottom substrate. Average pool size was larger and pools made up a greater proportion of the total habitat area in the lower section than in the middle and upper sections.

This example suggests that extrapolation from data collected in only one or several representative reaches could portray a highly biased and misleading picture of true trout abundance. The sampling design described here will be practical for estimating trout abundance and habitat areas in many small streams because the snorkeling technique for visual estimation of trout numbers requires less time than mark-and-recapture electrofishing techniques. Therefore, more areas can be sampled in less time. This technique, like all those described in this chapter, should be applied by experienced, professional biologists.

Inventories—A Final Note

Most inventory work is conducted in the summer or fall, but trout inhabit the stream year-round and experience changes in both the habitat and their habitat needs as the seasons progress. As water flows and temperatures decline during the late fall and winter, the trout begin to seek different areas for cover to help them survive. The stream is not the same as when the inventory work was conducted, and the trout in the stream use the available habitat in a different way.

How does the information collected in August relate to conditions in the stream in February? To answer this question, in-stream habitat inventories and trout-population studies should be conducted during each season. Although difficult and often uncomfortable to conduct, inventories are the only way to obtain a true understanding of the habitat factors that could be limiting the trout populations.

MONITORING AND EVALUATION

Monitoring and evaluation of a project after the work is completed will determine if the project brought about the physical habitat changes that were planned and if the trout population responded to the changes as anticipated.

When projects fail, it is likely that: (1) the factors that limit trout populations were not determined before the project was designed; and (2) the success of the project was not properly evaluated. The most basic fact of trout habitat rehabilitation is you cannot hope to increase production of trout unless you provide the kind of habitat—perhaps winter habitat for juvenile trout—that currently limits the population. The identification of limiting factors, which is the major topic of chapter 5, is absolutely crucial to the success of your project.

USFS research biologist Fred Everest stresses that evaluation of a project is also of paramount importance. Although the restoration of damaged habitats is well funded, the complex relationships between salmonids and their habitat are not well understood. Therefore, the chance of a project not succeeding is great. If you are to learn from initial mistakes, as well as successes, you must conduct postproject evaluations. The evaluation should include an analysis of:

1. Physical habitat—Did the physical habitat change as was planned?
2. Trout biology—Did the target species/life stage respond as anticipated?
3. Economics—Did the benefits derived justify the cost incurred?

These three essential elements of a project are usually short-changed because of a lack of funding or a lack of time. It seems incredible that program administrators—from federal and state governments to conservation organizations to private landowners—

would fund construction projects and then express no interest in their planning or, more astoundingly, in their success.

Robert Hunt has probably reviewed and evaluated more trout-stream rehabilitation projects than anyone in the United States. He developed the following two-level system to evaluate the success of completed trout-habitat rehabilitation projects.

Level I success is a 25 percent or more increase in a predetermined trout-population characteristic that could include one or a mix of the following: (1) total number of trout; (2) number of trout over six inches; (3) number of trout over ten inches; (4) total trout weight (biomass); or (5) angler hours and number of trout caught.

Level II success is a 50 percent or more increase in the same predetermined trout-population and sport-fishery characteristics.

As Hunt's system suggests, a reliable creel census can be an important aspect of a monitoring program. Too often the success of a completed habitat rehabilitation project can only be judged by a new well-worn path to the stream blazed by anglers. Although expensive, a reliable creel census would add a crucial element to any monitoring and evaluation agenda because the data generated by post-project population surveys that have not considered angling harvest, which usually increases, could render disappointing and misleading information.

Generally, however, an ongoing monitoring program will not be as extensive as initial inventories. The same methods are used, but the focus is limited to specific areas of interest—usually the physical habitat and the response of the trout population you are trying to increase.

An important aspect of the monitoring program is to establish a control section where stream treatments have not been applied. If the physical habitat and trout population in the treated reach show improvement but the control section deteriorates or remains stable, you may say with confidence that the treatment worked. Without the control section for comparison, an increase in the trout population could simply be attributed to normal annual variations.

How Long to Monitor?

Monitoring should continue every two to three years for at least five years, and preferably for ten years, following treatment. The importance of posttreatment monitoring cannot be overemphasized, because monitoring provides the data necessary to determine the success of a project. The information gathered after the completion of the project can help to teach you about the functioning of the system, which may lead to a more accomplished trout-habitat analysis, as well as better project design. In the meantime, you can use the inventory measurement information presented in table 4.4 to get a general idea of how to interpret the data you collect throughout the project.

Interpreting Results

Interpreting the results of an inventory program can be difficult. Because there is no standard number to render a habitat attribute excellent or poor, interpreting the results takes several years of experience.

Streams vary too much and too little is known about the interaction of trout with their habitat to develop hard and fast ratings of habitat. However, to provide some general habitat characteristics, table 4.4 was compiled to establish a rough starting point to help you better understand your inventory measurements. When using this table, do not rely upon the values for a single habitat attribute. Rather, look at the values of several attributes and particularly those habitat features that are closely related.

For example, if both streamside habitat and bank stability fall into the poor category, you may conclude that one problem with the stream is a lack of riparian vegetation. Similarly, if vegetation overhang, bank angle, and bank undercut are excellent, the stream bank must be healthy, so riparian vegetation is probably not limiting trout production.

Remember, it is possible to obtain seemingly conflicting results. For example, you may find diverse and abundant insect and periphyton communities, but also find that an entire age class of trout is consistently poorly represented in the stream reach. If that is the case, you must look at variables that may be influencing age class but are not influencing bugs or algae.

This table is not a substitute for experience. It is offered only to provide general guidelines that can give you a starting place to begin interpreting your stream inventory data.

In addition to interpreting data, a second approach to determine the state of the stream reach is to compare it to an undisturbed reach, to a similar stream nearby that is in good health, or to photos of the stream prior to disturbance or a description of the stream from longtime residents of the area. This will give you a picture of the unimpaired condition of the stream. Re-creating, or allowing the stream to re-create this unimpaired condition should be the goal of the restoration project.

Some states have programs that provide information on stream restoration and that offer various levels of technical assistance or funding. Table 4.5 lists a state-by-state accounting, including Canadian provinces, of restoration programs.

TABLE 4.4

INVENTORY MEASUREMENTS

Habitat Attributes	Excellent	Good–Fair	Poor
Riparian vegetation			
Streamside habitat type	Brush/sod	Boulder/rubble tree, root, brush	Bare soil
Vegetation overhang* (less than 1 ft. from water surface)	Greater than 1 ft. on 50% of bank	Greater than 1 ft. on 30%–45% of bank	Greater than 1 ft. on less than 20% of bank
Shading	40%–60%	Less than 25%	Less than 10%
Bank stability	80% stable	Greater than 75% 30%–60% stable	Greater than 90% Less than 30% stable
Channel characteristics			
Bank angle*	50% of bank less than 90 degrees	30%–45% of bank less than 90 degrees	Less than 20% of bank less than 90 degrees
Bank height	Ave. less than 1 ft.	Ave. 1–3 ft.	Ave. greater than 3 ft.
Bank undercut*	Greater than 6 in. on 50% of bank	Less than 6 in. on 20%–45% of bank	Less than 6 in. on less than 20% of bank
Water width:depth ratio†	5:1	20:1	40:1
Substrate composition	Gravel/rubble boulder	Gravel/rubble and/or sand/silt	Sand, silt, boulder (in any combination)
Embeddedness	Less than 20%	20%–40%	Greater than 40%
In-stream habitat			
Pool/riffle ratio	.5:1–1.5:1		Less than .5:1 Greater than 1.5:1
In-stream aquatic vegetation	Abundant		Not present
Woody debris	Abundant		Not present
Summer high temperature	58°–64° F	55°–70° F	Less than 50° F Greater than 72° F

Biology

Aquatic insects	Many species abundant	Many species	Few species
Periphyton	Many species abundant	Many species	Few species
Fish			
Species‡	1–trout 2–whitefish 3–sculpins	1–trout 2–sculpin/whitefish 3–sucker 4–dace	1–sucker 2–dace 3–trout
Age distribution	Each age class has at least 10% as many fish as previous age class	All age classes represented, some consistently poorly represented	–No adults –1 or more age classes not represented
Numbers§	More than 250 in 1,000 sq. ft. of stream surface	Range from 200 to 50 in 1,000 sq. ft. of stream surface	Less than 50 in 1,000 sq. ft. of stream surface

* Based upon idea that thalweg will be adjacent to any bank a maximum of 50% of the reach length as a result of meandering. Thalweg must be adjacent to bank to form undercut banks with overhanging vegetation.

† Based upon 20-ft. wide stream:
  Average 2 ft. depth—excellent;
  Average 1 ft. depth—good–fair;
  Average 0.5 ft. depth—poor.

‡ Numbers indicate relative abundance.

§ Includes all age classes of trout.

TABLE 4.5
STATE AND PROVINCE RESTORATION PROGRAMS

State/Province	Does the state/province have a trout-stream restoration or enhancement program?	Does this program provide technical assistance to organizations interested in a habitat restoration project?	Does this program provide funds for interested organizations to conduct restoration projects on public land?
Alabama	No	No	No
Alaska Division of Sport Fish P.O. Box 3-2000 Juneau, AK 99802-2000	Currently establishing a program		
Arizona	Plan to start		
Arkansas	No	No	No
California	No response		
Colorado Division of Wildlife 6060 Broadway Denver, CO 80216	Yes	Yes	No
Connecticut	No		
Delaware	Considering establishing a program		
Florida	No response		
Georgia	No response		
Hawaii	No trout		
Idaho	No response		
Illinois	No response		
Indiana	No		
Iowa Dept. of Natural Resources R.R. #2, Box 269 Manchester, IA 52057	Yes	Yes	No
Kansas	No		
Kentucky	Establishing a coop program on Daniel Boone National		
Louisiana	No		
Maine	Not a formal program		
Maryland	Not a formal program		

Does this program provide technical assistance to private landowners?	Does this program provide funding for projects on privately owned land?	Does this program require public access to streams on private lands that have received technical assistance or funding?	Does this state/province conduct restoration/ enhancement projects on its own?
No	No	No	No
No	No	No	No
Yes	Yes	Yes	Yes
Yes	No	No	Yes

Forest with USFS and Trout Unlimited

TABLE 4.5 (*continued*)
STATE AND PROVINCE RESTORATION PROGRAMS

State/Province	Does the state/province have a trout-stream restoration or enhancement program?	Does this program provide technical assistance to organizations interested in a habitat restoration project?	Does this program provide funds for interested organizations to conduct restoration projects on public land?
Massachusetts Div. of Fisheries/Wildlife Field Headquarters Westborough, MA 01581	Yes	Yes	Yes
Michigan Dept. of Natural Resources P.O. Box 30028 Lansing, MI 48909	Yes	No	No
Minnesota Dept. of Natural Resources 500 Lafayette Rd. St. Paul, MN 55155	Yes	Yes	Yes
Mississippi	No trout		
Missouri Stream Coordinator Dept. of Conservation P.O. Box 180 Jefferson City, MO 65102-0180	Yes	Yes	Limited
Montana Dept. Fish/Wildlife/Parks Fisheries Division 1420 E. 6th Ave. Helena, MT 59620	Currently establishing a program		
Nebraska Game & Parks Commission P.O. Box 30370 Lincoln, NE 68503	Yes	No	No
Nevada	Yes	No	No
New Hampshire	No formal program		
New Jersey	No formal program		
New Mexico	Not for streams		
New York Dept. of Environmental Conservation 50 Wolf Rd. Albany, NY 12233	Yes	Limited	No

Does this program provide technical assistance to private landowners?	Does this program provide funding for projects on privately owned land?	Does this program require public access to streams on private lands that have received technical assistance or funding?	Does this state/province conduct restoration/enhancement projects on its own?
Limited	No	N/A	Yes
Yes	Yes	Yes	Yes
No	No	N/A	Yes
Yes	No	No	Yes
No	No	N/A	Yes
No	No	N/A	Yes
Limited	No	No	Yes

TABLE 4.5 (continued)
STATE AND PROVINCE RESTORATION PROGRAMS

State/Province	Does the state/province have a trout-stream restoration or enhancement program?	Does this program provide technical assistance to organizations interested in a habitat restoration project?	Does this program provide funds for interested organizations to conduct restoration projects on public land?
North Carolina Wildlife Resources Commission 512 N. Salisbury St. Raleigh, NC 27611	Yes	Yes	Yes
North Dakota	No response		
Ohio	No response		
Oklahoma	No		
Oregon STEP Coordinator Dept. of Fish/Wildlife P.O. Box 3503 Portland, OR 97208	Yes	Yes	Yes
Pennsylvania Pennsylvania Fish Commission 450 Robinson Ln. Bellafonte, PA 16801-9616	Yes	Yes	Yes
Rhode Island	No response		
South Carolina Wildlife/Marine Resources Dept. Rembert C. Dennis Bldg. P.O. Box 167 Columbia, SC 29202	Yes	No	No
South Dakota Dept. of Game/Fish/Parks 3305 W South St. Rapid City, SD 57702	Yes	No	No
Tennessee	No		
Texas	No		
Utah Dept. of Natural Resources Wildlife Resources Div. 1596 W.N. Temple Salt Lake City, UT 84116-3154	Yes	Yes	Yes

Does this program provide technical assistance to private landowners?	Does this program provide funding for projects on privately owned land?	Does this program require public access to streams on private lands that have received technical assistance or funding?	Does this state/province conduct restoration/ enhancement projects on its own?
No	No	N/A	Yes
No	No	N/A	Yes
Yes	Yes	Yes	Yes
No	No	Yes	Yes
No	No	N/A	Yes
Yes	Yes	Yes	Yes

TABLE 4.5 (*continued*)
STATE AND PROVINCE RESTORATION PROGRAMS

State/Province	Does the state/province have a trout-stream restoration or enhancement program?	Does this program provide technical assistance to organizations interested in a habitat restoration project?	Does this program provide funds for interested organizations to conduct restoration projects on public land?
Vermont	No formal program		
Virginia	No formal program		
Washington	Yes	Yes	No
West Virginia	No response		
Wisconsin Dept. of Natural Resources Box 7921 Madison, WI 53707	Yes	Limited	Limited
Wyoming Wyoming Game & Fish Dept. 528 S. Adams Laramie, WY 82070	Yes	Yes	Yes
Alberta Forestry/Lands/Wildlife Fish & Wildlife Division N. Tower, Petroleum Plaza 9945-108 St. Edmonton, Alta. T5K 2G6	Yes	Yes	Yes
British Columbia Ministry of Environment Recreational Fisheries Parliament Bldgs. Victoria, B.C. V8V 1Y5	Yes	Yes	Yes
Manitoba Natural Resources Fisheries Branch Fisheries Enhancement Box 40; 1495 St. James St. Winnipeg, Man. R3H 0W9	Yes	No	No

Does this program provide technical assistance to private landowners?	Does this program provide funding for projects on privately owned land?	Does this program require public access to streams on private lands that have received technical assistance or funding?	Does this state/province conduct restoration/ enhancement projects on its own?
Yes	No	No	Yes
Limited	Limited	Yes	Yes
Yes	No	No	Yes
Yes	Yes	No	Yes
Yes	Yes	Yes	Yes
No	No	No	Yes

TABLE **4.5** (*continued*)
STATE AND PROVINCE RESTORATION PROGRAMS

State/Province	Does the state/province have a trout-stream restoration or enhancement program?	Does this program provide technical assistance to organizations interested in a habitat restoration project?	Does this program provide funds for interested organizations to conduct restoration projects on public land?
New Brunswick Dept. of Natural Resources Fish/Wildlife Branch Box 6000 Fredericton, N.B. E3B 5H1	Yes	Yes	Yes
Newfoundland	No, but do have program for salmon		
Nova Scotia Dept. of Fisheries Aquaculture/Inland Fisheries Division P.O. Box 700 Pictou, N.S. B0K 1H0	Yes	Yes	Yes
Ontario	No response		
Prince Edward Island	No response		
Quebec	No		

Saskatchewan
Saskatchewan Parks/
  Recreation and Culture
Fisheries Branch
Box 3003
Prince Albert,
  Sask. S6V 6G1
	Yes	Yes	Yes

Yukon	No		
Northwest Territories	No		

Does this program provide technical assistance to private landowners?	Does this program provide funding for projects on privately owned land?	Does this program require public access to streams on private lands that have received technical assistance or funding?	Does this state/province conduct restoration/ enhancement projects on its own?
No	No	N/A	Yes
No	No	N/A	No
Yes	Yes	Yes	Yes

SOURCES

Bisson, P.; Nielsen, J.; Paalmason, R.; and Grove, L. 1981. A System of Naming Habitat Types in Small Streams, with Examples of Habitat Utilization by Salmonids during Low Streamflow. In *Acquisition and Utilization of Aquatic Habitat Inventory Information*, ed. N. Armantrout, pp. 62–74. Portland, OR: Western Division Am Fish Soc.

Buell, J. 1986. Stream Habitat Enhancement Workshop; Level 1. U.S.D.A. Bonneville Power Administration Proj. no. 86–107.

Elliott, J. M. 1971. *Some Methods for the Statistical Analysis of Samples of Benthic Invertebrates*, Scientific Publication no. 25. Ambleside, GB. Freshwater Biological Assoc.

Hankin, D., and Reeves, G. 1988. Estimating Total Fish Abundance and Total Habitat Area in Small Streams Based on Visual Estimation Methods. *Can. Jrnl. Fish and Aquatic Science* 45(5): 834–44.

Helm, W. ed. n.d. *Aquatic Habitat Inventory Glossary and Standard Methods*. Logan, UT: Habitat Inventory Committee, Western Division AFS.

Hornig, T., and Pollard, M. 1978. *Macroinvertebrate Sampling Techniques for Streams in Semi-Arid Regions*. Washington, DC: U.S.E.P.A. EPA-600/4-78-040.

Hunt, R. 1988. *A Compendium of 45 Trout Stream Habitat Development Evaluations in Wisconsin during 1953–1985*. Wisc. Dept. of Nat. Resources Tech. Bull. no. 162. Madison, WI.

Kelly D., and Dettman, D. 1980. *Relationships between Streamflow, Rearing Habitat, Substrate Conditions, and Juvenile Steelhead Populations in Lagunitas Creek, Marin Co., 1979*. Prepared for the Marin Municipal Water District.

Kershner, J. In press. Planning Habitat Improvement Projects Using a Combination of Habitat Typing and Channel Typing. *N. Am. Jrnl. Fish Man.*

Miller, D. In prep. The Two Pin Method. In *Proceedings of the 1988 Am. Fish. Soc. Bioengineering Symposium*. Portland, OR, Oct. 24–28, 1988.

Ontario Ministry of Natural Resources. n.d. *Community Fisheries Involvement Program, Field Manual Part I: Trout Stream Rehabilitation*.

————. Stream Habitat Assessment Methodology. Unpublished xerox. Richmond Hill, Ontario: Ontario Ministry of Natural Resources, Central Region.

Platts, W.; Armour, C.; Booth, G.; Bryant, M.; Bufford, J.; Cuplin, P.; Jensen, S.; Lienkaemper, G.; Minshall, G.; Monsen, S.; Nelson, R.; Sedell, J.; and Tuhy, J. 1987. *Methods for Evaluating Riparian Habitats with Applications to Management*. U.S.D.A. Forest Service Intermountain Research Station, Gen. Tech. Rpt. no. INT-221. Logan, UT.

Platts, W.; Megahan, W.; and Minshall, G. *Methods for Evaluating Stream, Riparian, and Biotic Conditions*, U.S.D.A. Forest Service Intermountain Forest and Range Expt. Station, Gen. Tech. Rpt. no. INT-138. Logan, UT.

Wesche, T. 1980. *The WRRI Trout Cover Rating Method—Development and Application*. Water Resources Series no. 78. Laramie: Water Resources Research Institute, Univ. of Wyoming.

Winget, R., and Mangum, F. 1979. *Biotic Condition Index: Integrated Biological, Physical and Chemical Parameters for Management*. Ogden, U.S.D.A. Forest Service Intermountain Region.

Chapter 5

DETERMINING LIMITING FACTORS, DESIGNING, AND INITIATING THE PROJECT

I N the early 1980s an interest in restoring the mountain bluebird surfaced in areas of Montana where the bird's breeding habitat had been reduced or eliminated. Nest boxes were said to be the recovery key. Before you start shaking your head, a story about a boy's enthusiasm to recover the bluebird is particularly fitting to the subject of trout-habitat rehabilitation.

With the hope of seeing bluebirds from his own window, the boy built a nest box and proudly placed it on the backyard tree his parents said the bluebirds had once favored. He watched at the window for weeks, but the bluebirds never came.

The next spring the boy was determined to try again. With a little research he discovered that the birdhouse he had built did not meet any of the very specific requirements of mountain-bluebird nesting habitat. The materials were too flimsy. The nest-box entrance hole was too large and carved too close to the nest-box floor. He also learned that he had placed the box too low on the tree, with the entrance facing north instead of the bluebird's preferred southern exposure.

When he set out to build his second bluebird house, he followed the directions his research had uncovered. Within a few days the nest box was claimed by a pair of mountain bluebirds. That spring the boy proudly watched the pair successfully fledge two broods of mountain bluebirds from the nest box he had built.

This simple planning and construction lesson is relevant to your own trout-housing construction project, especially when you consider that by meeting the specific nesting habitat needs of mountain bluebirds, Montanans increased the bluebird fledgling rate 2,000 percent between 1981 and 1987. Similarly, your goal should be to meet the habitat needs of trout. If you achieve that goal, more often than not, the trout population will grow and prosper.

To help you reach that goal, this chapter will introduce the concepts you need to understand to complete the final five phases of a trout-habitat restoration project:

1. Identify the problems that limit trout production.
2. Design the project.
3. Finalize planning and preparation.
4. Estimate project maintenance.
5. Continue to monitor and evaluate the project.

WHAT IS A LIMITING FACTOR?

Just as adequate nesting habitat limited the bluebird population in Montana, one or more factors may be limiting the production of trout in your stream. Anything that impedes the potential rate of growth of any organism or population is said to be a limiting factor. Trout-habitat attributes that could be limiting factors include water quality, spawning habitat, summer- and winter-rearing habitat, cover, stream flows, and food.

The idea that a single factor can limit biological production began in 1840 when German chemist Justus Liebig discovered that farm-crop production was often limited by whatever essential element was in short supply. Today, Liebig's law of the minimum has come to mean that a population's rate of growth is dependent on the availability of basic requirements that are present in the minimum quantity it needs to survive and prosper. It is applied to the entire spectrum of ecological relationships.

The measurements and ratings described in chapter 4 will help you determine if your stream meets a trout's critical minimum requirements for survival. When you find an attribute that does not meet a trout's minimum requirement, you will have found a limiting factor, but it can be a tricky business.

The Bottleneck

The process of determining limiting factors can be a frustrating chore. Often, it is only after the enhancement of one seemingly deficient attribute that the real limiting factors become apparent. Consider a case where a trout-habitat rehabilitator worked for several years to successfully restore a spawning area only to discover that sufficient rearing habitat was the real limiting factor (figure 5.1).

In the upper portion of figure 5.1, you can see that five fry are produced from a number of eggs during the spring, but only two juveniles survive through the winter to the following spring. In the middle portion of figure 5.1, additional fry are the result of the spawning-area enhancement project. In winter, however, the population appears to have reached a bottleneck: Despite the increased number of fry, the number of yearling trout has not improved because there is not enough winter-rearing habitat to support increased numbers of juvenile trout.

The winter-rearing habitat also must be improved if the stream is to successfully produce more trout through the winter than when the project began. The bottom portion of figure 5.1 represents the result of such an improvement. A winter-rearing-habitat enhancement project successfully increased the overall production of yearling trout.

The bottleneck is a practical analogy, but the successful identification of the limiting factors in the trout stream you plan to rehabilitate may not be quite so elementary. Because the intricate relationships between trout and their environment are not well understood, many limiting-factor analyses can become complicated. Much of the detailed research of trout-habitat requirements has only been undertaken in the last 20 years. Consequently, many aspects of trout ecology are poorly understood, and others have yet to be studied. For example, if you know 5 percent of a stream provides suitable spawning, you might then want to discover: (1) the amount of habitat trout needed for suitable summer- and winter-rearing needs; and (2) the amount of habitat that must be provided to maximize the number of adult trout the stream can carry. As yet, no one has been able to precisely answer these important and seemingly basic questions.

On the other hand, in many cases the limiting factors can be very

BASELINE CONDITION

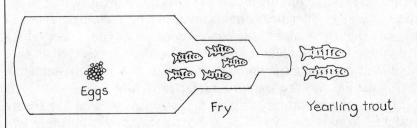

Eggs   Fry   Yearling trout

SPAWNING ENHANCEMENT

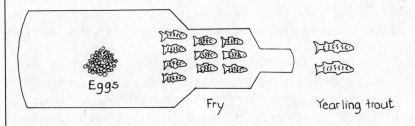

Eggs   Fry   Yearling trout

WINTER-REARING ENHANCEMENT

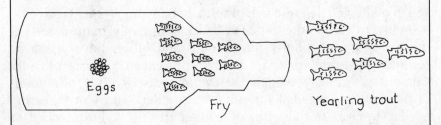

Eggs   Fry   Yearling trout

5.1 The limiting-factor bottleneck. *The bottleneck analogy for limiting-factor analysis.*

obvious, especially when streams have been severely damaged by channelization or other land-use practices. The initial remedy to improve trout production would probably require the restoration of diverse in-stream habitats.

Whether limiting factors are obvious or obscure, habitat inventories can help you to identify them. Potential limiting factors can be studied and systematically eliminated with good inventory information.

DETERMINING LIMITING FACTORS

If you follow the process presented in this book, a great deal of effort will be devoted to conducting seasonal land-use, stream-bank, and in-stream habitat inventories and trout-population estimates. There will come a time, probably in the dead of winter, when you will wonder what you are going to do with the mass of data you have collected. When that time comes, remember that a trout-stream ecosystem is a synthesis of the chemical, physical, and biological properties of a stream. The information you have gathered to determine what is limiting your stream's trout production must be considered as a whole, and not simply as a compilation of measurements and ratings.

The following two examples, and their accompanying habitat inventory ratings in tables 5.1 and 5.2, are provided to show you how that may be done.

Limiting-factor Analysis—Hypothetical Stream No. 1

Although you may have some suspicions, you will seldom be able to pinpoint a trout stream's limiting factor until you begin to analyze maps, interpret inventories, and crunch all the numbers and measurements you have collected. Take a look at the physical habitat inventory provided in table 5.1. The inventory shows that this stream reach has very little pool habitat and virtually no cover in the form of large substrate or woody debris. The measurements also show that the stream banks are three to four feet high with little or no undercuts or overhanging vegetation. The gradient is 0.6 percent, and the channel has a sinuous to meandering pattern.

Imagine that a review of land use shows that the project-area reach is located in a large pasture, where cattle spend the spring,

TABLE 5.1
PHYSICAL HABITAT DATA HYPOTHETICAL STREAM NO. 1
(AVERAGE VALUES FOR TEN HABITAT TRANSECTS
TAKEN FROM EACH AREA)

Habitat Attribute	Project Area	Downstream Control
Sinuosity	1.3	2.5
Gradient	.6%	.6%
Pool:riffle ratio	.3:1	1.1:1
Bank height	3.2 ft.	1.1 ft.
Bank angle	110°	40°
Bank undercut	3 in.	9 in.
Vegetation overhang	1 in.	6 in.
Water width	22 ft.	16 ft.
Water depth	6 in.	14 in.
Water temperature	70° F.	68° F.
Stream-bank vegetation stability	Poor	Good
Average pool depth	1.3 ft.	3.5 ft.
Pool-forming feature	Gravel deposit	Woody debris
Pool rating	Poor	Good
Embeddedness	45%	25%
Substrate composition		
Boulder	0%	5%
Rubble	5%	20%
Gravel	10%	40%
Coarse sediment	30%	20%
Fine Sediment	35%	10%
Silt	20%	5%

summer, and fall. Both within and upstream of the project-area reach, inventory maps indicate that heavy grazing pressure resulted in a stream channel that now supports little riparian or upland vegetation.

The map, however, also shows that a fence line divides the downstream control area from the project area. In the control area, which is only grazed in the spring, the habitat map shows that the stream banks are low with undercut banks, and they are covered with abundant overhanging vegetation. The map also shows that the large cottonwood trees and smaller shrubs that have fallen into the stream provide trout with a variety of suitable habitats.

Now, take another look at table 5.1. The control-area data show that the gradient is 0.6 percent, but the channel is meandering and there are deep pools, which are probably located at the outside meander banks. A comparison of the two areas' water-temperature readings shows that the downstream reach is one to two degrees Fahrenheit cooler than the project-area reach.

Imagine that the trout-population data reveal abundant fry and juvenile trout in the project-area reach during summer, but few juveniles in the winter. The downstream reach, however, contains a healthy population of fry, juveniles, and adults during all seasons, but increased numbers of juveniles overwintering in the control area's sheltered pools.

What is the problem with this stream? An initial appraisal should uncover the fact that grazing has eliminated the riparian and upland cover. This has resulted in increased flood-stage flows that probably caused channel down cutting and straightening. The local groundwater table also must have dropped as the channel became incised. This caused a change in streamside vegetation from willows and cottonwoods to dry-site vegetation (sagebrush, for instance). The trees contributed to stream-bank stability, but the vegetation has comparatively little root structure.

In the downstream reach, where grazing has been better managed, the stream channel has adjusted to flows, the incision has healed, the groundwater level has risen, the stream banks have naturally revegetated, and the stream's meandering pattern has been naturally restored. The downstream section provides good summer and winter habitat for resident trout, and also provides winter habitat for juvenile trout that leave the project-area reach in the fall in search of winter shelter. In the project area heavy grazing must be preventing the natural healing process.

Based upon this analysis, it is apparent that winter-rearing habitat and general habitat diversity are major limiting factors in the project area. It is clear that the root cause of the problem is an incompatible grazing practice. When all the data are considered, the first step toward a successful trout-habitat rehabilitation project on this stream should be to work with the landowner to bring about a change in grazing management.

Limiting-factor Analysis—Hypothetical Stream No. 2

Imagine a stream flowing through the heavily wooded Appalachian Mountains of North Carolina that appears to be perfect for brook trout. The stream's appearance, however, belies its reputation as a poor fishery. A trout-population inventory that showed the stream held abundant numbers of fry, juveniles, and yearling trout, but nothing larger than six inches, confirms that its lackluster reputation is justified.

The habitat inventory data presented in table 5.2 shows that the stream's problem is a lack of habitat diversity. Since the sinuous stream gradient is a moderate 1.2 percent, and because it flows through heavily forested hills, the lack of stream-bank cover is not of immediate concern. You assume that much of the habitat structure will be provided by large woody debris. However, your maps show many standing trees but no deadfall trees, and very little large woody debris in the stream. The banks are dished out, the substrate is too small to provide cover, the overhanging vegetation provides some

TABLE 5.2

PHYSICAL HABITAT DATA HYPOTHETICAL STREAM NO. 2
(AVERAGE VALUES FOR TEN HABITAT TRANSECTS
TAKEN IN PROJECT AREA)

Habitat Attribute	Project Area Value
Sinuosity	1.8%
Gradient	1.2%
Pool:riffle ratio	.4:1
Bank height	1.3 ft.
Bank angle	115°
Bank undercut	4 in.
Vegetation overhang	3 in.
Water width	15 ft.
Water depth	5 in.
Water temperature	66° F
Stream-bank vegetation stability	Excellent
Average pool depth	1.5 ft.
Pool-forming feature	Gravel bar/boulder
Pool rating	Poor
Embeddedness	30%
Substrate composition	
Boulder	7%
Rubble	23%
Gravel	40%
Coarse sediment	17%
Fine sediment	7%
Silt	6%

cover but not enough, and the major pool-forming feature is composed of gravel bars and rubble instead of woody debris. The area, remember, is heavily wooded. Why is there no woody debris in the stream?

A similar roadblock in your own data analysis will require some detective work. In this case, a little searching turns up the almost-forgotten fact that the now heavily wooded area was intensively logged and farmed until the 1930s. With that information it is safe to conclude that timber-harvest practices and farming caused many of the stream's problems. Once the timber harvests and farming ceased, the land began to revert to a forest. However, the young trees have yet to begin falling into the stream to create the diversity of habitat that trout need to survive in mountain streams.

The stream is on the road to a natural recovery, but a major limiting factor for trout production is an absence of habitat for larger trout. The somewhat unproductive nature of the stream may be caused, in part, by the lack of debris accumulations, which trap leaf litter and other organic material that form the base of the food web in this type of stream. The recovery of this stream may be hastened by the introduction of woody material to help the stream resemble its character prior to intensive farming and timber harvests. The new woody-debris accumulations would lead to trapping of leaf litter and possibly an increase in productivity.

In nearly all cases—including these examples—the limiting-factor analysis is not simply an exercise in identifying the potential limiting factors. Rather, it is a process that leads you to understand why particular habitat attributes are lacking. This understanding is crucial to the design of a restoration program.

Limiting-factor Analysis—A Black Art

It is unfortunate that a method for determining the factor or factors limiting trout production cannot be as easily described as a method for measuring undercut banks. At the risk of overemphasizing a theme of this handbook, the analysis requires three things of every trout-stream rehabilitator: (1) an understanding of the physical, chemical, and biological attributes of the stream; (2) the ability to analyze these diverse sets of data; and (3) experience in conducting this type of analysis.

Trout-stream-habitat restoration practitioners have been known to describe their science as a black art, ostensibly because the identification of limiting factors and the design of a program to try to correct the problem can appear to be arcane. Without a doubt experience in the art of trout-habitat rehabilitation is very important to its successful application.

Given the difficulty in identifying limiting factors in some situations, restoration efforts first should be concentrated on areas where the limiting factors are obvious. As these stream reaches are treated, results monitored, and experience gained, you will be better prepared to move to stream reaches where limiting factors are more obscure.

PROJECT DESIGN

The most important aspect of the limiting-factor analysis is to continue the process beyond the identification stage to discover the root cause of the problem. Sometimes, however, the limiting factor may not be amendable to treatment. If a stream is naturally plagued by constantly weak and intermittent flows, as is the case in many western streams, nothing short of flow augmentation can be done to treat that low-flow limiting factor and increase trout production. On the other hand, if general habitat diversity is identified as limiting the trout population, the question then becomes, "Why is diversity lacking?" Perhaps the stream was straightened to control flooding, or the rangeland has been so overgrazed that the stream banks have turned bald and weak.

The identified limiting factor is very often related to land use—an unfortunate product of land uses undertaken for other purposes. In most cases restoration efforts will not be successful unless land-use activities are altered.

Many of our finest trout waters can be found in alluvial valley streams, streams characterized by channels that shift back and forth between valley walls as they continue to adjust characteristics and locations in search of a state of dynamic equilibrium. Placing permanent structures in such a channel, whether the channel is severely degraded or well on the road to recovery, attempts to lock the stream into a relatively fixed location and condition. The stream focuses its erosive energy on these unyielding structures, and the result—often the loss of the structure—becomes especially troublesome when structures are placed unnecessarily.

Several recent studies warn that it is futile to use artificial in-stream structures to circumvent the real causes of stream degradation. The studies are a somewhat controversial call for patience and persistence. They represent an emerging conviction that artificial stream improvements must never be substituted for responsible stewardship of the surrounding watershed.

In 1988 trout-stream habitat experts Wayne Elmore and Robert Beschta suggested that the "construction of expensive structures allows managers to sidestep difficult management decisions. Often, the structural 'enhancement' of rangeland streams is viewed as the solution to inadequate riparian management." In other words a strategic fencing project to keep livestock away from the stream, as described in the Camp Creek case study in chapter 7, is often more effective and cost-efficient than an expensive, highly engineered approach.

At all costs you should avoid expensive and ineffective engineering approaches to trout-habitat rehabilitation. In most cases, when you conclude that an incompatible land use is your major problem, the land-use component of a stream rehabilitation plan may simply demand that activity be conducted differently, relocated, or eliminated to allow the riparian vegetation and stream channel to recover. Only after you consider the crucial question of land-use changes, will you be ready to design the in-stream structural work that may be necessary.

In-stream Structures

Despite the tone of the above statements, the intent is not to deny the usefulness of in-stream structures, such as dams, deflectors, and awninglike bank extensions that provide overhead cover for trout. The proper placement of in-stream structures can play an important role in overall project design.

However, if the stream you are working on suffers from an inappropriate land use, the best advice is to take steps to change the land use to allow the stream to heal. Once the stream has begun to heal, you should be able to identify where in-stream structures will be most effective. If you don't wait for the stream to mend, you may find your structures located several yards or more away from the new channel the stream carved as it begins to heal itself. Dams can break, floodwaters can rip deflectors out of the bank, and artificial bank covers can be left high and dry or fill with sediment as the stream searches for a new equilibrium after all the structures are in place.

When evaluating potential in-stream structures, you must consider not only how they will restore limiting habitat attributes but also the type and condition of the stream channel. The moment you place a structure in a channel, you will change the dynamic equilibrium of the stream and set a series of natural forces into action in response to the structure. If you want the trout-habitat enhancement structures to meet your expectations, you must anticipate how the stream channel will adjust to them.

Channel-type Considerations and In-stream Structure Selection

The structure under consideration must not only provide the limiting habitat attribute but also be compatible with the stream channel. If it is not compatible, chances are it will fail or create new problems rather than eliminate the original one. This occurred in the Rocky Mountains following the publication of White and Brynildson's *Guidelines for Management of Trout Stream Habitat in Wisconsin*. Well-intentioned fishery biologists, with little understanding of stream dynamics, attempted to place structures designed for the low-gradient, sand-bottomed streams of Wisconsin in the high-gradient, gravel-cobble-boulder streams of the Rockies. At high flows many of the structures were washed out along with stream banks.

To avoid similar project-planning mistakes, the stream classification concepts introduced in chapters 3 and 4 can be particularly helpful. The stream classification system developed by hydrologist David Rosgen, and the fish-structure selection guide derived from it by Rosgen and fishery biologist Brenda Fittante, can help you determine the suitability of various in-stream structures.

For example, imagine that cover is a limiting factor in a hypothetical stream with a gradient of 1.5 to 2.5, a sinuosity of 1.3 to 1.5, a width to depth ratio of 8 to 20, and a substrate dominated by large cobble mixed with small boulders and coarse gravel. In Rosgen's classification system, the stream is classified as a B-2 channel. The fish-structure selection guide suggests that the cover-providing structure most suited for a B-2 channel is half-log cover.

The use of Rosgen's channel classification system in conjunction with stream-habitat inventories is highly recommended. Rosgen's system can help you select the structures best suited for very specific problems encountered in many stream reaches. Two words of caution, however, are advised. First, although you may want to attempt to interpret the classification system and structure selection guide, it will be necessary for you to double-check your conclusions about the stream channel and the in-stream structures most appropriate for it with an expert before work is commenced. Second, the guides should not be used as a prescription. If you determine that you have a B-2 channel, it doesn't necessarily mean you should construct half-log covers. The guides are designed to determine suitability of particular structures for a given channel type. They are not substitutes for a comprehensive analysis of the stream.

Fish-housing Design Specifications

The structures you select and design must meet the habitat needs of trout, as well as the hydraulic characteristics of the stream. If, for instance, your limiting-factor analysis identifies a need to create summer-rearing habitat, your structure must provide the depth, velocity, cover, and substrate the trout species needs for summer rearing. In short, you need fish-housing design specifications.

These design specifications are provided in large part by the habitat suitability criteria curves described in chapter 2. These curves describe the habitat preferences of rainbow, brook, and brown trout according to their various life stages.

The habitat suitability curves should be augmented by a trout-population inventory. One of the real benefits of conducting a trout-population inventory using the habitat-partitioning method described earlier is the information you obtain about the habitat preferences of the trout in your stream. Be cautious, however, of a potentially interpretive pitfall: It is possible, and often likely, to find trout congregated in marginal habitat because it is the best habitat they can find in a degraded stream. Or the trout might have collected in areas that provide security in response to the snorkeling or electrofishing crew. Since your goal is to provide good or excellent habitat—not to increase the amount of marginal habitat—you should study the trout habitat suitability curves that have been published for the species and life stage of interest for your geographic area. If the curves exist, you should be able to obtain copies from the National Ecology Center, 2627 Redwing Road, Creekside Building #1, Fort Collins, CO 80526-2899. In addition, the experience and advice of a local fishery biologist can be most valuable, especially when tempered by your own observations of trout-habitat preferences in your stream.

General Design Considerations

Of course, the pitfall mentioned above is not the only one you may encounter. Whenever one attempts to make an adjustment to a natural system, the adjustment has the potential to adversely affect an associated component of the natural system. The *Stream Enhancement Guide*, published by the Province of British Columbia's Ministry of the Environment, offers the following tips for installation of in-stream habitat enhancement structures:

1. A project designed to affect one species of salmonid may adversely affect another species or another life stage of the target species. Measures to improve spawning habitat, for example, could cause a loss of rearing habitat if the importance of pools, undercut banks, logs, boulders, and other cover features are not taken into consideration.
2. All stream devices must be constructed in low profile to permit free passage of drifting logs and debris at high flows. The low profile will also enhance the durability of the structure.
3. Construction materials should be of natural materials durable enough to withstand freeze-thaw cycles and hydraulic forces, and reasonably resistant to decay.
4. Structures designed to improve a specific section of stream should be constructed so that they will not damage adjacent areas of high value to fish.
5. Construction should be timed to minimize impacts to streambed and banks and to avoid conflict with spawning and incubation periods of salmonids. Late winter or early spring, before the

ground thaws and the spring runoff begins, is a good time in northern climates. Much stream work can be safely undertaken during late summer as well.

6. Stream banks must be well protected, either naturally or with placed revetment (riprap) if a device accelerates the flow or turns the flow toward a bank, in order to minimize bank erosion.

Chapters 6 through 9 describe and critically analyze a wide variety of project designs that have been used around the country.

FINAL PLANNING AND PREPARATION

Final planning and preparation for the project include:

1. Obtain any necessary permits and/or landowner approval. Check with your state fish and game and natural resources agencies to determine the type and number of permits you may need to acquire to conduct in-stream construction. A U.S. Army Corps of Engineers 404 permit for stream-channel dredge and fill may also be required.
2. Identify and obtain all necessary materials and equipment. The structures you have designed and the tools necessary to put them together will determine your materials list. Logs, rocks, chain saws, and steel-reinforced rods should be some of the items you may need to complete a project.
3. Determine labor needs. Most projects requiring in-stream structures require three to four laborers. The time involved depends entirely upon the extent of the project. Labor requirements are described in several of the upcoming case histories in chapters 7, 8, and 9.

PROJECT MAINTENANCE AND MONITORING

When you have completed the construction project, in many ways, your work has just begun. Maintenance of the structures will be an ongoing job. Without maintenance the structures may stop functioning and may even lead to further stream degradation. For example, boulders, gravel, sand, or debris transported during high flows may fill in a bank overhang built to provide cover and thwart all your hard work. Debris trapped in a structure could also deflect flows toward the bank, resulting in significant erosion that could quickly destroy the bank and the structure. Extremely high flows may damage the structures.

Monitoring of habitat changes and trout-population response will be a continuing obligation. Analysis of the monitoring data will lead to changes in future project designs, as illustrated by the bottleneck in figure 5.1.

PUTTING IT ALL TOGETHER

Your job is now to synthesize all the information presented into a plan that will result in increased trout production. The following example describes how Fred Everest, Jim Sedell, Gordon Reeves, and John Wolfe approached the problems presented by Fish Creek, a stream near Estacada, Oregon, that was not producing the steelhead trout many felt it was capable of producing.

Fish Creek Drainage Land Use

The entire Fish Creek drainage basin lies within the Mount Hood National Forest on the west side of the Cascade Mountains in north-central Oregon. The stream begins at an elevation of about 4,600 feet and flows for about 13 miles to its confluence with the Clackamas River. The channel gradient is steep, generally exceeding 5 percent except for the last four miles, where gradient eases to 2 percent. The steep gradient and volcanic geology have created a stream with mostly riffle habitats and boulder substrates.

The basin is heavily forested, and the land use consists of timber harvests and public recreational activities. Six clear-cuts straddle the stream and contribute to the higher water temperatures in the unshaded reaches.

Habitat Surveys

During the habitat surveys of five 0.3-mile stream reaches, workers noted that woody debris had been greatly reduced as a result of timber sales. Each reach selected was representative of the overall habitat conditions in Fish Creek. A map of each reach included obstructions (logjams, culverts, falls); diversion structures; landslides; debris torrents (fallen trees); springs; bank erosion; and wetland habitat. The substrate was also mapped.

In addition to the mapping, stream-habitat transects were established, in-stream habitat measurements were taken, and photo points were established.

In-stream Habitat and Trout-Population Surveys

In-stream habitat and trout abundance by habitat type were determined throughout the stream length by using the visual estimation methods described at the conclusion of chapter 4 and reported in 1988 by David Hankin and Gordon Reeves.

Limiting-factor Analysis

The limiting-factor analysis proceeded continuously from 1983 through 1986. Each year the effects of the structural treatments were evaluated to direct the project-design efforts the succeeding year. Essentially, all the information obtained became a part of an ongoing monitoring and evaluation process that drove the following year's construction projects.

Based upon three years of data, the biologists concluded that either winter habitat for young-of-the-year steelhead (those hatched that spring) or summer habitat for yearling steelhead (those hatched the previous spring) was limiting the number of yearling steelhead in Fish Creek. The conclusion was based upon the observation that despite large annual variations in numbers of young-of-the-year steelhead, which were directly related to the number of adults that returned from the ocean to spawn, the number of yearling fish remained remarkably constant.

An analysis of the habitat area and its use indicated that the availability of pool habitat was limiting summer rearing of yearling steelhead because, although pool habitat was not abundant, it was heavily used by yearling steelhead. The addition of deep boulder pools appeared to be the factor most likely to enhance summer-rearing capability of the stream for yearling steelhead.

Because the stream was used by coho and chinook salmon, a similar habitat area and use analysis was made for these species. From it an enhancement plan—in addition to the deep boulder-associated pools—was developed. The plan included: (1) an off-channel pond to provide winter-rearing habitat for coho; (2) development of a side channel to provide additional spawning habitat, as well as juvenile winter habitat (pools with associated woody debris and roots); (3) insertion of boulder berms to trap gravel for spawning habitat; (4) planting of two-year-old cottonwood trees in clear-cut areas to reestablish riparian vegetation on four streamside acres; and (5) restoration of woody cover to five habitat sites by using explosives to fall trees into the stream. (Dynamite was used rather than a chain saw to leave the root wad attached to the tree.)

Following this elaborate construction phase, an extensive monitoring program was established to observe changes in fish populations and in overall habitat, as well as to gauge the success of efforts to create additional habitat. In just two years, the workers were able to conclude the following:

1. Initial prototype habitat enhancements made changes in overall availability of four types of habitat in Fish Creek basin. As a result, riffle habitat decreased by 4 percent, pool habitat increased by 3 percent, beaver-pond habitat increased 15-fold, and side-channel habitat increased by 2 percent.
2. Immediate changes in trout production associated with the boulder berms, the side channel, and the alcove trees were minimal.
3. Trout response to improvements was often delayed, so extended evaluations were required.
4. Some habitat manipulations designed to improve spawning habitat appeared to have had a negative impact on winter habitat.
5. Factors limiting production of anadromous salmonids were difficult to identify.
6. At least three years of data will be needed to understand species interactions and habitat usage.

7. The risk of failure to achieve biological objectives of enhancement is high without a thorough pre- and post-project inventory evaluation.

CONCLUSION

The Fish Creek example is noteworthy because the biologists conducted an intensive preproject inventory of land use, in-stream habitat, and fish population. They essentially covered all the bases, which is seldom done, and still were not totally successful. However, the Fish Creek project is still being monitored, and new information is being used to further develop trout-habitat improvements. Today, the trends show that all the work is beginning to pay off in more steelhead trout. The workers' thorough and systematic approach to trout-stream rehabilitation provided them with precise information to better define other factors that limit steelhead-trout production.

Because the Fish Creek workers identified the factors limiting trout production after the preproject inventory, the project design was based upon the limiting-factor analysis and the hydraulic characteristics of the stream. Following construction of the project, an extensive monitoring program led to new limiting-factor discoveries and subsequent changes in future project designs.

When it is done correctly and patiently, the whole process becomes a precise computational procedure in which a cycle of inventories and measurements is repeated until the results begin to more and more closely approximate the desired and expected outcome. The prospect of creating a thriving, healthy trout population where an abused stream channel now exists stirs the youthful enthusiasm in most of us. As difficult as it may be, however, that enthusiasm must be tempered with a thorough, scientific analysis of the stream.

SOURCES

Elmore, W., and Beschta, R. 1988. The Fallacy of Structures and the Fortitude of Vegetation. Paper presented at the California Riparian Systems Conference; September 22–24, 1988; at Univ. of California at Davis, CA.

Everest, F., and Sedell, J. 1984. Evaluating Effectiveness of Stream Enhancement Projects. In *Pacific Northwest Stream Habitat Management Workshop*, ed.

T.J. Hassler, pp. 246–56. Arcata, CA: California Cooperative Fishery Research Unit, Humboldt State Univ.

Everest, F.; Sedell, J.; Reeves, G.; and Wolfe, J. 1984. *Fisheries Enhancement in the Fish Creek Basin—An Evaluation of In-Channel and Off-Channel Projects, 1984.* Bonneville Power Administration Project no. 84–11. Portland, OR.

Hankin, D., and Reeves, G. 1988. Establishing Total Fish Abundance and Total Habitat Area in Small Streams Based on Visual Estimation Methods. *Can. J. Fish. Aquat. Sci.* 45(5):834–44.

Hutchinson, G.E. 1973. Eutrophication—The Scientific Background of a Contemporary Practical Problem. *Am. Sci.* (3):269–79.

Odum, E. P. *Ecology.* 1966. New York: Holt, Rinehart and Winston.

Platts, W., and Nelson, R. L. 1985. Stream Habitat and Fisheries Response to Livestock Grazing and Instream Improvement Structures, Big Creek, Utah. *Jrnl. Soil and Water Cons.* 40(4):374–79.

Platts, W., and Rinne, J. 1985. Riparian and Stream Enhancement Management and Research in the Rocky Mountains. *N. Am. Jrnl. of Fish. Man.* 5(2A):115–25.

Province of British Columbia. 1980. *Stream Enhancement Guide.* Vancouver, BC. Province of British Columbia, Ministry of the Environment.

Rosgen, D. 1985. A Stream Classification System. In *Riparian Ecosystems and Their Management: Reconciling Conflicting Uses. First North American Riparian Conference.* USDA-FS Gen. Tech. Rpt. no. RM-120. pp. 91–95.

Rosgen, D., and Fittante, B. 1986. Fish Habitat Structures: A Selection Guide Using Stream Classification. In *Fifth Trout Stream Habitat Improvement Workshop*, ed. J. Miller, J. Arway, and R. Carline. pp. 163–79. Loch Haven, PA.

White, R., and Brynildson, O. 1967. *Guidelines for Management of Trout Stream Habitat in Wisconsin*, Wisc. Dept. of Natural Resources Technical Bulletin no. 39. Madison, WI.

Chapter 6

THE ROLE AND FUNCTION OF
IN-STREAM STRUCTURES

T HE first five chapters have focused on the theory of trout-stream restoration. Land use has been emphasized as a critical element of trout-habitat rehabilitation and management because it is one of the major factors that controls the vitality of a trout stream. By design, little has been said about the role of in-stream devices in trout-habitat restoration projects. Nonetheless, one shouldn't ignore the important contribution well-placed and well-researched in-stream structures have made to the field of trout-habitat rehabilitation. To that end, some general information regarding generic structure types is presented with the understanding that structural elements are one piece of the stream rehabilitation puzzle. In a successful rehabilitation project all the puzzle pieces must be used.

DAMS

There is almost an infinite variety of designs for dams used in stream restoration work. The primary purpose of a dam is to mimic a debris jam or gravel bar in a step-pool or pool-riffle sinuous stream. Upstream of the dam, the water velocity is reduced and a portion of the stream's sediment load is deposited. This can have either good or bad consequences, depending upon the purpose of the dam and the nature of the sediment load. If the intent of the dam is to create additional spawning areas and the stream transports sufficient quantities of gravel, deposition of the gravel load upstream of the dam

133

may be beneficial. If the stream carries a substantial sand or silt load, the area upstream of the dam may quickly fill with silt and eliminate insect and trout habitat.

Downstream of the dam, a pool is usually formed where the water drops over the structure and attacks the streambed. The pools can provide cover for adult trout and overwintering habitat for both adult and juvenile trout.

Dams are generally not suitable in low-gradient meandering streams. Often these stream types are marginally warm for trout. Water ponded behind a dam has additional opportunity to warm to levels that can be lethal to trout. Even a low dam can pond water for some distance upstream in a low-gradient stream. In addition to warming, the ponded water may spread out and begin to eat around the edges of the dam, which can lead to catastrophic dam failure.

If a dam is being considered as a limiting-factor prescription, it should be remembered: (1) it can restrict trout migration; and (2) it can present a hazard to rafters and canoeists.

DEFLECTORS

Water-current deflectors are used to force the stream into a more meandering pattern and to create pools. Deflectors have also been used to scour fine sediments from the streambed in order to reveal the streambed's gravel substrate.

Like dams, deflectors come in a variety of shapes and sizes. The basic design consists of a triangle with an apex angle of 30 to 60 degrees. The partial barrier to water flow deflects the current toward the opposite bank. By partially blocking flow, the deflector causes water to back up or pile up to some degree, which results in increased water depth and velocity. The water scours a pool just downstream and opposite the deflector. A portion of the stream's sediment load is deposited in the lee of the structure. Thus, a bar forms downstream of, and on the same bank as, the structure.

The wing deflector is an early design that is seldom used in modern trout-habitat restoration work, primarily because it can lead to severe bank erosion. Its design consists simply of a wall, rather than a triangle, composed of log, boulders, or other materials that deflect the current. The problem is that a wing deflector can work too well. When water flows over an obstruction, such as a riffle or a deflector, it leaves the obstruction flowing at a right angle to it. In figure 6.1 you can see how water flowing over a wing deflector at high flow is directed toward the stream bank. Water flowing over a triangular deflector is directed back to the middle of the channel by the downstream edge of the structure.

Through the creative work of several researchers, deflectors have evolved into multipurpose structures that not only enhance the natural meandering of a stream but also provide cover and stream-bank protection as well.

Deflectors are best suited for low-gradient meandering streams. It is rather futile to attempt to force a high-gradient sinuous stream into a meandering pattern. In addition, the armored bottom of the mountain stream is not as susceptible to scouring as the generally more soft-bottomed bed of a meandering stream.

White and Brynildson state that deflectors are the best all-around devices for restoring or enhancing low-gradient meandering stream channels. They urge that the use of deflectors be guided by two important principles: (1) Deflectors should guide the current rather than dam it; and (2) deflectors should be built in low profile with no protrusions upon which drifting debris can accumulate.

COVER

Cover is provided naturally by undercut banks with overhanging vegetation, debris jams, root wads, boulders, aquatic weed beds, turbulence, and sufficient depth.

Historically, cover structures have been constructed of logs placed along the bank opposite and downstream from a deflector. This is done in an attempt to mimic an undercut bank on the outside meander bend.

Wooden cover structures have also been designed for, and placed in, mid-channel locations, but they are seldom used there today because they have not been particularly successful at attracting trout and they tend to direct the current at the stream banks. If the banks happen to be unstable, the structure can cause stream-bank erosion.

The placement of trees, root wads, and boulders to provide

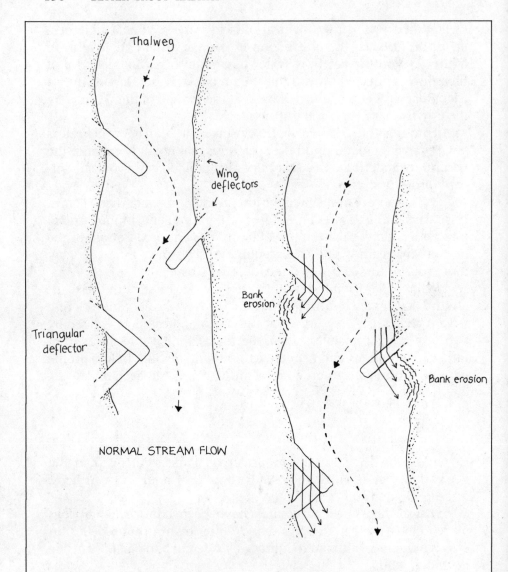

6.1 Wing deflectors cause bank erosion. *Wing deflectors, which appear to function as well as triangular deflectors during normal flows, can cause bank erosion during flood or high flows, as shown on the right side of the drawing. This is because when water flows over an obstruction, it leaves the object flowing at a right angle to it.*

cover and focal points, or lies, has become increasingly popular. Half-log structures have been used in both sinuous and meandering streams to provide cover. These are very natural materials and unobtrusive to the eye. To avoid bank erosion, both the method and location of such cover should be important considerations in high-gradient, high-velocity streams.

STREAM-BANK PROTECTION/STABILIZATION

The best form of bank protection is to keep man's and domestic animals' activities well-removed from the bank. Where man's encroachment upon the riparian corridor has already resulted in bank instability, the best solution is to move those activities away from the bank and allow the channel to stabilize naturally. Where this is not possible, such as in urban areas or along major transportation corridors, structural approaches to stream-bank protection/stabilization must be employed to speed the natural healing process. In these areas placement of rock revetment and jetties and construction of log cribs are common structural techniques used to help the stream recover.

Stream-bank revetment is generally constructed from rock, evergreen trees, or brush bundles. Rock revetment can take the form of a continuous blanket of rock or a series of jetties. Both types of riprap can provide trout cover, as well as stream-bank stabilization. Large evergreen trees with branches or brush bundles will also provide bank protection and will provide more cover than rock riprap. Trees and brush also are more natural-looking than the rock. However, the effective life span of trees and brush bundles is far shorter than that of well-placed rock.

FENCES, LIVESTOCK CROSSINGS, AND PEOPLE GATES

In riparian areas where livestock grazing needs to be controlled, fences can be used to fence the animals either out of the riparian area or to create a riparian pasture. There are three types of fences used to

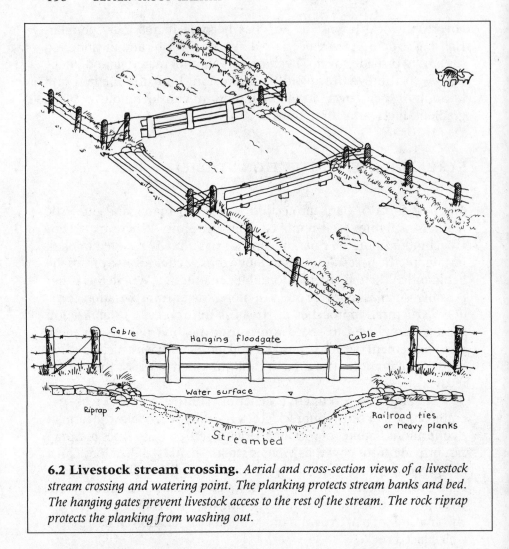

6.2 Livestock stream crossing. *Aerial and cross-section views of a livestock stream crossing and watering point. The planking protects stream banks and bed. The hanging gates prevent livestock access to the rest of the stream. The rock riprap protects the planking from washing out.*

fence livestock. The basic three- to four-strand barbed-wire fence is the most widely used. It is relatively inexpensive ($5,000 to $6,000 per mile) but requires at least annual maintenance. Cattle can lean against these fences, stretching wire and breaking the fence posts.

The split-rail or jackleg fence is more aesthetically pleasing and requires less maintenance, but is considerably more expensive than barbed-wire fencing.

A third and increasingly popular alternative is the one-strand, solar-powered electric fence. This type of fence is competitively priced, easily erected and taken down, and apparently very effective.

Fences, however, create two problems, in addition to the maintenance they require: (1) They limit livestock access to streams for watering; and (2) they limit angler access.

Figure 6.2 illustrates a livestock watering-access point along a fenced portion of stream. The railroad ties or planking minimizes the erosion of banks and the introduction of silt into the stream. The hanging floodgates are designed to prevent livestock access to the rest of the stream from the watering point. The rock riprap, both upstream and downstream of the planking, prevents the planking from washing out.

Figure 6.3 shows two approaches that afford anglers access to a barbed-wire fenced section of stream.

CONSTRUCTION MATERIALS

Whenever possible, naturally occurring materials should be used for construction. The use of native materials enhances the aesthetic quality of the structures and helps keep costs in line. When wood is used, it is important that it remain under water at all times. If the

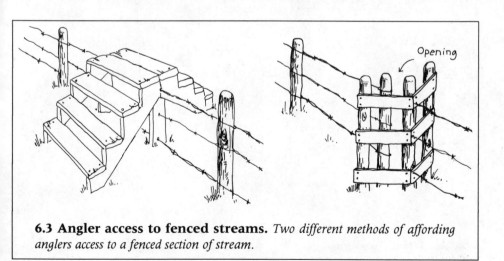

6.3 Angler access to fenced streams. *Two different methods of affording anglers access to a fenced section of stream.*

wood is periodically wet and dry, it will rot more quickly and reduce the structure's effective life span.

Although gabions, or rock-filled wire cages, are widely used to construct dams and deflectors, they are not natural in appearance, and many workers feel their use should be discouraged. Gabions, like all structures, will eventually fail. When the gabion fails, it leaves behind rusting pieces of the wire cage, which are dangerous to recreationists, as well as unsightly. The logs and boulders of a failed structure constructed of native materials can be incorporated into the stream's natural organic material load. The steel pins and reinforcement bar used in constructing log structures can create many of the same problems as failed gabions, although to a much lesser degree.

Because the construction of some structures requires the use of heavy equipment that can disturb the streambed and banks, care should be used. It is often a good practice to do much of the heavy equipment work in winter when banks are frozen. In addition, all permits necessary for working in and along streams should be obtained before construction begins.

Chapter 7

STREAMS AFFECTED
BY AGRICULTURE

T HE following three chapters will show how trout-stream restoration theory and its many variations have been put into practice
over a broad range of geographic areas, land uses, stream-channel
types, and for different factors that limit trout production.

Much of the background research for this book took the form of
extended on-site visits to several regions of the country to observe
contemporary trout-habitat restoration projects. Those observations
are chronicled in 14 case histories that range from the forested
Appalachian streams of northern Georgia to the low-gradient sand
streams of Wisconsin to the rangeland streams of eastern Oregon.

Because workers in different regions address different problems,
specific methods for conducting restoration and habitat enhancement projects have evolved to meet the problems each region offers.

Table 7.1 cross-references the case histories by geographic area.
Such referencing clearly indicates how workers in specific areas have
approached their streams.

Each case history describes the stream setting, preproject inventory, limiting-factor analysis, design, implementation/construction,
monitoring, and degree of success for each project. In addition,
sources for further information are provided for each example.

The case histories are presented as they relate to specific land-
use problems that have affected trout habitat. They are also cross-
referenced according to stream location.

TABLE 7.1
CASE HISTORIES
(BY GEOGRAPHIC AREA)

Southeast
  Jones Creek, Georgia

Midwest
  Lawrence Creek, Wisconsin
  Little Plover River and Lunch Creek, Wisconsin
  Rapid Creek, South Dakota

Intermountain West
  Confederate Gulch, Montana
  Irrigation Ditch/Spring Creek, Montana

West Coast
  Bear Creek, Oregon
  Camp Creek, Oregon
  John Day River, Oregon
  Yellow Creek, California

East Coast
  Cranberry River, West Virginia
  Left Branch Young Woman's Creek, Pennsylvania
  Little Crabby Creek, Pennsylvania
  West Valley Creek, Pennsylvania

The land-use priority was selected for several reasons:

1. The predominant land use(s) in a drainage often is responsible for the degraded state of trout habitat. Land-use considerations will be an important aspect of limiting-factor identification and restoration-project planning.
2. Sections of streams flowing through forested lands often have similar problems and solutions, regardless of whether they are in Georgia, Maine, or Oregon. The same is true of streams flowing through agricultural and suburban landscapes.
3. In addition to having similar problems, streams flowing through the same land uses will have similar physical properties, such as gradient and channel type. For example, most streams draining forested watersheds will be step/pool or pool/riffle sinuous streams. Streams flowing through agricultural and rangelands are usually low-gradient meandering streams. These physical proper-

ties play a large role in determining the type of structures that will succeed or fail in a particular setting.

The case histories are presented with the hope that some of the problems and solutions encountered may be similar to those in trout streams yet to be restored. At the very least, it is hoped that an idea or treatment approach that has already been developed will suggest a solution for another restoration plan. There will no doubt be strong inclinations to read the case histories that present information on the land use or geographic area that is of immediate interest. However, it is very likely that each stream project will offer insightful solutions to the problems that confront trout-habitat rehabilitators.

CAMP CREEK, OREGON

Location	*60 miles southeast of Prineville*
Project status	*Public*
Project leader	*Wayne Elmore*
Landowner	*BLM*
Rehab. length	*Five miles*
Limiting factor	*Unstable soils and lack of vegetative cover*
Problem	*Summer livestock grazing*
Prescription	*Exclude livestock from project area*
Begin date	*1965*
End date	*Ongoing*
Current status	*Research project on water storage and aquifer recharge*
Estimated cost	*Unavailable*

Background

Camp Creek is located in north-central Oregon, east of the Cascade Mountains. The main stem of this low-gradient 20-mile-long stream meanders through very erodible soils that contain high proportions of silts and clays. Camp Creek drains high-elevation (roughly 4,000 feet) rangeland. Although the region averages only 12 to 14 inches of rain per year, the discharge regime of the stream is characterized by wide fluctuations in flow. Out-of-bank flows generally occur in the spring during snow-melt runoff, but they also periodically occur at other times of the year in response to heavy rains.

In 1875 the surveyor general of Oregon described the Camp Creek valley floor as a wet meadow with several marshes. By 1903, however, the U.S. Geologic Survey (USGS) reported that Camp Creek and its tributaries were gullies measuring 15 to 25 feet deep and 25 to 100 feet wide. The changes were thought to be the result of extensive overgrazing by cattle and a major flood that probably occurred in 1889. The USGS report suggests that overgrazing reduced the once-abundant vegetation cover, thus rendering the soil incapable of soaking up and holding rainwater. The result was increased runoff and, ultimately, a significant channel incision in Camp Creek. As the channel became incised, the water table dropped dramatically, and the landscape's vegetation gradually changed from a lush marsh and meadow to sagebrush and bunchgrass.

In December 1964, in an attempt to restore the degraded channel, an eight- to ten-foot-high detention dam was installed on Camp Creek. The dam, however, did not last long. It was washed out within the month by a storm of a size that occurs every 100 years.

The current condition of Camp Creek, after 100 years of cattle-grazing pressure in areas where restoration is not underway, is shown in figure 7.1. The incised channel is at least 20 feet deep and 100 feet wide. The stream carries very little flow and obviously does not contain trout. There is virtually no riparian vegetation.

Inventory Methods

A standardized, repeatable inventory was not conducted prior to the initiation of restoration efforts in 1965. At the time, although a few scattered grasses and forbs could be found, the stream banks and floodplain were composed almost entirely of silt, and the stream channel was essentially devoid of vegetation.

Limiting-factor Analysis

Virtually every aspect of trout habitat was lacking from Camp Creek. The stream provided no cover, there was no habitat diversity, water quality was poor, and during the summer there was often no water at all. Based upon the 1875 report of the surveyor general of Oregon,

7.1 Camp Creek, Oregon, 1988. *Unrestored section at Camp Creek as it looks today, after 100 years of grazing pressure, upstream of the restoration project. The incised channel is approximately 20 feet deep and 100 feet wide.*

the biologists working on Camp Creek knew that prior to the onset of heavy grazing the stream had been a very different place. They concluded that heavy grazing was the cause of the degraded state of the channel.

Project Design and Implementation

In 1965 the Bureau of Land Management (BLM) and the Oregon Wildlife Commission initiated a fencing project on Camp Creek to help restore riparian wildlife habitat. Approximately one-tenth of a mile of barren gully was fenced to exclude livestock and permit vegetative recovery. To speed recovery, tall wheat grass and sweet clover were seeded within the fenced area.

Since 1965 additional fences have been built and maintained on Camp Creek. Of the nine miles of Camp Creek that are in public ownership, the BLM has fenced approximately four miles of main stem Camp Creek and one mile of tributary. Today, seeding is no longer an aspect of the fencing projects because native plants reestablished quickly and have proven more rigorous than the seeded species within the riparian zone.

Monitoring

Permanent photo points were established in 1968 by the BLM and Harold Winegar of the Oregon Department of Fish and Wildlife. The BLM began intensive monitoring surveys of Camp Creek in 1978.

The inventory methods initiated in 1978 measured the quality of riparian and adjacent vegetation along a linear transect where vegetation community types were identified. The length, width, and acres of each vegetation community type were measured, as were other attributes. The data were summarized for an entire reach or tributary.

PHYSICAL

A stream-habitat and channel-stability inventory was conducted utilizing methods described by Dale Pfankuch. Variables measured include slope mass wasting or failure; debris-jam potential; vegetative-bank protection; channel width and capacity; bank cutting; bank-margin deposition, substrate size and distribution, and scouring and deposition.

An in-stream habitat inventory was used to evaluate large and small structural material such as boulders, tree trunks and limbs, organic debris, escape cover, pool class and area, spawning area, and pool to riffle ratio.

BIOLOGICAL

In addition to water samples collected and analyzed to determine water quality, aquatic insects were collected, and the data were analyzed using the biotic condition index (BCI) described by Robert Winget and Fred Mangum. By using BCI, workers can rate the quality of the stream based upon the insects collected when compared to an optimum insect community for the stream. The optimum insect community for the stream is based upon its gradient, substrate, and water quality (alkalinity and sulfate).

The stream also was electrofished to determine the fish species and numbers present.

The water quality and aquatic-insect monitoring are repeated every two to three years. The photo points and remaining monitoring studies are completed roughly every five years (1969, 1978, 1984, 1989, etc.).

Summary of Findings

The reaches of Camp Creek that have been protected from grazing offer textbook examples of the natural recovery of an incised channel as described in chapter 3.

For a few years after fencing, even though the grasses along the stream bank grew well enough to provide some stream-bank protection during high flows, the stream remained wide and shallow and exhibited little habitat diversity. The new grasses, however, trapped waterborne silt and clay during floods, and the deposition of the silt built the banks and the floodplain higher. Since 1965, in the area where fences were initially erected, the banks and floodplain of Camp Creek have built up three to six feet. The increased volume of the floodplain also has allowed it to soak up water like a sponge during high flows and assist the uplands in recharging the valley aquifer. Now these moist, silty soils are perfect for the sedges and rushes that have gradually replaced some of the grasses. In combination with the grasses, the sedges and rushes, with their dense, fibrous root systems, are even more effective than the grasses at providing stream-bank stability, as well as building banks and floodplain.

As the vegetation succeeded from grasses to sedges and rushes, the nature of the stream began to change dramatically. As a result of the narrowed channel, water velocity has increased, and silt has been scoured out to reveal gravels suitable for aquatic-insect production.

Although longnose and speckled dace have become established in the enclosure areas, trout do not yet live in Camp Creek. Wayne Elmore, principal investigator for this project, has attempted to obtain a rare rainbow-trout subspecies for introduction. He is confident the rainbow-trout subspecies—redband trout, which are native to the region—would survive in the stream's current improved conditions.

The building of banks and floodplain has brought about another benefit as well. The floodplain sponge releases water to the low-flowing stream through most dry seasons while in downstream areas, where grazing has continued and riparian recovery has not occurred, the flow disappears into the dry streambed.

Today, within the fenced area, the stream more closely resembles its 1875 character. Although the meadow and marshlands are confined to a 100-foot-wide gully bottom as the channel continues to aggrade and the water table rises, the benefits may eventually spread out and affect an even wider area.

Even with these improvements, however, all is not rosy at Camp Creek. In the early 1980s, after 15 years of significant progress in restoring portions of the stream through land-use changes, an impatient federal land manager tried to apply a structural solution to Camp Creek's problems by placing large gabion dams across the stream outside the enclosures. The intent was to speed the healing process by trapping more sediment than the naturally restored streamside vegetation could hold. Unfortunately, the gabion dams lasted less than six months before a flash flood washed them out and caused the soil around the ends of the structures to erode away.

A continued reliance on quick-fix solutions to problems—even in the face of data showing that instant gratification is not as effective as a long-term solution—may be our most persistent human foible. For many trout-habitat rehabilitators, Camp Creek should be testimony that patience will often prove a most rewarding virtue.

BEAR CREEK, OREGON

Location	*25 miles south of Prineville*
Project status	*Public and private*
Project leaders	*Earl McKinney and Wayne Elmore*
Landowner	*BLM*
Rehab. length	*Six miles*
Limiting factor	*Rapid runoff, poor upland and riparian conditions*
Problem	*Season-long livestock grazing*
Prescription	*Three-pasture late-winter/early-spring grazing*
Begin date	*1976*
End date	*Ongoing*
Current status	*Dramatic recovery*
Estimated cost	*$25,000 for creek and fencing work and about $480,000 for upland clearing and burning*

Background

The Bear Creek drainage, which is located near Camp Creek in north-central Oregon, was once dominated by willows and birch trees with areas of wide, wet meadows. Today, the 26-mile-long stream flows through a mix of private and public lands that have been heavily grazed by cattle for more than 100 years. The public lands are administered by the U.S.D.A. Forest Service and the Bureau of Land Management.

Bear Creek, in the restoration-project areas, is a low- to moderate-gradient stream that meanders through sandy loam soils. Although there are wide fluctuations in the discharge regime, and out-of-bank flows generally occur each year, portions of the stream still run dry during droughts.

The channel itself is incised to a depth of about 10 feet. It is roughly 100 feet wide. The potential riparian area, outside the restoration areas, is dominated by sagebrush. Juniper, a tree that transpires a remarkable amount of water into the atmosphere (35 gallons per day when soils are saturated), apparently invaded the area over the past 100 years and still dominates upland portions of the drainage.

Inventory Methods

Restoration work on this stream began in 1976 with an intensive inventory of existing conditions. The techniques used to inventory the condition of Bear Creek are the same as those used to monitor changes in Camp Creek.

PHYSICAL

1. Linear transects were established and riparian-vegetation community types were inventoried to determine species present, extent of the community types, and their contribution to streambank stability.
2. Stream-habitat and channel-stability inventories were taken using transect methods.

3. In-stream habitat inventories were taken to quantify the amount of escape cover, number, size and quality of pools, spawning areas, and pool to riffle ratios.
4. Water quality was described through analysis of water samples.

BIOLOGICAL

1. Aquatic insects were collected and analyzed using the biotic condition index.
2. The trout community was sampled using electrofishing.

Limiting-factor Analysis

Bear Creek, like Camp Creek prior to restoration efforts, was a stream in a state of total disrepair. The stream was wide and shallow with very little habitat diversity or cover. Stream banks were unstable, the channel was deeply incised, and water quality—as a result of high sediment loads—was poor. Aquatic insects were poorly represented, and there were no fish, let alone trout, to be found in the stream.

Project Design and Implementation

The restoration program called for three distinct management approaches:

1. Grazing management—cattle were excluded from six miles of the stream by fencing for the period 1976 through 1981. This allowed the vegetation to begin to recover in a manner similar to that described for Camp Creek. As the banks and floodplain were rebuilt by vegetation-trapped sediments, and the alluvial aquifer rose, the dryland-grass community types were replaced by sedges and rushes. This led to increased stream-bank stability and continued improvement in the stream. By 1982, six years after cattle had been excluded, the lower three and one-half miles of the six-mile project area were again opened to grazing.

Although this area had historically been subjected to season-long grazing in the riparian and upland areas, the new grazing plan—designed by BLM range conservationist Earl McKinney—established separate riparian and upland pastures. Today cattle are herded into the riparian three-pasture system for approximately six weeks in late winter. Livestock are not permitted on the pastures until spring runoff has started and the riparian vegetation is covered with water—a time when the upland vegetation is still dormant but beginning to turn green. After six weeks of grazing, the cattle are moved to upland pastures. This reduces use of the riparian zone and by offering it the late spring and summer months to grow ungrazed by livestock, the riparian vegetation is allowed to recover from the late-winter grazing. The beneficial effects of this ungrazed vegetation carry until the following spring as it influences stream processes, for example, by protecting stream banks and trapping the spring's flood-borne sediment load.

2. Upland vegetation management—the small tributaries rising in the uplands, which could contribute to the flow of valley streams, are generally dry in summer.

In 1979 a program of juniper cutting and burning was undertaken in conjunction with the new grazing management techniques, to reduce the competition with juniper for water and afford newly seeded grasses time to become established in the uplands. The root structure of the grasses is eventually expected to increase the permeability of the soils, which will allow rain and melting snow to percolate into the soil.

The combined result of these upland management techniques has led to: (1) a reduction in runoff, which had caused damaging erosion and the incision of the tributary channels; (2) a more spongelike soil that stores water—this is released later to help maintain the late-summer base flows of the tributaries, which, in turn, contribute to valley stream flows; and (3) palatable grasses for improved upland grazing conditions.

3. Bank protection—in 1982, when grazing management had been in effect for six years, juniper revetment was placed on Bear Creek to protect selected high, cut banks from further erosion. An unusual aspect of the juniper revetment is that the large trees were simply dropped over the edge of the bank and were not held in place with cable. This was done because the workers felt that the

large-sized trees would remain in place. So far, this has proven to work. Because the researchers knew that many bank-protection efforts had failed as the stream moved away from the raw bank in response to changes in land management, they chose to wait for the stream-channel changes to become established before they embarked on a bank-protection project.

Monitoring

The habitat attributes measured during the inventory continue to be measured, with the same techniques, every five to six years. Photographs shot from permanent photo points, an important aspect of monitoring this project, are also taken at five- to six-year intervals (1976, 1984, 1989, etc.). Water-quality and aquatic-insect monitoring is conducted every two to three years.

Summary of Findings

The recovery of the stream channel in the intensively managed riparian pasture is another textbook example of the natural restoration of an incised channel. The streambed and floodplain have aggraded approximately three feet over the past 12 years. The sedge-rush-grass riparian vegetation has replaced the dryland-grass community that inhabited the area prior to restoration efforts. The stream channel has narrowed by 30 to 40 feet. The stream is now narrow and deep, and the dense fibrous root mats provide undercut banks for trout, which are present for the first time in generations.

In addition to providing increased trout habitat, the riparian vegetation plays an important role in maintaining water quality. For example, during a recent major flood, the improved riparian area captured about 24,000 cubic yards of sediment. Rather than flowing downstream into a reservoir, this sediment immediately began to build the stream banks and floodplain to further encourage the recovery of Bear Creek.

As the volume of the floodplain has increased with the capture of additional sediment, so has its ability to store water. Today, even during a drought, this reach of stream maintains flows year-round. However, in stretches where recovery efforts have not taken place, the stream still dries up or becomes intermittent.

The Bear Creek restoration project will likely bring smiles to the faces of trout anglers, but they are not the only ones who have benefited. The rancher who grazes his cattle in the pasture and surrounding uplands is now smiling as well. The rancher's benefits include a more than fourfold increase in animal unit month (AUMs), a yearlong water supply on the creek, and a healthier, heavier herd. This herd now spends less time grazing the water-laden riparian areas and more time grazing the nutrient-rich upland vegetation. The rancher needs less hay because he can graze his livestock in late winter.

Clearly, the upland vegetation management is an important component of the Bear Creek project. Its success demonstrates that the physical condition of the uplands can have a direct influence on the outcome of riparian and in-stream habitat enhancement projects. In November 1988, under the siege of six months of drought, a small upland tributary was still flowing. Grasses, too, were thriving in the stream bottom and actually obscuring the stream itself. The willows, grasses, and forbs had begun to stabilize the steep, incised banks.

The juniper revetment also played a role in the restoration of Bear Creek by protecting the high cut bank from further erosion. The dense tangling of branches actually caused a decrease in water velocity and a deposition of sediment that has been invaded by bank-stabilizing grasses, sedges, and rushes.

The dramatic response of Camp Creek and Bear Creek is a result, in part, from the soils of the area and the streams' widely fluctuating discharge regimes. The building of new banks and a floodplain requires riparian vegetation, silt, and regular out-of-bank flows to transport the silt to the building sites. Accordingly, this type of response could not be expected in a low-silt stream that seldom has out-of-bank flows.

Camp Creek and Bear Creek project leader Elmore feels very strongly about a stream's ability to restore itself in response to management changes. His beliefs are reflected in his patient approach to trout-stream habitat rehabilitation. For Elmore, structural approaches to trout-stream habitat work are too often employed for the worst reasons. He says that although an elaborate structural solution gives the appearance that an agency or landowner is actively trying to solve a problem, it often fails to treat the real disease—

inappropriate land use. In Elmore's view, the large sums of money and hours of labor that are expended on stream structures doomed to failure would be better spent to bring about proper land-use management.

In addition, Elmore feels that structural approaches can inhibit a stream from restoring itself. He has seen streams change location dramatically and often in response to positive land-use changes. These channel movements occur as the stream tends toward dynamic equilibrium. Structures, however, lock the channel into place, limiting the flexibility of the stream as it moves toward dynamic equilibrium.

LAWRENCE CREEK, WISCONSIN

Location	*Adams and Marquette counties in central Wisconsin*
Project status	*Public*
Project leader	*Robert L. Hunt*
Landowner	*Wisconsin Department of Natural Resources*
Rehab. length	*One mile*
Limiting factor	*Lack of permanent trout hiding/resting cover*
Problem	*Long-term bank degradation as a result of cattle grazing*
Prescription	*Intensive installation of bank cover/deflectors structures*
Begin date	*Spring 1964*
End date	*Fall 1964*
Current status	*Structures still 90 percent functional*
Estimated cost	*$26,200 (in 1964 dollars)*

Background

The sand counties of central Wisconsin have been the home and inspiration to some of America's best-known and most influential conservationists. John Muir spent his childhood in the sand counties and Aldo Leopold's *Sand County Almanac* is based on his experiences at his beloved sand-county farm.

In *Sand County Almanac* Leopold writes:

The sign says, "You are entering the Green River Soil Conservation District." The sign is neatly painted. It stands in a creek-bottom pasture so short you could play golf on it. Nearby is the graceful loop of an old dry creek bed. The new creek bed is ditched straight as a ruler; it has been "uncurled" by the county engineer to hurry the run-off. On the hill in the background are contoured strip-crops; they have been "curled" by the erosion engineer to retard the run-off. The water must be confused by so much advice.

Lawrence Creek, too, must have been similarly confused. Figure 7.2 shows an undisturbed stretch of Lawrence Creek. The narrow, deep channel with undercut banks and overhanging vegetation would undoubtedly look inviting to a trout angler. Yet the background of figure 7.3 reveals the effects farming and cattle grazing had on Lunch Creek, a neighboring sand-county stream. Because the bed and banks of Lawrence Creek are composed largely of sand, the banks can become very unstable if the vegetation that holds them together is disturbed. As illustrated in figure 7.3, re-

7.2 An undisturbed reach of Lawrence Creek, Wisconsin.

7.3 Agricultural influence on Lunch Creek, Wisconsin. *The effects of agriculture on nearby Lunch Creek. Note the change in riparian vegetation between the foreground and background of the photograph. Where do you think the trout are in this picture?*

moval of riparian vegetation and subsequently weakened banks resulted in a laterally unstable channel and an unnaturally wide and shallow stream.

Lawrence Creek, like most of the sand streams of central Wisconsin, is a very low-gradient (less than 0.5 percent) meandering stream. The sand that composes most of the soil in this area was deposited by the great continental glaciers. It effectively soaks up the abundant snowmelt and the annual average 30-inch rainfall and slowly releases the water into the stream. The result is extremely stable stream flows that resemble a steady spring creek.

With so little gravel or rubble habitat available, the sand bed of Lawrence Creek does not immediately appear to be capable of supporting abundant trout populations. Where do trout spawn and where do the aquatic insects grow?

Robert Hunt found that in Lawrence Creek only about 5 percent of the stream's total substrate provided suitable spawning habitat, but that small amount was enough to fully seed the four-mile-long stream with fry. These streams are also highly productive (alkalinity is generally 150 ppm or greater), and they harbor abundant watercress (an aquatic plant) and large populations of freshwater shrimp. Burrowing mayflies, blackflies, and caddis flies also do well in Lawrence Creek and round out the diets of the native brook trout.

Nevertheless, Lawrence Creek, like most other sand-county streams, contains trout in only its first few miles. As it moves away from its cool headwaters, the water temperatures in most sand-county streams become too warm for trout, or the stream channels are disrupted by shallow, warm impoundments—remnants of mill ponds built by pioneer settlers.

Inventory Methods

PHYSICAL

For three years before habitat development work was scheduled to begin, Hunt collected data on the physical habitat, the trout populations, and the sport fishery of a treatment reach and three reference, or control, reaches.

Detailed maps (figure 7.4A) of the stream were drawn to scale (1 inch = 25 feet) and show channel width, water width, substrate type, pools, and permanent bank cover.

Permanent bank cover was defined as all undercut stream banks that provided at least 6 inches of overhang and had at least 12 inches of water beneath it. This was measured in a continuous transect along both banks and expressed as a percentage. A homemade device of wood and dowels was used to measure permanent bank cover.

Gradient was also measured. Water-surface area, pool area, area of individual substrate types, and channel volume were quantified from the stream maps.

BIOLOGICAL

Trout-population information was obtained using electrofishing techniques. Each study section was divided into 100-yard segments that were electrofished in April, June, and September.

(Although not used in the Lawrence Creek study, fisheries man-

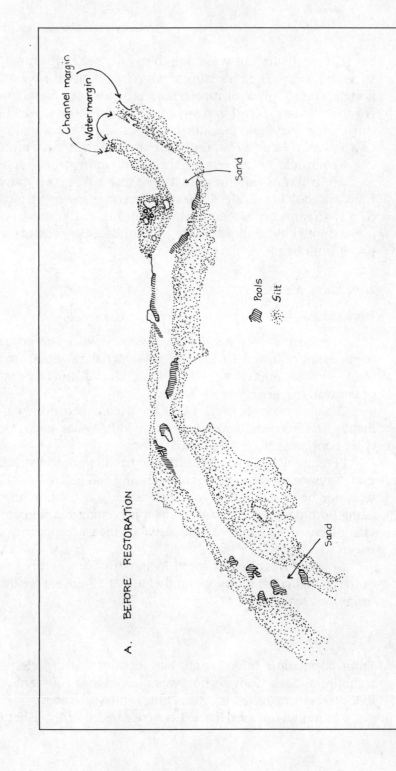

A. BEFORE RESTORATION

Channel margin

Water margin

Sand

Pools

Silt

Sand

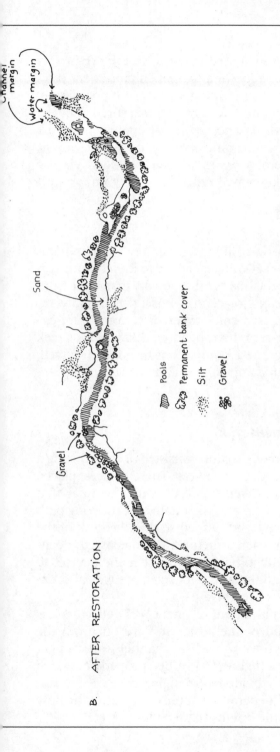

B. AFTER RESTORATION

Channel margin

Water margin

Sand

Gravel

Gravel

Pools

Permanent bank cover

Silt

Gravel

7.4 Lawrence Creek, Wisconsin; habitat maps. *These two maps show the same reach of Lawrence Creek before (A) and after (B) restoration. Following restoration, the channel and water width are greatly reduced, as is the amount of sand and silt found in the channel. The permanent bank cover, pools, and gravel is much increased following construction. Notice that the pools and permanent bank cover are found together on the outside bank of meander bends where the cover/deflector structures were placed.*

agers in Wisconsin have recently added a new aspect to pre-project inventory work. In order to qualify for a habitat enhancement project, a stream must be capable of sustaining a wild-trout population. Alkalinity and other water-quality indicators are measured to determine the fertility of the stream. The stream also must have the potential for natural reproduction, angler use, and public access. Because the habitat development work is largely funded via the Wisconsin trout stamp, the latter two criteria are very important.)

Limiting-factor Analysis

Hunt and others had been working at Lawrence Creek and on habitat development in general for several years prior to undertaking this study in 1964. Data from previous work showed that wild-trout populations in the sand streams of central Wisconsin usually responded dramatically to increased bank cover. Therefore, Hunt expected that his detailed, long-term investigation at Lawrence Creek would shed new light on why these populations responded so well. Neither food nor spawning area appeared to limit the trout population in Lawrence Creek.

Project Design and Implementation

Habitat alteration in the treatment section consisted of constructing a series of bank cover/current deflector devices. These devices, placed alternately on each bank, narrowed the stream in a manner that guided the newly confined flow in an accentuated meandering path down the channel. The devices were placed so that the bulk of the flow passed along the face of each structure. The narrowed, deepened flow scoured the streambed beneath and near the devices to form pools. In some cases additional gravel substrate was also exposed as sand and silt were scoured away.

In the construction and placement of such cover/deflectors it is important that the lower end of the structure flare out from the original bank and direct the flow across the channel to the upper one-third of the next structure (figure 7.5). When properly designed and placed, these structures provide overhanging cover at the upstream end, where the pool is generally scoured, and deflect the flow toward the next structure at the downstream end.

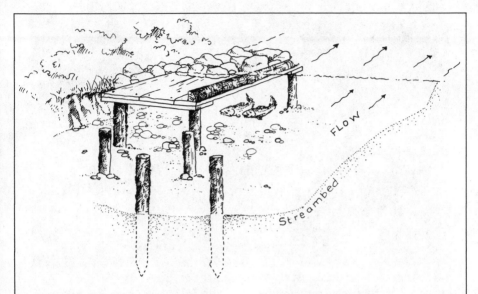

7.5 Cover/deflector structure construction. *Cover/deflector structure showing the various stages of construction prior to placement of sod.*

The maps prepared from the inventory work were used to plan the locations and dimensions of these devices. Construction began by securely embedding five-foot-long wooden pilings into the stream bottom. This was accomplished by using a pressurized water jet to bore a hole in the substrate as the piling was pushed into the hole. Green-cut hardwood stringer planks were nailed at right angles to the bank on top of each pair of pilings. Then green hardwood planks were nailed to these stringers parallel to the natural stream flow. The result was a complete underwater platform—typically three to five feet wide—that was positioned to effectively narrow the channel by an average of 50 percent (figure 7.6).

The underwater deck was covered with stones. A final layer of dirt and grass seed or sod completed construction of the platform. In later applications where fieldstone or quarry rock were not available, geoweb (a polyethylene grid) or polyethylene sandbags (figure 7.7) have been used instead.

The area between the platform and the old stream bank was filled with fieldstone to prevent erosion of the bank. This rock, too,

7.6 Cover/deflector construction sequence at Radley Creek, Wisconsin. *The underwater platform of the cover/deflector structure has been completed in this photo of Radley Creek, near Lawrence Creek. The structure is built to narrow the stream by approximately 50 percent. The area between the eroding bank in the foreground and the cover deflector will be filled with rock to create a new bank and prevent further erosion.*

7.7 Sandbags used to cover deck of cover/deflector. *Polyethylene sandbags are used to cover the underwater deck of the cover/deflector structure in this project on Fordham Creek.*

was covered with dirt and grass seed or sod. In the humid Midwest these structures quickly vegetate and look quite natural (figure 7.8).

Monitoring

Stream-mapping techniques used to assess preconstruction conditions were repeated to monitor the Lawrence Creek rehabilitation project during the postdevelopment phase (figure 7.4B). This work was done only once following construction. Detailed mapping measurements were confined to the treatment section and one control section.

Trout-population monitoring continued for ten years following construction in all study sections.

A compulsory creel census was conducted for each fishing season three years prior to, and six years following, the habitat development work. Information obtained included length, weight, age, and sex of trout caught. Fishing method, hours of fishing per trip, and number of trout released were also recorded.

7.8 Revegetated cover/deflector. *After dirt and grass or sod is placed on the structure, it quickly assumes a very natural appearance.*

Summary of Findings

Habitat alteration reduced the water-surface area of the treatment section by 50 percent and increased average depth by 60 percent. Stream bottoms classified as sand and silt were reduced by 40 percent and 70 percent, respectively. Gravel stream bottom increased by 11 percent. The number of pools was increased by 52 percent, but, more importantly, the area of streambed covered by pools increased by 170 percent (figure 7.4B). The greatest measured change was in the amount of permanent overhanging bank cover, which increased 400 percent.

Changes in the brook-trout population were reported by Hunt for six years following development. The average weight of trout in the study reach in April for the first three years following development was 242 pounds, as compared to a 130-pound average for the three years prior to development. The production of Lawrence Creek trout was even greater during the second three years following restoration work, when total weight of trout in the spring increased to an average of 363 pounds. Similarly, the average number of legal-sized brook trout in April grew from 562 to 1,130 in the first three-year interval following development and to 1,638 during the second. Similar trout-population increases were not observed in the control sections.

The brook-trout population in the treatment section steadily increased, despite the nearly 200 percent increase in angler harvest rates. Lawrence Creek anglers also showed a preference for fishing where the improvement work had been done. During the three years preceding improvement, only 18 percent of the anglers fished in that section. After the reach was improved, 46 percent of all anglers chose to fish in the treatment section.

Data from Hunt's long-term evaluation indicate the value of monitoring for several years following habitat alteration. They also show the value of planning a three- to four-year rest period following construction before beginning monitoring work if financial constraints prevent intensive monitoring.

A review of the trout-population data from Hunt's studies revealed that increased biomass (total weight of trout in a reach) and numbers largely resulted from increased survival of trout after the ninth month of life. The average number of age class 0 brook trout in the treatment section in September was about the same after habitat development as before. In April, however, this section held approximately 40 percent more age class I trout during the postdevelopment period than it did during the predevelopment period. The habitat alteration had greatly increased overwinter survival of full-age classes of brook trout.

An interesting sidelight of similar habitat evaluations on other Wisconsin trout streams has been mentioned by Hunt. In those streams that contain brook and brown trout prior to habitat alteration, the browns invariably dominate following construction. Hunt believes this is because these two species have very similar habitat preferences (especially during the adult life stage) that are well-served by the cover/deflector structures. The browns, however, are more aggressive and smarter than the brookies, so they outcompete them in these altered reaches. Increased fishing pressure and greater harvest after habitat enhancement place additional burdens on the easier-to-catch brook trout.

Hunt also conducted a cost/benefit analysis of the habitat enhancement work at Lawrence Creek. The cost of the development in 1964 dollars was $26,200 for 6,550 feet of stream. Because it is anticipated that the work will remain in place with very little maintenance for at least 25 years, the average annual investment is about $1,050 per year. Using a very conservative recreational value of only $5 per angler trip, and factoring it into the observed increase of 300 angler trips per season, it is clear that this project was cost-effective. The project will be paid off in 17 years.

NATURAL VERSUS STRUCTURAL RESTORATION

The work of Elmore in Oregon and a number of fish managers and habitat crews that were evaluated by Hunt in Wisconsin provide dramatic juxtapositions that ought to raise difficult questions. These workers investigated totally different approaches to stream-habitat problems, which had been created by similar land uses. Both described solutions that have been extremely successful. Elmore decided to work on land-use management changes because he knew that with the silty soils and widely fluctuating discharge regimes in his region, streams would begin to heal themselves quickly once the watershed's poor grazing management was changed. He also knew that structural approaches would not work well because: (1) of the incised nature of the streams; and (2) the streams' discharge regimes would wash out structures and cause significant channel changes from year to year.

Most of the projects evaluated by Hunt, on the other hand, deal with streams that have very stable flows and very low silt loads. These streams cannot build and narrow their banks as quickly as those of eastern Oregon. In Wisconsin, therefore, banks can only be built as fast as the vegetation grows, dies, and grows anew. The stable flows, however, lend themselves well to in-stream structural modifications of channel shapes. Damage to structures from flood events that exceed bankfull flows are not a major tactical concern in Wisconsin. However, because much of the habitat enhancement work in Wisconsin consists of in-stream structures, making the structures appear as if they occur naturally is a major aesthetic concern.

As shown in the evaluation work reported by Hunt and Elmore, one who is interested in trout-habitat rehabilitation must understand not only the habitat needs of the trout species present but also the geomorphic and hydrologic systems that affect the stream in which salmonid-habitat enhancements are being considered.

Postscript

Since completion of the Lawrence Creek trout-habitat restoration project, some rather innovative work has been done by fisheries managers in Wisconsin with the basic cover/deflector structure. Most notable are the skyhooks and Little Underwater Neighborhood Keepers Encompassing Rheotactic Salmonids (LUNKERS) that have been developed for rocky-bottomed streams that won't easily accept water-jet-driven pilings.

SKYHOOKS

Eight-foot sections of skyhook cover are prefabricated during the winter and then stockpiled. Following inventory work, construction begins by laying out the line the structures will follow in the stream channel (figure 7.9). A backhoe is then used to dig a trench along this line. The skyhook (figure 7.10) structures are placed on the bottom along this trench, so that half of the width of each structure is suspended out over the trench to provide hiding cover. Dredge mate-

7.9 Skyhook-structure construction sequence. *A line is staked out for placement of a series of skyhook structures, which will narrow this channel by 40 to 50 percent.*

7.10 Skyhook-structure placement. *The prefabricated skyhook structures are placed in the stream.*

rial is placed on top of the back-half portion of each structure to hold it in place. A sill, which runs along the underside length of each platform, prevents dredge material from flowing back into the trench. The dredge material is sodded at the edge and the rest is seeded. The area between the new bank and the old bank is low and wet, and quickly vegetates. A secondary feature of this technique is that it forms good waterfowl habitat in backwater reaches.

LUNKERS

The LUNKERS structure evolved in the coulee region of southern Wisconsin. The jetted post/plank structures used in the sand counties were not suitable to this area because of the rocky stream substrates. Construction of LUNKERS (figure 7.11) involves nailing oak planks to the top and bottom of six- to eight-inch oak spacer logs. These planks form stringers, which tie into the stream bank at right angles. Oak planks are nailed to the top and bottom stringer boards. These planks run parallel to the stream bank. The entire structure forms a crib, which can be constructed onshore and moved by a loader or backhoe to the installation site.

Once in the stream, the LUNKER is placed in position and anchored by driving five-foot lengths of steel-reinforcing rod through predrilled holes in the structures and then into the streambed. As with the cover/deflectors and skyhooks, these structures are set in a line that simulates the outside bend of a meander. They generally are placed to narrow the stream by as much as 50 to 60 percent. The structures provide 24 to 30 inches of 12-inch-deep overhanging bank. After the structures are in place, the area behind them is filled with rock riprap, which also is used to cover the structure, and then the entire area is covered with soil. The first two to three feet of soil is sodded. The remainder of the bank is seeded. (For additional construction details see Vetrano [1988] in Sources.)

BRUSH BUNDLES AND BOULDER RETARDS

Two other adaptations are brush bundles and boulder retards. In many areas trout-habitat construction crews in Wisconsin install brush bundles on the inside meander bends opposite the bank covers. The brush bundles are anchored to wooden stakes with polyester twine. These bundles are designed to trap silt, which is then in-

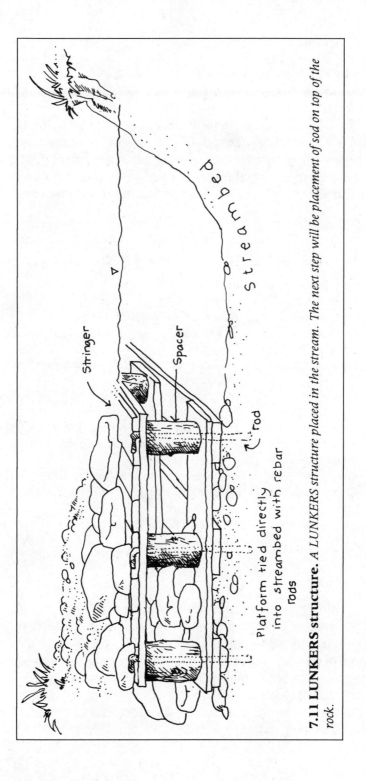

7.11 LUNKERS structure. *A LUNKERS structure placed in the stream. The next step will be placement of sod on top of the rock.*

vaded by encroaching vegetation that causes a further narrowing of the stream. Brush bundles also provide excellent habitat for brook-trout fry.

The use of boulder retards to create additional mid-channel pocket-water feeding sites and provide lanes for trout movement has also been combined with the cover/deflector structures (figure 7.12). Turbulence created by the boulder retards causes local scouring of sand and silt and often reveals gravels suitable for spawning.

IRRIGATION DITCH/SPRING CREEK, MONTANA

Location	*Southwestern Montana*
Project status	*Private*
Project leader	*Dave Odell/Curlew Consulting*
Landowner	*Private ranch*
Rehab. length	*Ten miles*
Limiting factor	*Lack of water depth, clean gravel, and bank vegetation*
Problem	*Overgrazing by livestock and siltation from irrigation return flows*
Prescription	*Fencing, channel narrowing, silt removal, log cabling, and revegetation with native shrubs*
Begin date	*1984 through 1987*
End date	*Ongoing*
Current status	*Fishery improving, natural reproduction occurring in creek*
Estimated cost	*$10,000 to $20,000 per mile for complete rehabilitation*

Background

As the title suggests, this narrative describes a fairly unusual situation. This spring creek begins at a large irrigation headgate on one of the big rivers in west-central Montana. The creek—an old overflow channel of the river that is used to convey irrigation water—flows for approximately seven miles before it reaches the private ranch where the restoration work took place.

Just upstream of the ranch, the ditch/creek divides into two smaller channels, which meander and braid through the property

7.12 Boulder retards at White River, Wisconsin. *Boulder retards are used to create feeding focal points and provide lanes for fish movement. Do you see the cover/deflector structure in this photo?*

until they return to the river. The channels are very low gradient, and they convey their highest water flows during the summer's irrigation season. The soils in the area are river-deposited alluvium. Therefore, cobbles, gravel, sand, and silt are all present. The rainfall in the area is generally 12 to 15 inches per year.

Upstream of the ranch, three smaller ditches tap into the creek and deplete its flow; still other ditches discharge silt- and sediment-laden irrigation return flows to the ditch/creek flow. Springs located along the ditches replenish the flow with water that is sufficiently warm to keep the creek from freezing in the winter yet cool in summer.

The ranch was purchased by the current landowner in the early 1980s. At that time the pastures were extremely overgrazed and dominated by spotted knapweed, a highly noxious weed. In addition to causing a change in the pasture vegetation, heavy cattle grazing on this ranch reduced the vigor of the riparian vegetation, which led to the lateral instability of the channels. The continual input of silt from irrigation return flows compounded the channels' lateral instability problem and directly contributed to the overall lack of in-stream habitat diversity.

Dave Odell, a local fishing guide and restoration consultant with a master's degree in environmental science, estimates that more than two feet of silt covered the gravel and rubble substrates in the pools of more than half of each channel. Based upon the landowner's own fishing log, only three pools on the property contained trout when he first acquired the ranch. He had never observed fry or small juvenile trout in any of the channels.

The landowner, an avid fisherman, recognized the potential spring-creek nature of these irrigation ditches. He set about to turn the wide, shallow waterways with very little bank vegetation or cover into productive fishing waters. He retained Odell to help design and implement the restoration plan.

Inventory Methods

PHYSICAL

Aerial photographs, crossed-checked with informal on-site surveys, supplied information on land use, the extent and condition of the riparian vegetation, and stream length and width.

While walking the channel, Odell evaluated its condition on the basis of: (1) the amount of clean spawning gravel present; (2) the variety of in-stream cover; and (3) the state of the riparian vegetation.

Transects were established at channel cross sections to estimate the amount of silt in the channel and to measure stream flows.

BIOLOGICAL

Because attempts to observe trout when snorkeling were thwarted by the murky water, the Montana Department of Fish, Wildlife and Parks was asked to conduct electrofishing surveys. Although quantitative estimates of the population were not made, the electrofishing surveys confirmed suspicions that few or no fry were being produced in the stream and that several of the young-age classes were not present or very poorly represented.

Limiting-factor Analysis

The limiting-factor analysis, as is often the case, was not a formal process. The landowner and consultant felt that the wide, shallow channels lacked cover and suitable substrate to support a healthy, naturally reproducing trout population. They wanted to narrow and deepen the channels, create cover, and better manage the silts, which were smothering the channels' clean gravel habitat.

Project Design and Implementation

Project design was directed toward improving streamside vegetation, narrowing the channel, providing additional cover, and managing silt.

The first step was to remove cattle from the property and install a sprinkler irrigation system in the pastures. These steps would not have been economically feasible if the property was to remain a working ranch. But, as a recreational property, these land-management changes became logical long-term improvements.

The removal of the cattle allowed the stream-bank vegetation to grow back virtually unimpeded, and because knapweed cannot tolerate constant moisture, the irrigation of the pastures has helped reduce knapweed from the area. The pastures, which were seeded to alfalfa hay, now support a few horses that are fenced away from the streams.

As baseline data were gathered, the removal of cattle and the installation of the sprinkler irrigation system were the only steps taken during the first two years of the study. The efforts to narrow the stream and provide additional cover to enhance natural meanders were slow and deliberate by design.

Overall, the landowner and consultant have taken a very incremental approach toward this project. Each year one or two treatments have been applied and then evaluated to determine if they are working as planned and if they will be used again. The construction is generally carried out in the late winter or early spring when the ground is still frozen. This helps to protect the existing banks and vegetation from degradation during construction.

GRAVEL-BAR DEFLECTORS

To narrow the channel and enhance some natural meanders, a backhoe or track hoe was used to pull silt and sediment off the gravel/rubble bottom. The silt and sediment was then deposited along the low-velocity inside bank of a meander bend. Gravel was subsequently placed along the outside edge of backhoe-deposited silt to create a stable bar that deflects flows to the concave bank. The gravel bars are built low in profile so that they will remain subirrigated. This subirrigation leads to very rapid invasion by native riparian vegetation, which further stabilizes the bar. These point-bar deflectors narrow and deepen the flow. The resulting increased water velocity keeps the freshly exposed gravels scoured clean. In this way the channel cross section is manipulated to direct the swifter flow through the areas where deep water, rubble bottoms, undercut banks, and healthy riparian vegetation combine to form prime trout habitat.

Although silt and gravel are the preferred materials for constructing wing deflectors, large cottonwood logs were also used in some instances. When logs were used, they were placed in a line on the convex bank of the bend, where if necessary they were cabled together to deflect the flow toward the opposite bank.

To build this type of deflector, the first log was buried 10 to 12 feet into the stream banks. Additional logs—if necessary—were cabled to the first, and the area behind the deflector was then filled with streambed silt and seeded. Figure 7.13 shows a newly constructed log deflector and how it forces the water flow toward the opposite bank. The men in the photograph are standing on the silt-filled and seeded area, an area that will continue to grow as the slow waters drop their sediment load behind the deflectors.

Logs were placed along the opposite bank to provide overhead trout-cover habitat. The logs are cabled to a deadman (any heavy, bulky object) buried 2 feet deep and at least 15 feet back from the stream bank.

These simple deflectors and bank covers have been used in several locations along the ditch/creek to narrow, deepen, and enhance the natural meander of the channels. The structures also direct the flow to the lateral scour pools and the cover associated with the outside meander bank.

In addition, small islands have been created by placing the

7.13 Deflector and cover logs at Spring Creek, Montana. *A newly constructed deflector directing flow toward cover logs placed along the opposite bank. The area behind the log deflector where the men are standing consists of sediments and silt that were pulled from the area of the cover logs and seeded.*

material dredged from beneath cover logs. Logs were placed in a V-shape on the upstream side of the material, which was then seeded. The channel obstruction created by the island caused scouring of the two newly created side channels. Island structures should only be created where it appears that the flow has already concentrated along the banks rather than in the middle of the channel.

Each spring thousands of cuttings from native shrubs, such as willow and red osier dogwood, are collected. These are placed in buckets of water until roots begin to form. Then they are planted along the point bars that have been built with silt and gravel. Wire cages are placed around this woody vegetation to help protect it from, in this case, browsing by an abundant population of white-tailed deer.

DREDGED POOLS

Another technique used to create additional cover has been to backhoe pools beneath several of the few remaining large shrubs along the bank. Again, as evidenced by the fact that several pools have refilled with silt, this was only successful in areas where the current is rapid enough to keep the pool scoured clean.

SEDIMENT BASINS

An important aspect of silt management has been the use of sediment basins. These basins collect silt and sand. They are periodically cleaned out with a backhoe. Odell has taken some of the guesswork out of properly locating these basins by using naturally occurring ones. During his inventory work, he located several pools that had totally filled with sediment. These pools were cleaned out and began to fill again with sediment. Now they are sediment traps and are cleaned regularly.

BANK STABILIZATION WITH LOGS

A unique approach has been used to rehabilitate several high (three feet) eroding stream banks. A backhoe was used to peel back streambank sod and remove underlying gravels. Then, again with the backhoe, the slope of the bank was fashioned to a gentle, more stable angle. For each foot of bank height, the incline of the bank from the stream bed was extended three feet to create a slope with a ratio of three to one. Cottonwood logs or rubble was placed along the base of the new bank to resist further cutting action. Finally, the sod was replaced by packing it down with a backhoe. Bare areas were re-seeded and planted with shrub cuttings. The result is a low, stable bank that provides good lateral bank cover for trout.

Monitoring

Aside from photographs, there has not been a formal program of monitoring stream morphology or trout-population changes. The landowner's detailed fishing log, however, seems to indicate increased fishing success. In addition, he now sees large numbers of fry and small trout.

Summary of Findings

It is difficult to evaluate the success of this project because there is little posttreatment data to examine. The landowner, however, is pleased with the work done to date and believes the channels are now producing more trout. In addition, he feels that trout are reproducing within the channels. When Odell was asked to evaluate the success of the project, he said, "Last summer, after we took seven trout over 22 inches in an evening's fishing, I could judge it by the smile on the landowner's face."

The gravel-bar deflector and bank-cover approach removed silt and clearly led to a narrower, deeper channel with more trout cover. Similarly, the technique for rehabilitating the banks has reduced erosion and increased trout cover. These changes should lead to improved trout populations. However, stream habitat changes are not always reflected in increased trout production.

Postscript

All things considered, several aspects of this work are noteworthy. The deflector/cover structures used are much less engineered than others observed, particularly when compared to those used in Wisconsin at Lawrence Creek and South Dakota at Rapid Creek. However, they appear to work with the very stable flows found in this spring creek, which reinforces the adage that every stream is unique and that restoration project design must recognize and incorporate each stream's unique qualities.

There are some interesting parallels and contrasts between Odell's work and the work of Elmore and Hunt. In each project agricultural land use led to sediment-related habitat problems. Elmore was able to deal with the land-use issue directly because his agency, the BLM, is the manager. Neither Hunt nor Odell was so lucky. Hunt had no control over land use, and although Odell and the landowner could treat problems on the ranch, much of the silt was being transported to the creek by irrigation return flows.

The soil and discharge regime of Bear Creek and Camp Creek allowed Elmore to take a nonstructural approach to his restoration project. A similar approach by Odell in Montana or Hunt in Wisconsin would have been quite slow—50 years or more according to Odell. The structural and sediment management techniques were used to accelerate the natural processes.

Hunt and Odell each stressed the need to manage and manipulate the cross section of the stream so that the greatest flow is placed next to the best trout habitat. An undercut bank with overhanging vegetation is of little value if the current is not flowing along its face and scouring the gravels clean.

At Lawrence Creek the flow and habitat were made to coincide with highly engineered cover/deflector structures. At the Montana spring creek, silt and gravel point bars were constructed to deflect the current toward outside meander bends where cabled logs provide cover. In each project channels were narrowed and deepened, and creation of pools and escape cover was an important consideration. Hunt, however, used a structure that underwent several modifications as its successful placement in Wisconsin streams evolved. Odell, on the other hand, needed to remove large volumes of silt and sediment from the stream. The creation of gravel bars with this material allowed him to solve several problems at once. (The Rapid Creek case history presented in chapter 9 illustrates a project in which both techniques were used.)

In each case the techniques appear to work. Hunt and Elmore have collected the monitoring data that prove their success. The spring-creek success is reflected by the landowner's smile. The message is: Take the time to understand how the stream functions in its drainage and design a treatment that will work for that stream. The incremental approach used on this stream is a very effective way to evaluate and modify treatments to obtain the best results.

JOHN DAY RIVER, OREGON

Location	*Grant County*
Project status	*Private*
Project leader	*Stephen H. Williams*
Landowner	*Private cattle ranches*
Rehab. length	*12.5 miles*
Limiting factors	*High water temperature, and lack of adult-salmonid holding pools and hiding cover*
Problem	*Stream channelization, no bank vegetation*
Prescription	*Create cover, stabilize eroding banks, exclude livestock to allow vegetation recovery*
Begin date	*June 1985*
End date	*August 1989*
Current status	*Project will be maintained at least until year 2000*
Estimated cost	*$422,250*

Background

The John Day River rises as a small stream in the mountains of central-eastern Oregon, approximately 100 miles east of Bear Creek and Camp Creek. The river supports runs of anadromous chinook and steelhead, and flows north through an arid (11 to 15 inches of precipitation per year), largely volcanic landscape to its confluence with the Columbia River.

By the time the stream reaches the low-gradient (.75 percent) privately owned agricultural land near the town of John Day, it is a fair-sized river. During low-flow months in the fall, stream-water width is approximately 40 feet.

As described in chapter 1, prior to 1964 the river meandered down the valley. The state highway connecting the town of John Day to the rest of the world was linked together by a series of bridges that crossed the river's meandering course. The small hay fields, interspersed with dense stands of cottonwood and willows dotted along the floodplain, were subirrigated by the alluvial groundwater aquifer. The hay fields then, as now, played an important role in the local ranching economy. During the spring and summer, when hay is grown and cut on these meadows, the ranchers graze their cattle in the mountains on U.S.D.A. Forest Service and BLM grazing allotments. In winter, the cattle are moved to private, riparian meadows, where they are fed summer-grown hay and graze uncut hay and riparian vegetation.

A flood in 1964 eroded some of the hay fields. In response the U.S. Army Corps of Engineers channelized, but did not riprap, a section of the river to speed floodwaters out of the valley. The state highway was rebuilt parallel to the straightened river, and large, contiguous hay meadows replaced the small hay fields and the stands of willows, hawthorne, and cottonwoods.

Because of the channelization and consequent increased water velocities, the John Day River began to cut at bed and banks. The channel quickly became an incised wide, shallow riffle. The ranchers found that as the alluvial groundwater level dropped 10 to 12 feet along the incised channel bed, they were forced to irrigate more. As irrigation increased, the protein content of their hay began to decrease. The irrigation water apparently leached important plant nutrients from the hay-root zones.

Riparian vegetation was lost as the larger hay meadows were created and grazed. The ranchers were spending up to $15,000 per year snagging downed cottonwoods out of the river and placing rock riprap on the banks in an attempt to reduce the erosion of their lands.

The end result of the Army Corps of Engineers' project was a wide, shallow, straightened incised river that consisted of one large riffle. Very little large woody debris was found in the stream. Stream water temperatures increased because of a lack of shading vegetation. Important rearing habitat for chinook and steelhead was lost. The ranchers had more land in production, but it required irrigation and produced a less valuable, low protein hay. In sum, what had been a lovely and fairly harmonious relationship between the river and surrounding land use was completely disrupted to the detriment of all, including the trout and salmon.

Inventory Methods

In this case the pre-project physical habitat inventory consisted of walking the length of the study section to visually estimate pool to riffle ratios, streamside vegetation, and usable trout cover.

Limiting-factor Analysis

A limiting-factor analysis was not undertaken. It was clear that the channelization and ensuing incisement had severely reduced the habitat diversity in the river. The lack of shade created intolerable water temperatures and of particular concern to district fish biologist Errol Claire of the Oregon Department of Fish and Wildlife (ODFW) was the lack of river-edge pocket water for juvenile steelhead and chinook. After years of conducting in-stream habitat and trout-population surveys in the area, Claire felt that this habitat type was critical to the survival of juvenile steelhead and chinook. Because the river was a large riffle for most of its length, it lacked this shoreline pocket water.

The general lack of habitat diversity and high water temperatures caused by channelization and the removal of in-stream woody debris and riparian vegetation were deemed to be limiting the anadromous and resident fisheries.

Project Design and Implementation

The project design was driven by two main considerations. First, ODFW wanted to restore the river to a more natural geomorphic regime. The reestablishment of a healthy, functional riparian area was ·considered key to this goal. In particular, ODFW wanted to curtail the removal of large woody debris from the channel and the grazing of the riparian zone. Each activity was limiting in-stream habitat. The agency realized that a widespread education and information campaign would be required to effect these changes.

As a second consideration, ODFW wanted to maintain the genetic diversity of the river's different strains of wild steelhead and chinook. This required the reestablishment of habitat diversity that would benefit wild trout and provide trout habitat in as natural a way as possible. Such habitat included the use of natural materials for all in-stream structures.

EASEMENTS AND EDUCATION

The keystone of the ongoing restoration plan is to obtain 15-year conservation easements on 100-foot-wide riparian corridors immediately adjacent to the stream. The easements are obtained from individual ranchers who become interested in the benefits provided by a healthy riparian area.

To entice participation in the program, ODFW describes how a healthy riparian area stores water in the alluvial groundwater aquifer, which is later discharged to the stream during late-summer low flows. This can be a compelling message to a rancher who has difficulty obtaining sufficient irrigation water during the late summer.

In exchange for the riparian-corridor easement, ODFW agrees to correct erosion problems along the banks, provide offsite water developments, and rearrange pasture fencing. Offsite water developments lead to better distribution of cattle, and pasture fencing allows better plant growth through rotation grazing. Since erosion control can cost the rancher up to $15,000 per year, the easement is often a good business deal for the rancher.

FENCING

Once the easement is obtained, a stout livestock fence is constructed to keep livestock out of the riparian corridor. The fences are made of four-strand barbed wire with a tamarack fence stay placed every 5 feet and a metal fence post placed every 15 feet. The fences are built stout because after a few years the riparian-corridor forage begins to look very tempting. Cattle will break a fence down if it is not well constructed. "If the cows get through the fence, they can ruin three years of recovery in three weeks," said ODFW biologist Jeff Neal.

In areas of high snow and/or heavy elk, round, high-tensile wire is used. This fence wire can withstand the pressure of heavy snow and persistent elk better than barbed wire.

EROSION CONTROL

To meet the obligation to control bank erosion, ODFW uses bank sloping, rock jetties, and, in some cases, rock riprap to stabilize raw and eroding banks.

Upon the removal of grazing cattle, the response of riparian vegetation led to a narrower and deeper channel (as described in the Camp Creek and Bear Creek case histories). In one area the bank has grown to narrow the channel 10 to 15 feet over a two-year period.

ROCK STRUCTURES

In addition to fencing the riparian corridor and providing protection for eroding banks, ODFW has done some structural work with rock to create habitat for anadromous chinook and steelhead. In many areas several boulders have been placed along the margin of the stream where overhanging grasses provide cover. These boulders break up a long riffle and provide rearing habitat for juvenile trout. The combination of slow, shallow water and cover to protect against predation provides excellent rearing habitat.

Boulder berms—placed only at one-mile intervals because each one that is built reduces habitat available for juvenile rearing—create pools where adult steelhead and salmon can rest as they travel upstream to spawn. Figures 7.14 and 7.15 are close-ups of a boulder berm and the downstream pool it created. Claire prefers boulder

7.14 & 7.15 Boulder berm and pool at John Day River, Oregon. *Views of a boulder berm and the long, deep downstream pool created by water flowing over the berm.*

berms to log dams for creating pools because he feels if log dams break up, the loose logs can cause erosion problems. As a precaution, ODFW utilizes riprap both upstream and downstream of these boulder berms to protect them from washing out at high flows. He also believes that the boulder berms create a longer pool and more holding water than log dams.

The total cost of this work ranges from $30,000 to $60,000 per mile of stream, not including ongoing maintenance.

Monitoring

Monitoring consists of maintaining a photo-point history of each project, and of inspecting the fences, banks, and structures to be certain that they are functioning as designed.

Trout-population estimates—through redd counts and limited electrofishing surveys—are made annually to determine the response of trout to the structural work.

Summary of Findings

If the landowner agrees, the easements that ODFW obtains from landowners can be renewed after 15 years. The program has not been in existence long enough for an easement to be renewed. Claire, who views this as an educational program, is optimistic that the benefits provided by a healthy riparian area will persuade participating landowners to renew their easements.

It is not yet known if the structural habitat work has increased production of anadromous salmonids. The data collected to date indicate that the habitat created by boulders placed along banks in riffles contains juvenile chinook and steelhead. Similarly, the adult trout and salmon are using the boulder-berm pools for resting as they travel upstream to spawn.

Claire explains that it could take 100 years for this river to return to a normal geomorphic regime with a dense riparian forest. The recovery of the riparian zone has been encouraging, but it is only the beginning in a long process that will include the gradual rise of the streambed and the alluvial groundwater aquifer.

Postscript

The work being done on the John Day River is an interesting contrast to the approach taken 100 miles away at Camp Creek and Bear Creek, where restoration has affected a virtual drainage-wide change in land management with a minimum of structural work. On the John Day River the change in management has consisted of the total exclusion of livestock from within a narrow riparian corridor. A great deal of effort is put into structural work to prevent further erosion and to provide some of the habitat diversity that has been lost. The structural work is seen as a short-term measure as the stream heals and returns to a more natural geomorphic regime.

These differences in restoration strategy result, in large part, from land-ownership patterns and how that land is used. Portions of the lands along Camp and Bear creeks are rangelands owned by BLM. The riparian pasture lands along the John Day River are privately owned, and their production of hay for winter feeding of cattle is a very important aspect of the ranch operations. Thus, the regulation of cattle grazing, and similar restrictive land-management options in the John Day River valley, are limited by cooperation of the private landowners. ODFW has no management authority over the lands it is trying to influence. Furthermore, the hay these riparian lands produce is critical to the ranching community's economy.

Claire believes that the principal drawback to the work on the John Day River, as compared to the work at Bear and Camp creeks, is the fact that his work is restricted to a narrow 100-foot-wide corridor. He recognizes that Elmore is able to work with the entire floodplain.

The other difference is Claire's use of boulders to create habitat, where Elmore prefers to let the stream create and provide the habitat as it heals itself. This is a simple philosophical difference in the way these two men approach stream rehabilitation. Despite these differences both men see their programs as being largely educational in nature. Each is depending on the ranchers with whom they are working to eventually understand the benefits—particularly the increased late-summer stream flow—provided by a healthy riparian area. Once this lesson is learned, they hope the proper riparian management will supplement the current management practice. If these educational programs are successful, the streams will be protected and able to produce trout and salmon as they have historically.

An interesting facet of the work of Claire and Neal is their commitment to maintain the genetic diversity of the John Day River's wild trout and salmon. They insist that hatchery trout not be introduced to the system and that the stream's habitat diversity be maintained. According to Neal, "Wild trout are going to make much better use of our improvements than hatchery trout would because we are keying in on the egg-to-smolt life stage. Hatchery trout are dumped in river as smolts and don't have to worry about juvenile rearing conditions."

YELLOW CREEK, CALIFORNIA

Location	*80 miles northeast of Redding*
Project status	*Private and public*
Project leader	*Robert Franklin*
Landowner	*Pacific Gas and Electric Company, Dye Creek Cattle Company, and the U.S. Forest Service*
Rehab. length	*Three miles*
Limiting factor	*Lack of cover, sediment deposition*
Problem	*Livestock grazing, channelization, sedimentation*
Prescription	*Stream-corridor fencing, willow planting, instream structures*
Begin date	*1978*
End date	*Ongoing*
Current status	*Construction and land management changes proceeding gradually*
Estimated cost	*Unavailable*

Background

Big Springs bubbles up out of the ground at an elevation of 4,300 feet in the Humbug Valley of northern California's Cascade Range. It is a beautiful spring creek, which flows over a gravel streambed between low, wet undercut banks (figure 7.16).

7.16 The Big Springs, Yellow Creek, California. *The Big Springs with the newly constructed fence. Notice the low, lush banks.*

This half-mile stream has been protected from grazing by a split-rail cedar fence installed in 1988 by volunteer members of California Trout (CalTrout). It represents the ongoing efforts of the management cooperative of CalTrout, California Department of Fish and Game, Pacific Gas and Electric Company, Dye Creek Cattle Company, Plumas County Fish and Game Commission, and the U.S.D.A. Forest Service. The aim of this unusual cooperative is to return Yellow Creek to its former glory.

At the end of the fence built in 1988 and the beginning of the first experimental fence, which was installed in 1978, the character of Big Springs changes. Big Springs is a tributary of Yellow Creek, which drains the heavily grazed upstream meadows. These upstream meadows somewhat tenuously store large amounts of very fine alluvial soils. The root systems of the dryland grasses in this upstream section provide little bank stability to Yellow Creek; the channel is incised and there is little undercut bank or in-stream cover.

Near the confluence of Big Springs and Yellow Creek there is a gap between the new and old fences. This spot is used as a crossing by grazing cattle. The banks are grazed contiguous to the edge, and the continual trampling by cattle has caused the banks to cave in.

Slightly downstream, where the stream banks are somewhat higher than at the confluence of Big Springs and Yellow Creek, it is clear the banks are slowly recovering. Why are these banks, which have been fenced for 10 years, higher and still recovering, yet the banks of the newly fenced reach are in such wonderful condition? The lands in the immediate vicinity where the spring emerges are very wet. This alone probably deters cattle use, which has likely helped to maintain the vegetation and banks in this headwater area.

Farther down Yellow Creek's meandering course, streambed and banks seem to be recovering well, but not for long. Approximately one-quarter of a mile downstream, Yellow Creek was diverted out of its old meandering channel into a short, straight channelized reach. From this point the stream has been channelized for approximately one-half to one-quarter of a mile downstream. No one knows when or why the stream was diverted.

The channelization, combined with the overgrazed stream banks, caused channel incision and bank sloughing. Now the stream in this reach flows between three- to five-foot-high exposed banks of fine alluvium. Here, despite the fencing, riparian vegetation consists of dryland grasses rather than sedges and rushes, because the groundwater level dropped as the channel became incised. The gravel streambed, weed beds, and undercut banks that characterize the upstream section are not found here. The undercut banks have collapsed and the gravels that supported the roots of the aquatic plants have been scoured and replaced with a hard-packed clay. Figure 7.17 shows the nick point, or the point of active channel cutting.

Beginning in 1980 several in-stream structures, mostly half logs and brush bundles, were installed along stream banks in areas where cover appeared to be limited. Partly because of improper placement, little improvement of stream habitat was realized. In some places bank erosion was actually accelerated by improper placement of structures.

Overharvest of the brown-trout population, as well as habitat degradation, has contributed to the decline of the Yellow Creek fishery. In 1983, in an attempt to increase the number of 10- to 16-inch trout, the California Fish and Game Commission prohibited the

7.17 Nick point in Yellow Creek. *Point of active channel cutting in Yellow Creek.*

killing of trout under 16 inches. To facilitate the safe release of undersized trout, only artificial lures with single-point barbless hooks are allowed.

Inventory Methods

In 1986 CalTrout retained a consultant to develop a long-range management plan for restoration of Yellow Creek.

PHYSICAL

The stream profile began with a review of geological maps and aerial photos to develop an understanding of the land and how it was being used. Then, using an engineering transit and stadia rod, water-surface and streambed elevations were taken at a number of points along the stream. Water depths were also measured. These data were used to develop a streambed and water-surface profile that shows changes in gradient along the channel.

Portions of the old meander channel were also surveyed to

determine if Yellow Creek flows could be reintroduced, but it soon became clear that channel incision had lowered the elevation of the streambed for a substantial distance upstream of the old channel. Therefore, to reintroduce Yellow Creek flows to the old channel, a diversion would have had to be built upstream of the original fence to supply the downhill elevation needed to get flows into the old channel. This was deemed not to be a feasible alternative.

The in-stream habitat survey was conducted by walking the entire reach of the stream and photographing, measuring, estimating, and sketching a variety of in-stream habitat attributes. These included water-surface width, substrate composition (percentage of area covered by silt, sand, gravel, etc.), small aquatic plants (percentage of area covered by each species), thalweg depth, presence and extent of undercut banks, water temperature, status of channel (aggradation/degradation of bed, bank sloughing), and stream-bank angle. Riparian vegetation, water temperature, and discharge regimens were measured at several locations.

On the basis of this survey, three distinct habitat zones were identified (figure 7.18). Zone 1 consisted of the section above the diversion from the old channel. This section was characterized by high sinuosity, low gradient, abundant submerged weed beds, gravel-dominated streambed, high aquatic-insect production, and well-vegetated, stable banks with numerous undercuts.

Zone 2 extended from the diversion to downstream of the point where the old channel re-enters the channelized section. It was characterized by decreased sinuosity, moderate to steep gradients, few submerged weed beds, clay substrates and alternating patches of gravel, patchy aquatic-insect production (associated with gravel bottoms), and bare, unstable banks with very few undercuts.

Zone 3 extended from the end of zone 2 to the end of the CalTrout fence. This section is still healing and contains increased sinuosity, decreased gradient, moderate numbers and extent of weed beds, substantial areas of gravel substrates, high aquatic-insect production, and a mixture of unstable and stable banks, which generally lack substantial undercuts.

Sediment Storage in Upper Meadow. The researchers suspected that sediment problems in the project area were related to erosion in the upper meadow. In order to better understand this relationship, approximately one and one-half miles of stream channel, upstream of

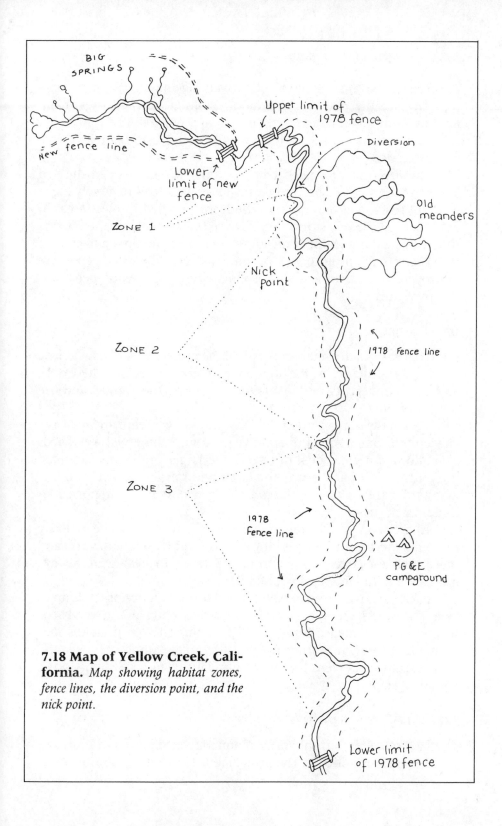

7.18 Map of Yellow Creek, California. *Map showing habitat zones, fence lines, the diversion point, and the nick point.*

Within the image: BIG SPRINGS, New fence line, Upper limit of 1978 fence, Diversion, Lower limit of new fence, Old meanders, ZONE 1, Nick Point, ZONE 2, 1978 Fence line, ZONE 3, 1978 Fence line, PG&E campground, Lower limit of 1978 fence the project area, were inventoried by walking and sketching to determine the occurrence and extent of sediment storage sites, bank failures, gully erosion, and other potential problems. The volumes of sediment both in storage (sandbars) and lost to erosion (gullies) were also estimated.

The inventory revealed large volumes of sediment in the bed and banks that would be easily transported from this relatively high-gradient reach and deposited in the lower-gradient project area. In February 1986 heavy storm runoff caused some of the fine sediments that were held in the upper meadow to settle in and on top of aquatic weed beds in the project area. In some instances the weed beds were destroyed, and in others the productivity of the weed beds was greatly reduced.

BIOLOGICAL

A biologist snorkeled the upper half of the project area to take a close look at the structure of the submerged banks, especially the extent and size of undercuts, and to qualitatively assess the number and size range of trout.

Undercuts that afforded the most trout cover were always associated with some type of riparian vegetation. Submerged weed beds also afforded a great deal of cover. The larger undercuts extended three to six feet back under the bank and ran for eight to ten feet along the bank. In some places a single willow bush supported an undercut of these dimensions.

All trout observed were 8- to 24-inch brown trout. The majority of trout were 10 to 14 inches long and used both undercut banks and weed beds for cover. Larger trout (18 to 24 inches) were always associated with large undercut banks.

A kick net was used to collect qualitative aquatic-insect samples from riffle areas with gravel/rubble substrates and aquatic weed beds in low-velocity areas. Large mayflies, stone flies, and caddis flies dominated the community in the riffle areas. Small mayflies and small crustaceans were the most abundant trout-food items in the aquatic weeds.

Limiting-factor Analysis

The lack of cover—in the form of aquatic weed beds and undercut banks—was identified as the principal factor limiting trout production. The continued introduction of sediments from cattle stream crossings and the upstream meadow was also identified as a major problem. In addition, there was some concern that the limited extent of gravels and weed beds in some stretches of the project area would limit insect production. These problems were caused by heavy cattle grazing that led to stream-bank instability and increased sediment production in the riparian zone throughout the valley. Channelization of the stream resulted in channel incision and a drop in the water table.

Project Design and Implementation

Robert Franklin, the project consultant, suggested that CalTrout and Pacific Gas and Electric consider purchasing the grazing rights to Humbug Valley to either exclude cattle or alter the range-management scheme by introducing more compatible grazing techniques. In addition, the stream-enhancement master plan states:

> We recognize the fact that artificial stream enhancements cannot act as substitutes for the wise management of the watershed. It is the intention of this master plan to facilitate a coordinated effort between Yellow Creek landowners, resource managers and user groups that will result in: (1) the preservation of high quality trout habitat where it now exists; (2) the accelerated recovery of degraded trout habitat; and (3) the protection and enhancement of aesthetics.

In the master plan a number of treatments are prescribed for implementation by CalTrout. The prescribed treatments are presented below in order of priority.

FENCING PROJECTS

The first fencing project was to take place on the main stem of Big Springs, from the upstream end of the existing fence to the origin of the springs at the edge of U.S. Forest Service property. It was constructed in the fall of 1988 and described earlier in this case history.

The second fencing project is suggested for the main channel of Yellow Creek, from the confluence of Big Springs to the top of the Humbug Valley. The intent is to allow revegetation of the stream banks that will, in turn, lead to a reduction in the transport of fine sediments to the downstream project reach. It will also lead to recovery of in-stream habitat in the upper-meadow reach of Yellow Creek.

WILLOW PLANTING

In 1987 and 1988 willows were planted along bare and unstable banks throughout the project area, as well as in the upper-meadow reach. Willow planting, however, has been restricted to one bank—the outside of bends or one side of straight sections—to facilitate fly casting.

The willows, which have become established in several areas, will eventually help stabilize banks and lead to the development of undercut banks.

BRIDGE CONSTRUCTION AND ARMORING OF CATTLE CROSSINGS

The two crossings now used by cattle will be realigned to follow the natural, diagonal trend of riffles across the stream. These crossings will be armored against continued disruption by cattle with one-foot-deep layers of six- to eight-inch rock placed with a backhoe or other suitable equipment.

The two existing crossings will ultimately be replaced by a single bridge. In addition to decreasing erosion rates at cattle crossings, the bridge will provide easy access to both banks for anglers.

PLACEMENT OF BOULDERS

The placement of a series of single boulders, approximately one cubic yard in volume, is scheduled for a long, straight stretch of channel. The boulders should be placed adjacent to the thalweg, and five to ten feet apart to provide low-velocity resting areas and overhead cover in the form of surface turbulence. They will cause both scouring of the bottom downstream and deposition upstream, it is hoped, of gravel.

An advantage of boulders over other types of structures is that they continue to be effective even after minor shifts in position. Care must be taken, however, that the placement of boulders does not direct flows toward already unstable banks.

BOULDER GROUPS WITH ATTACHED COVER

To provide cover in two large pools that contain no overhead cover, the CalTrout master plan suggests that groups of four boulders, each approximately one cubic yard in volume, be positioned in the chan-

nel and large root wads be attached to the boulders with a cable/
polyester anchoring system (figure 7.19). In this technique the ends
of galvanized polyester fibercore cables one-half inch in diameter are
inserted into holes 9/16 by 10 inches deep drilled into the rocks and
glued in place using cartridge-dispensed C-10 polyester resin. The
drilling is done on land; the gluing is done by divers working under
water.

ENHANCEMENT OF AQUATIC-INSECT PRODUCTION

The channelized section of stream contains channel segments characterized by smooth, unproductive substrates of hard-clay steep gradients and high velocities. These are all inhospitable habitat
attributes for trout and aquatic insects. The consultant, however,
believes the potential exists to increase the production of aquatic
insects in these areas through the construction of a series of cobble
beds with stabilizing log-sill structures (figure 7.20). The area recommended for this treatment is shown in figure 7.17.

OVERHANGING BANK COVERS

Appropriate sites for overhanging bank covers are limited by channel
geometry. For Yellow Creek this type of cover must be constructed

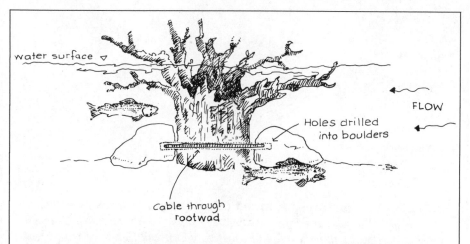

7.19 Boulder grouping. *Side view of a boulder group with an attached root wad to provide cover.*

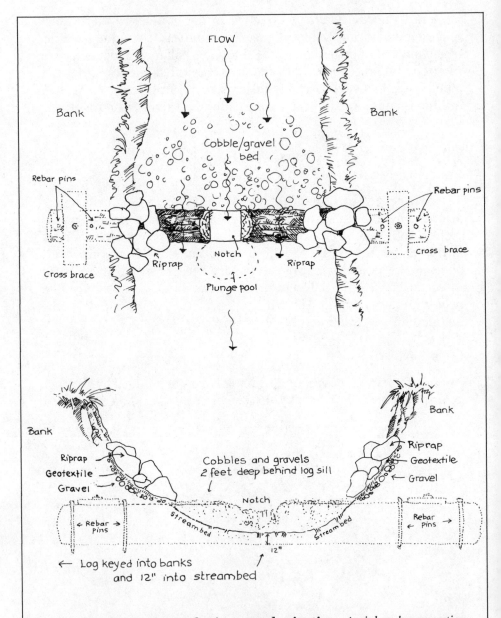

7.20 Log-sill structures for insect colonization. *Aerial and cross-section views of log-sill structures with upstream cobble/gravel substrate. It is hoped these cobble/gravel beds will be colonized by insects, which will lead to increased food production for trout.*

on an outside bend with stable banks (figure 7.21). The bank covers will be constructed of three or four fir or cedar logs 18 to 24 inches in diameter. These are lashed or pinned into a bundle, keyed well into the bank at either end, and supported at six- to eight-foot intervals with 18-inch-diameter cantilever logs. The bank cover may then be covered with a layer of gravel, filter cloth, and sod. Buried portions of this and all wooden structures must be constructed of highly rot-resistant wood, such as cedar or redwood.

LOG-CRIB BANK PROTECTION

This structure is recommended to protect a rapidly eroding bank near a campground. The consultant notes that the erosion of channel banks is a natural feature of all alluvial streams, but given the value of the improved campsites, bank protection is warranted in this case.

The log crib will be constructed of half logs cut from trees approximately 12 inches in diameter and arranged in a wall-like structure. The log wall will be supported at both ends by wood pilings 12 inches in diameter driven well into the stream bottom. The

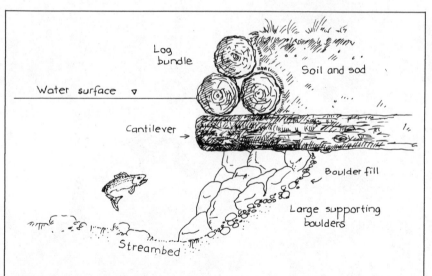

7.21 Overhanging bank cover. *Cross-sectional view of the planned overhanging bank cover. Appropriate sites for this structure type are limited on Yellow Creek because of channel geometry.*

half logs will then be pinned into place with the upstream end of the wall buried 20 feet into the bank. Kicker logs will be attached to the face of the crib below the water surface to deflect flow away from the crib and provide overhead trout cover (figure 7.22).

Monitoring

The only construction effort to date has been the extension of the fence from the Yellow Creek mainstream to Big Springs. Although a trout-population monitoring survey hasn't begun, photo points to document changes in riparian vegetation, the condition of the in-

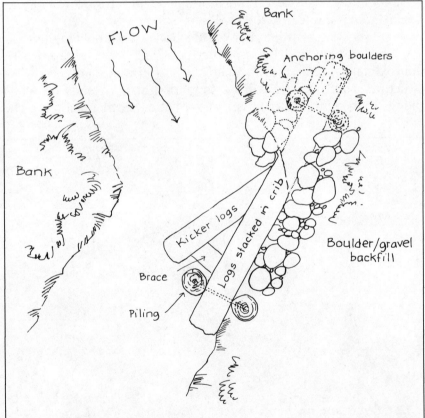

7.22 Log-crib bank protection. *Aerial view of a log-crib structure designed to protect a rapidly eroding stream bank near a campground.*

stream structures, and changes in the number and extent of aquatic weed beds have been established.

The intent of the trout-population monitoring is to determine changes in the number and size distribution of trout in the enhanced reaches and reaches where no restoration efforts have taken place, that is, the control sites. By using this method, changes in the trout population attributable to the restoration work can be differentiated from natural, annual variations in trout populations. Data collection efforts could include a regular angler creel census, electrofishing surveys in shallow-water areas, and direct underwater counts by divers in deeper pools.

Summary of Findings

Because the restoration program designed by the consultant has not yet been fully implemented, it is too early to judge the results.

It is apparent, however, that the original fence, built in 1978, has allowed riparian vegetation to recover. Dry grassland vegetation and raw bare banks have been replaced by sedges, rushes, and some willow. These banks now provide cover in the form of overhanging vegetation and undercut banks, which have formed at the rate of one to two inches of undercut per year.

Unfortunately, the four-foot-high split-rail cedar fence has not been a complete success, because cattle have tried to hurdle it. When the cattle land on the top rail, it breaks, and they then gain quick and easy access to the lush, riparian vegetation. It does not take the cattle much time to graze this vegetation down, which underscores the importance of maintenance to any structural solution including fences.

It is noteworthy that the main emphasis is placed on land management and revegetation with lesser emphasis on permanent structural solutions, such as log bank cover and crib deflectors.

The consultant's plan does not directly address the channel incision. As discussed in chapter 3—and in the Camp Creek case history—structural solutions to incised channels are rarely successful unless they are preventive in nature. Thus, the only realistic course of action is to allow the incision to heal naturally. Sometimes the lack of overt action is the best restoration strategy.

SOURCES

Camp Creek, Oregon

Most of the information for this case study was provided by Wayne Elmore, Bureau
    of Land Management, State Riparian Specialist, Prineville, Oregon.
Written sources include:
Pfankuch, D. 1975. *Stream Reach Inventory and Channel Stability Evaluation* Missoula,
    MT: U.S.D.A. Forest Service Northern Region.
U.S. Bureau of Land Management. Prineville, OR. n.d. Camp Creek Watershed
    Facts. Unpublished xerox.
Winget, R. and Mangum, F. 1979. *Biotic Condition Index: Integrated Biological, Physical
    and Chemical Stream Parameters for Management.* Logan, UT: U.S.D.A. Forest
    Service Intermountain Region.
Winegar, H. 1975. Camp Creek: Rebirth of a Section. *Oregon Wildlife* 30(11):6–7.

Bear Creek, Oregon

Most of the information for this case history was provided by Wayne Elmore,
    Bureau of Land Management, State Riparian Specialist, Prineville, Oregon.
Written sources include:
Pfankuch, D. 1975. *Stream Reach Inventory and Channel Stability Evaluation.* Missoula,
    MT: U.S.D.A. Forest Service Northern Region.
Winget, R., and Mangum, F. 1979. *Biotic Condition Index: Integrated Biological, Physi-
    cal and Chemical Stream Parameters for Management.* Logan, UT: U.S.D.A. Forest
    Service Intermountain Region.

Lawrence Creek, Wisconsin

Ed Avery, Max Johnson, and Dave Vetrano provided expert information.
Written sources include:
Hunt, R. L. 1969. Effects of Habitat Alteration on Production, Standing Crops and
    Yield of Brook Trout in Lawrence Creek, Wisconsin. H.R. McMillan Lectures in
    Fisheries, Univ. of British Columbia, Vancouver, BC.
————. 1971. *Responses of a Brook Trout Population to Habitat Development in
    Lawrence Creek.* Department of Natural Resources, Tech. Bull. no. 48. Madison,
    WI.
————. 1976. Long-term Evaluation of Trout Habitat Development and Its Rela-
    tion to Improving Management-Related Research. *Trans. Am. Fish. Soc.*
    105(3):361–64.
————. 1987. *Glossary of Wisconsin Trout Habitat Development Techniques.* Madison,
    WI. Department of Natural Resources.
————. 1988. *A Compendium of 45 Trout Stream Habitat Development Evaluations in
    Wisconsin during 1953–1985.* Department of Natural Resources, Tech. Bull. no.
    162. Madison, WI.
Leopold, A. 1949. *A Sand County Almanac.* New York: Oxford Press.

Vetrano, D. 1988. *Unit Construction of Trout Habitat Improvement Structures for Wisconsin Coulee Streams*. Bureau of Fisheries Management, Department of Natural Resources, Administrative Rpt. no. 27. Madison, WI.

Irrigation Ditch/Spring Creek, Montana

All of the information for this case history was obtained from the landowner and his consultant.

John Day River, Oregon

All of the information for this case history was provided by Errol Claire and Jeff Neal of the Oregon Department of Fish and Wildlife, John Day, Oregon.

Yellow Creek, California

Mr. Robert Franklin, formerly a fisheries biologist with the consulting firm of Entrix of Walnut Creek, California, provided most of the information presented.
Written sources include:
Franklin, R., and Baldridge, J. 1987. *Master Plan for the Enhancement of Brown Trout Habitat in Yellow Creek, California* Walnut Creek, CA: Prepared for California Trout, Inc. by Entrix.

Chapter 8

FORESTED STREAMS

JONES CREEK, GEORGIA

Location	*Chattahoochee National Forest, Lumpkin County*
Project status	*Public*
Project leader	*Monte E. Seehorn*
Landowner	*U.S.D.A. Forest Service*
Rehab. length	*0.5 miles*
Limiting factors	*Lack of deep water, cover, and food*
Problem	*Low-gradient stream as a result of past management practices under private ownership*
Prescription	*Add 90 in-stream structures at specific locations*
Begin date	*July 1984*
End date	*August 1988*
Current status	*Project will be maintained indefinitely*
Estimated cost	*90 structures at three work-days per structure*

Background

Jones Creek is typical of the streams I visited in north Georgia and North Carolina with Monte Seehorn, Jim Kidd, and Larry Neuhs. To better understand Jones Creek, some knowledge of the region's history and geology is helpful.

During the early 1900s the timber industry in the southern Appalachian Mountains was big business. The rivers and streams of the Appalachians were used to transport logs from the mountains to the mills in the valleys. However, because of the streams' relatively small size, dams were built to store sufficient water to transport the logs. Once the area behind a dam filled with logs and water, the dam was blown up and the water and logs rushed downstream. The sudden release of such a large volume of impounded water and tumbling logs must have had a devastating effect on the stream channels.

The loggers were followed by subsistence farmers, who removed the remaining trees, planted crops, and let their livestock roam freely through the hills. This way of life continued until the Great Depression, when most of the farmers lost their farms. Following the depression, much of this land came under the ownership of the U.S.D.A. Forest Service.

Streams like Jones Creek were likely very wide and shallow with laterally unstable banks. Their lack of riparian vegetation and woody debris probably added to a lack of habitat diversity, and with few trees to shade the stream the water was probably fairly warm.

In the intervening 60 years, with the aid of 60 or more inches of annual precipitation, the forest has regenerated tremendously. Rhododendrons, hemlock, pine, and a variety of hardwood-tree species form a lush and beautiful forest today.

Jones Creek, like many of the streams draining these forested hills, is small (less than 20 feet wide), shallow (less than six inches deep at riffles), of moderate gradient (1.5 to 3.0 percent), sinuous, and not very productive. Jones Creek has low alkalinity (10 mg./l. or less) and is slightly acidic (pH 6.0−7.0). Insects are not abundant, and electrofishing surveys yield relatively low numbers of small trout.

However, this has not dampened the enthusiasm of the region's trout anglers. In fact, several of the North Carolina and Georgia chapters of Trout Unlimited are annually among TU's top fund raisers, and much of the money raised is used to fund in-state trout-habitat enhancement projects.

The best-known stream-habitat restorationist in the Southeast is Jones Creek project leader, Monte Seehorn. Seehorn's habitat-enhancement philosophy is to observe and imitate nature. He also tries to think like an experienced angler, because he has come to believe that anglers almost instinctively know the types of habitat larger trout tend to prefer.

Inventory

PHYSICAL

The pre-project habitat inventory of Jones Creek was limited to a walk-through survey. The existing habitat features of the stream channel were noted on a hand-drawn map.

BIOLOGICAL

At Jones Creek the pre-project electrofishing survey turned up a total of 44 brown trout in a 600-foot reach of stream. Of the 44 trout, 11 were over six inches long. The largest trout was less than ten inches long.

Limiting-factor Analysis

A formal limiting-factor analysis was not conducted for the Jones Creek project. Yet because Seehorn has been working in the southeastern United States for nearly 30 years, he believes that the two factors generally limiting the production of larger trout in these streams are the lack of deep water and cover.

The lack of deep water, cover, and habitat diversity is attributed, in large part, to the lack of in-stream woody debris. Despite the fact that the forest has regenerated tremendously since the 1930s, it is still young. Consequently, few trees have died and fallen into the stream.

The lack of undercut banks probably is related to the type of stream-bank vegetation that grows along Jones Creek. Seehorn says if the stream was "opened up to sunlight" its ability to support grassy banks would help to produce more undercut banks. Grasses and sedges have extremely dense, strong root systems that hold soil much better that the larger but less dense tree root systems.

Finally, the substrate is composed largely of gravel and rubble with few boulders available to provide cover or to promote the scouring action needed to dig pools.

Project Design and Implementation

Although a formal process of project inventory and limiting-factor analysis was not conducted for this project, proper planning procedures were stressed. The following action plan was instituted to implement the Jones Creek project:

1. Examine and identify limiting factors.
2. Prescribe activities to correct deficiencies and tailor them for individual stream needs that are based upon overall goals.
3. Treatment by prescription. Base priorities on overall management objectives.
4. Evaluate project to determine if short-term goals are met.
5. Maintain project to ensure completion of long-term goals.

The combination of Seehorn's experience in the region and the information obtained during the walk-through survey yields his prescription.

A second walk-through survey of the project area was conducted with the management prescription in mind. Structures were sketched onto the map, as were dimensions of the structures and the stream.

Stakes were placed at the locations of the proposed structures. Materials were delivered to the site. Construction was usually completed by a Youth Conservation Corps crew or volunteer labor of the local TU chapter. The work was conducted under the direction of the local U.S.D.A. Forest Service fisheries biologist or technician.

Jones Creek, like many of Seehorn's projects, included a mixture of deflectors associated with log covers, channel constrictors, cover logs, boulders, and small dams. Seehorn, however, prefers the deflectors and channel constrictors to dams because dams have a higher potential for failure and are more expensive to build. "However," Seehorn says, "anglers love them." He notes that if he was working in higher-gradient streams with rubble substrate he might use more dams. This is because maximum scouring action provided by a dam is needed to keep the developed pool free from the large rubble moved during high flows.

DEFLECTORS

Deflectors were constructed to narrow, deepen, direct, and increase the velocity of the stream flow. The objective was to create or enhance lateral scour pools and form a more meandering, or sinuous, channel. Deflectors were often constructed to direct flow toward naturally occurring cover, such as a tree root mass, boulders, or a stable and overhanging bank. If natural cover was not present, a cover log was used to hold and stabilize the bank and to provide cover for trout.

The deflectors were constructed of logs, such as black locust, oak, yellow poplar, eastern hemlock, and white pine, with diameters ranging from 14 to 20 inches. The front log of the triangular structure was generally placed at an angle of 40 degrees or less to the stream flow. Figure 8.1 presents an overhead view showing position of cover log. The downstream brace log was pinned to the front log at an angle of approximately 90 degrees. This angle can vary as long as it is sufficient to direct waters topping the structure toward the center of the stream rather than toward the bank.

The deflectors, as well as all other structures, were built low in profile. The low-profile construction technique not only increases the structures' life spans. It also recognizes that they must function during high flows. The finished deflector should rise 6 to 12 inches above normal summer flows, but it should never equal or exceed bank height.

The two logs that form the structure are laid in trenches that are at least three to four inches deep and extend into the stream bank four to six feet. The apex of the triangle generally narrowed the channel by as much as 70 to 80 percent (figure 8.1).

A two-foot-long section of 5/8- or 3/4-inch steel rebar was driven through the logs at the apex to help hold the structure in place. In streams over ten feet wide, to help secure the log, at least one or two 4-1/2-foot-long pieces of 3/4-inch rebar are driven through the main log, three to six feet from the apex of the triangle.

The Fine Art of Driving Rebar. Many of the in-stream structures used in habitat restoration include steel rebar for securing logs to each other and the streambed. Driving rebar through a log and into the stream-bed with a sledge hammer while standing knee-deep in rushing water presents a serious challenge. Some pointers from the pros are:

1. Whenever possible, predrill holes for the rebar while still on the bank.
2. Holes can be made with a large drill or with the tip of a chain-saw blade.

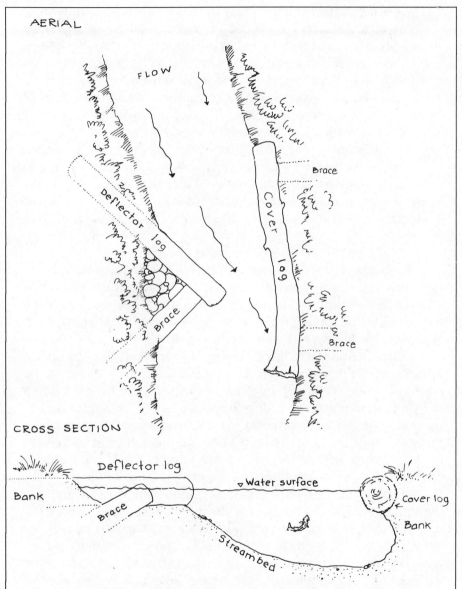

8.1 Deflector and cover log. *Aerial and cross-section views of a deflector and associated cover log. The deflector is positioned toward the lower third of the cover log. This creates deeper water along the upper two-thirds of the cover log. The downstream end of the cover log should either flare out, as in this drawing, or be placed at an angle to the flow to keep it scoured free of sediments.*

3. Have a rebar driving head made from a six-inch piece of two- to three-inch diameter cold-rolled steel stock. A three-quarter-inch hole should be drilled four inches into the end. The driving head is placed over the end of the rebar to provide a bigger target to strike. Always wear safety goggles when driving rebar.
4. An air hammer, rather than a sledge hammer, can be used to drive the rebar if a compressor can be used near the site. Portable gasoline-powered jackhammers work well in less accessible sites.
5. Although some workers drive the rebar until the end is flush with the log, others leave six to eight inches to bend over the log to keep the structure from floating up. This approach is a good one, but the rebar must be bent flush with the log. If not, it will trap floating debris or pose a hazard to anglers and other recreationists.

The area within the triangle was filled with hand-placed boulders. It is important to use large material because this rock can be plucked from within the structure at high flows. Seehorn has toyed with the idea of leaving these areas open to provide shallow, low-velocity areas for fry, but he has yet to try it.

When attempting to direct the flow toward boulders, stumps, or other short, stable objects, the apex or tip of the deflector should be placed opposite or slightly upstream of the objects. Where cover logs or extensive root mats provide a longer surface, the tip of the deflector should be located approximately one-third of the distance above the lower end of the log or root wad. By placing the deflector toward the lower end, the constriction, or damming effect, of the deflector can create deeper water along the upper two-thirds of the log.

When using a cover log in association with a deflector, it is important that the log flare out at the downstream end. This can be accomplished by using a naturally curved cover log or by placing the log at a slight angle to the flow (figure 8.1). This ensures that the flow will keep the area under the log scoured and free of sediments. If the log is parallel to, or angled away from, the flow, the lower end will fill with sediment and render it useless as cover.

The scouring action created by the deflectors has caused several of them to become completely exposed (figure 8.2). This picture was taken in July 1988, during one of the worst droughts in memory. Despite the low flows, and the fact that the structure is no longer bedded in the stream bottom, it is still functioning.

8.2 Exposed deflector at Jones Creek, Georgia. *Scouring action of Jones Creek, induced by the deflector on the left, has completely exposed the structure during an extreme low-flow situation. The deflector and cover log continue to function as designed.*

CROSS LOG AND REVETMENT

Seehorn first saw the cross-log and revetment structure in *Guidelines for Management of Trout Stream Habitat in Wisconsin.* He then adapted it for use in southeastern streams. Although this structure is very similar to the deflector with cover log, there are some important differences.

The brace log of this structure extends across the stream and into the opposite bank. The end of the brace log, where it meets the revetment or cover log, should be six to eight inches lower than the other end. The trench for this log should be as deep as the log itself so that it is entirely covered. The revetment and brace logs are pinned together and into the stream bottom with 48-inch by 3/4-inch rebar.

As water flowing over the brace log that crosses the stream creates a lateral scour pool, the revetment log(s) provide overhead cover and bank protection (figure 8.3). Because these structures are best located in low-gradient streams—and at existing stream bends that lack pools and cover—potential sites are somewhat limited.

8.3 Cross log and revetment at Jones Creek, Georgia. *Cross log and revetment create a lateral scour pool with cover at a naturally occurring bend in the channel.*

Only one site appropriate for this type of structure was found at Jones Creek.

CHANNEL CONSTRICTORS

Channel constrictors are modified deflectors that are designed to scour and deepen the streambed and provide overhead cover similar to that provided by undercut banks. They are generally best placed in long, straight, low-gradient stream stretches.

Channel constrictors can be placed alone or in pairs, such as the two under construction in figure 8.4. If the placement of only one channel constrictor is being considered, the bank opposite its placement should be stable and provide natural cover in the form of root masses, boulders, etc. A cover log can be placed on the opposite bank.

Each channel-constrictor structure in Jones Creek consists of a main channel log with two brace logs pinned to it at approximately

45-degree angles (figure 8.5). The main log was generally 10 to 30 feet long and as large in diameter as a crew of three could handle. A rough, crooked log provides the best cover and helps promote self-cleaning.

Construction. Construction of these devices was similar to that of deflectors. Trenches were dug and the logs were placed so that 6 to 12 inches of the log was exposed during summer low flows. Steel rebar was used, as shown in figure 8.5, to pin the logs together. The area within the log structure was filled with boulder material.

Since completion of the Jones Creek project, Seehorn has modified the channel constrictor. Filling the crib area with rock was expensive and the rock kept sloughing off and filling the undercut. To solve the problem, he now adds one or two more logs behind the main channel log, which provides more room for undercut. The area behind these extra logs is filled with slash held in place by poles (figure 8.5).

There are two keys to the successful construction of a channel

PHOTO COURTESY OF MONTE SEEHORN.

8.4 A channel constrictor under construction.

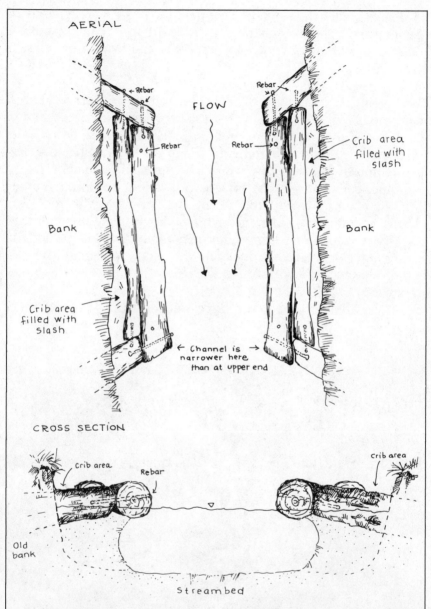

AERIAL

← Rebar

Rebar

Rebar

Rebar

FLOW

Crib area
filled with
slash

Bank

Bank

Crib area
filled with
slash

← Channel is →
narrower here,
than at upper end

CROSS SECTION

crib area

Crib area

Rebar

crib area

Old
bank

Streambed

8.5 Channel constrictor. *Aerial and cross-section views of a channel constrictor. When constrictors are built, the logs are embedded in the stream channel. The constriction of the flow increases velocity and cutting action, creating a narrow, deep channel with new banks.*

constrictor. First, upon completion the stream must be sufficiently narrowed (up to 80 percent) to increase the water velocity needed to scour out the streambed rubble and gravel, thus creating a narrow, deep lateral-scour pool. Cover will be provided by the main log along its entire length.

Second, the constrictor must be 6 to 12 inches narrower at the downstream end than at the upstream end (figure 8.5). This keeps the water velocity building throughout the length of the structure and prevents siltation of the device. If the constrictor(s) are parallel or narrower at the top end, a deposition area will be created in the lower, downstream part of the structure.

COVER LOGS AND BOULDERS

Both cover logs and boulders were used in Jones Creek to provide overhead cover and resting areas. Boulders can create additional depth because of the scouring caused by the channel's reduced capacity and increased water velocity.

The classic cover log, as described by White and Brynildson, consists of a half log with blocks to hold it off the stream bottom (figure 8.6A). The half log and blocks are secured to the stream bottom with rebar.

Seehorn used two adaptations on Jones Creek. He prefers to use whole, large (over 16 inches in diameter) crooked trees (figure 8.6B). The trees provide an irregular surface that causes turbulence along the edge of the log. This keeps the edges scoured free of silt and gravel. Logs with limb stubs and large stumps are also used because their irregular shape leads to self-scouring.

If large, irregular logs are not available, smaller, straight logs can be used. However, logs less than ten inches in diameter should not be used. A benchlike slab can be cut with a chain saw from the bottom of the log, creating a cover log that is secured to the stream bottom with rebar (figure 8.6B).

If placed improperly, cover logs accumulate silt and gravel and are soon rendered ineffective. The best and easiest locations for cover-log placement are along banks in stream meander bends. In these areas the log was placed at a slight angle to the flow to enhance scouring action. However, despite years of experience in placing cover-log structures, both Seehorn and Hunt report cases where the

8.6 A variety of cover logs.

Log placement in stream

FLOW

A. The classic Wisconsin cover log.

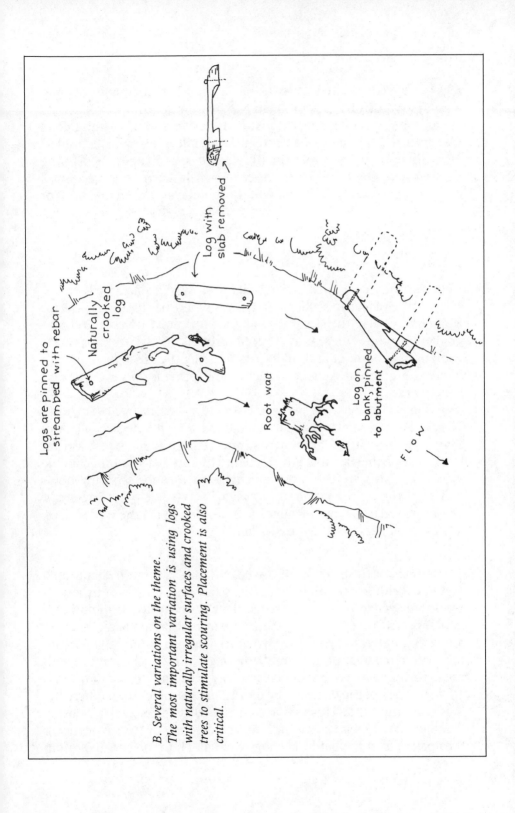

Log with slab removed

Naturally crooked log

Logs are pinned to streambed with rebar

Root wad

Log on bank, pinned to abutment

FLOW

B. Several variations on the theme. The most important variation is using logs with naturally irregular surfaces and crooked trees to stimulate scouring. Placement is also critical.

logs have become silted in. By using naturally irregular logs, stumps, and logs with stubs, this problem can be minimized.

Although boulder placement is not as critical, it is still a good idea to use the largest, most irregular boulders available. Boulders were used in Jones Creek in riffles, glides, and open pools. The greatest benefits are likely to be achieved in currents exceeding 2 cubic feet per second (cfs) and when boulders are placed in groups or clusters.

DAMS

Deflectors are less expensive to build than wedge dams or K-dams. They can be placed in sections of streams where banks are too low for a dam and where the stream is too wide for one. However, in high-gradient reaches where flows exceed three cfs and where substrate is composed of boulder and rubble, dams generally are better suited to break the gradient, reduce velocity, and provide more cover and resting areas.

Dams are the least preferred structure according to Seehorn. They are the most expensive to build, have a higher degree of failure than other structural approaches, and require high, stable stream banks. Nevertheless, in high-gradient streams with boulder/rubble substrate, dams are the most effective structure for scouring pools and breaking up the gradient to provide low-velocity resting areas. Seehorn used two types of dams on Jones Creek: (1) the wedge dam, which he prefers; and (2) the K-dam.

Wedge Dams. Construction of a wedge dam is shown in figure 8.7. Figure 8.8 shows the three-foot-deep scour hole produced by a two-week-old wedge dam. The wedge dam is an upstream-pointing V structure. The two main logs of the dam face upstream at a 45-degree angle to the stream flow. The two brace logs are pinned to the main logs with rebar at approximately a 90-degree angle. The butts of both the main and brace logs extend three to six feet into the stream bank.

The apex of the V should be 6 to 12 inches lower than where the logs enter the bank. This was accomplished at Jones Creek by using the taper of the log to advantage, and by digging the trench deeper at the apex than at the bank. The logs were dug into the stream bottom

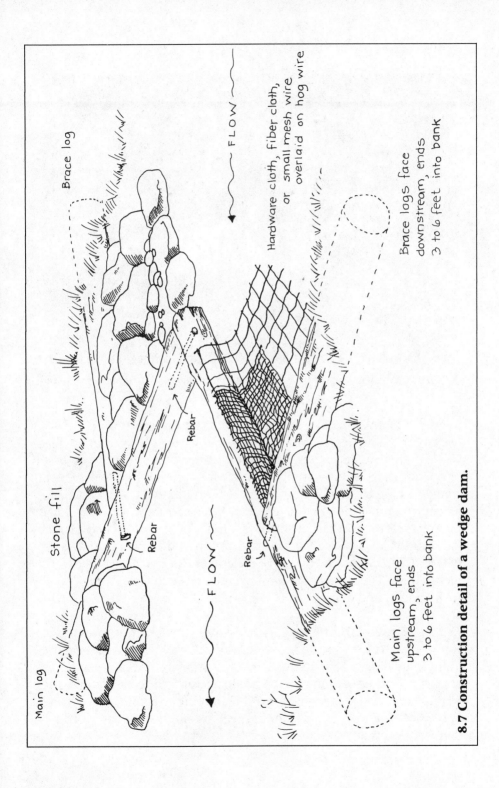

Brace log

FLOW

Hardware cloth, fiber cloth,
or small mesh wire
overlaid on hog wire

Brace logs face
downstream, ends
3 to 6 feet into bank

Stone fill

Rebar

Rebar

FLOW

Main log

Rebar

FLOW

Main logs face
upstream, ends
3 to 6 feet into bank

8.7 Construction detail of a wedge dam.

8.8 Wedge dam. *Deep scour pool created by a newly constructed wedge dam.*

as deeply as possible. The logs should also be as large as possible—at least 10 to 12 inches in diameter for small streams (less than ten feet wide) and 14 to 16 inches for larger streams.

Once the logs were in place, hog wire, or other heavy wire, was stapled to the upstream side of the logs and extended three to four feet upstream. This was covered with a layer of hardware cloth, fiberglass cloth, or synthetic highway underlayment. A layer of large, flat rock followed. Next, a layer of gravel was added and a final layer of large rock was placed on top of the gravel. The spillway was 6 to 12 inches high. The cribs at the bank were filled with a mixture of large rock, gravel, and dirt.

K-Dams. The K-dam (figure 8.9) is used for the same purposes as the wedge dam. It is best suited to streams less than 15 feet wide because a single log is used to span the entire stream. This main log should be at least 16 inches in diameter. It should be dug four to six feet into the stream bank and as deeply as possible into the streambed. Hog wire, hardware cloth, large rock, and gravel are applied as described for the wedge dam.

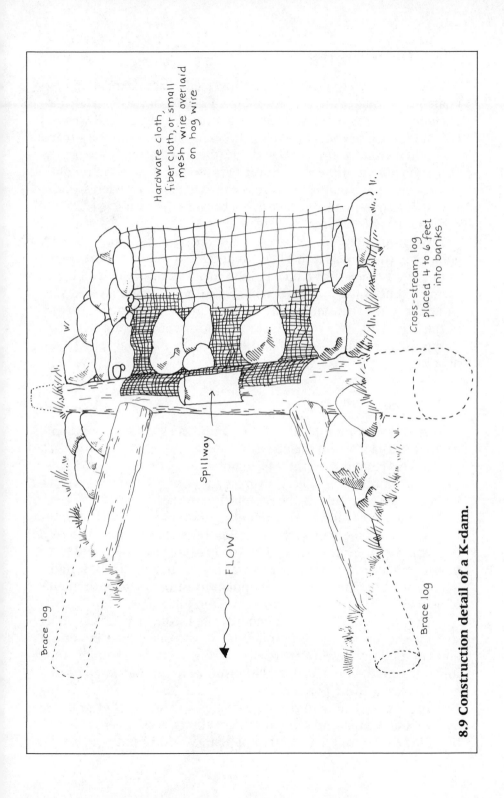

Hardware cloth,
fiber cloth, or small
mesh wire overlaid
on hog wire

Cross-stream log
placed 4 to 6 feet
into banks

Brace log

Spillway

FLOW

Brace log

8.9 Construction detail of a K-dam.

Brace logs were placed on the lower side of the dam at approximately a 45-degree angle to the main log. These brace logs were also anchored into the bank and stream bottom. Finally, a spillway was cut into the log to concentrate low flows in the center of the stream.

When compared to wedge dams, the installation of K-dams is more difficult and time-consuming because the excavation required to properly set the main log in the stream bank is more extensive. The K-dam is also more likely to wash out because the main log is usually not seated as deeply into the stream bottom.

Washout often occurs as a result of the scouring action of water going over the dam as it cuts back under the structure. Failure occurs as this scour hole—like a nick point—migrates upstream and under the dam. Either the hog wire, which is suspending the layered substrate above the scour hole, fails, or the scour hole migrates upstream of the hog wire. When this happens, the stream bottom upstream of the dam collapses, and water flows under the dam rather than over it.

Monitoring

Postconstruction monitoring of the Jones Creek trout population a year after construction yielded 104 trout of which 27 were over 6 inches. This compares to the 44 trout of which 11 were over 6 inches taken during the pre-project inventory phase. A few trout over 14 inches were taken during the monitoring studies.

Cognizant of the lack of monitoring studies completed on trout-habitat enhancement projects in the Southeast, Seehorn undertook a five-year monitoring study of five Appalachian streams in 1983. An interim evaluation of the projects was completed in 1984. Monitoring consisted of obtaining trout-population estimates, measurements of pool area (in square feet), and cover (in linear feet).

The results of this interim report were inconclusive. Two of the streams showed consistently more trout in treated than in control areas despite significantly increased fishing pressure. The remaining three streams did not show a relationship between increased habitat and increased trout populations. It was felt that increased fishing pressure was probably responsible for the apparent lack of response by the trout population to enhancement efforts. A creel census was to be added to the study in an attempt to answer this question.

Summary of Findings

It is difficult to evaluate the success of the described enhancement efforts without pre- and post-project monitoring data. Seehorn and local anglers obviously feel that their efforts have been rewarded.

The structures designed and constructed are simple and built to last. The aesthetic appeal of these structures is enhanced by the emphasis on creating lateral scour pools associated with cover made from natural materials. This creates a more natural appearance than a series of dams constructed perpendicular to the flow. Seehorn emphasizes the need to constantly provide maintenance to ensure that the structures function properly.

LEFT BRANCH YOUNG WOMAN'S CREEK, PENNSYLVANIA

Location	*North Bend*
Project status	*Public*
Project leader	*David F. Houser*
Landowner	*Pennsylvania Bureau of Fisheries*
Rehab. length	*Five miles*
Limiting factor	*Lack of cover for adult trout*
Problem	*Flood and heavy-equipment damage*
Prescription	*Provide improved cover and pool areas*
Begin date	*July 1984*
End date	*Ongoing*
Current status	*To be completed in 1990*
Estimated cost	*Unavailable*

Background

The Pennsylvania Fish Commission's (PFC) Adopt-a-Stream program provides technical assistance and, in some cases, materials to persons and groups interested in undertaking trout-stream habitat restoration projects. The service group, club, or individual receiving assistance must provide the labor necessary to complete the project.

The projects range from picking up trash along a stream to heavy construction—as in the case of Left Branch Young Woman's Creek in north-central Pennsylvania.

In exchange for assistance from PFC, the group working on a public-access stream is obligated to provide maintenance of the project's structural aspects for ten years. If the project is on a stream reach surrounded by private land, the landowner must provide public access to the stream for ten years following the project's inception.

The Adopt-a-Stream program was initiated in 1978 and currently has approximately 100 projects underway. No projects have been completed because the commission encourages a long-term, incremental approach. Each year one or two new structures are designed and constructed, and existing structures are evaluated to improve the design of the previous year's efforts. This incremental approach, plus the fact that most groups continue to find new project ideas, has led to ongoing, long-term projects.

Clinton County, in north-central Pennsylvania, is one of the state's most scenic areas. Like many scenic areas, however, the economy, which is based upon agriculture and the timber industry, has been depressed for some time. To help boost the economy, the local people decided to enhance the area's reputation as a tourist/recreation spot by enhancing nearby mountain-stream fishing opportunities.

In 1984 county officials, working with PFC, adopted Left Branch Young Woman's Creek to rehabilitate. PFC has provided technical assistance, and the county has paid for a work crew.

Left Branch Young Woman's Creek is a sinuous mountain stream with a gradient of approximately 1.5 percent. The stream drains state-owned forestland that has helped support the local timber industry for many years. The stream is clear, cold, and not very productive, yet the 45 to 50 inches of precipitation per year produces a lush hardwood forest.

When Hurricane Agnes tore through this area in 1972, it dumped devastating amounts of rain, and the floods caused considerable damage. The flood damage, however, paled in comparison to the damage done by the heavy-equipment operators who, almost predictably, set about to straighten the streams in the misguided belief that this would prevent future flooding.

Left Branch Young Woman's Creek is a productive nursery

stream that harbors many young-of-the-year trout. However, in 1984 there were very few two- to three-year-old trout to attract anglers to the area. The local PFC biologist felt that this was because of a lack of pools and cover necessary to provide habitat for larger trout.

PFC normally depends upon its area biologist for advice on the appropriateness of each project. In this case the area biologist was opposed to the project. He feared that the attempt to create a recreational fishery would eliminate the nursery value of the stream.

Inventory Methods

PHYSICAL

The physical habitat inventory consisted largely of walking and observing the stream. A systematic habitat inventory was not undertaken.

The informal survey showed that the naturally occurring pools had been scoured from bedrock and large boulders. In general these pools were shallow, small, and lacked woody debris. Consequently, they provided little in the way of escape cover for larger trout.

The survey also identified a point where the channel divided into three smaller channels for approximately three-eighths of a mile. During late summer none of these channels contained very much water. One of the channels was cutting into the steep road fill, thus threatening the road and contributing silt to the stream.

BIOLOGICAL

An electrofishing survey revealed abundant young-of-the-year trout, but few adult trout.

Limiting-factor Analysis

Given the lack of quality pool habitat and cover in the stream, and the lack of adult trout, it was determined that pools and cover were needed to produce the adult trout that would attract anglers to the area.

In addition, PFC decided that the three channels should be

consolidated into one channel to increase flow during low-flow periods, reduce danger to the road, and reduce the stream's sediment load.

Project Design and Implementation

The project design consisted of two components: (1) a series of jack dams, and (2) a large channel block.

Jack dams are known by a variety of names including low-flow channel structures and Hewitt ramps. These dams are effective at producing deep scour pools, but their use should be limited to moderate- to steep-gradient streams because a high-gradient stream minimizes the size of the upstream pool. It is important to keep these pools small because they tend to trap silt and sediment that render the pools unsuitable for aquatic insects and larger trout. Also, the larger the pool upstream of the dam, the more opportunity for warming of the water.

In addition, the stair-step profile created by dams mimics the natural configuration of moderate- to steep-gradient streams, not low-gradient ones.

It is important that the banks be high enough to contain the upstream ponded water. If the banks are low, ponded water or high flows can go over the bank and around the structure, washing out the entire structure. At Left Branch Young Woman's Creek several variations on the jack dam were constructed.

JACK DAMS (LOW-FLOW CHANNEL STRUCTURES)

Construction of the jack dams began with the placement of upstream and downstream bottom logs. Each log was at least 10 to 12 feet longer than the width of the stream so that each end of the log could be buried five to six feet into the stream bank (figure 8.10).

The trench dug for the upstream log was at least as deep as the full diameter of the log. This log was completely embedded in the stream bottom. The dam spillway was to be 12 to 16 inches high. The trench for the downstream log was only about half the depth of diameter of the log because the logs were 12 to 16 inches in diameter.

The second step was to use dimension lumber for flooring between the two bottom logs. The lumber was placed on top of both logs and then driven into the upstream substrate. The intent was to develop, as much as possible, a watertight ramp for the water to flow over. After the boards were driven into the upstream substrate, they were nailed to the bottom logs. The ramp extends from bank to bank. A layer of plastic sheeting or other waterproof material was placed on top of the flooring, and a second layer of flooring was added.

The next step was the construction of the wing walls. The wing walls were designed to narrow the channel as the water flowed over the structure, thus increasing the velocity and hydraulic force of the water. This energy actually digs the downstream pool. The distance between the wing walls must be adequate to convey normal flow and still provide for this narrowing. The average annual high flow and 10-, 20-, and 50-year flood flows are important design considerations.

The wing walls were constructed in a manner similar to that described for deflectors. The upstream leg of the wing wall was constructed of a single log buried five to six feet into the bank. This log rests on top of the upstream bottom log at some point in the bank (figure 8.10). The log rests on the wood flooring of the structure. The downstream wing wall was constructed of two to three logs, depending upon the height of the dam and the diameter of the logs. It was built high enough so that the top log was the same elevation as the log that formed the upstream wing wall. The logs used for the downstream wing wall were also butted five to six feet into the bank. The two wing walls meet at an angle of 120 to 150 degrees.

Board facing was placed on the outside of the logs to complete the upstream wing wall and inside of the logs to complete the downstream wing wall. The area within the wing walls was filled with stone to complete the structure.

Some of the jack dams on Left Branch Young Woman's Creek did not have wood flooring. Instead, the very flat angular rock in the area was shingled into place. One of these dams failed, and water flowed through the stones rather than over the lip of the dam. However, PFC fisheries habitat enhancement specialist Dave Houser hopes that following future high flows, silt will be deposited in the shingled rock area and the dam will reseal. Still, the flooring was a critical aspect of the design of these dams. As water flowing over the dam scours a hole downstream of the structure, this hole migrates

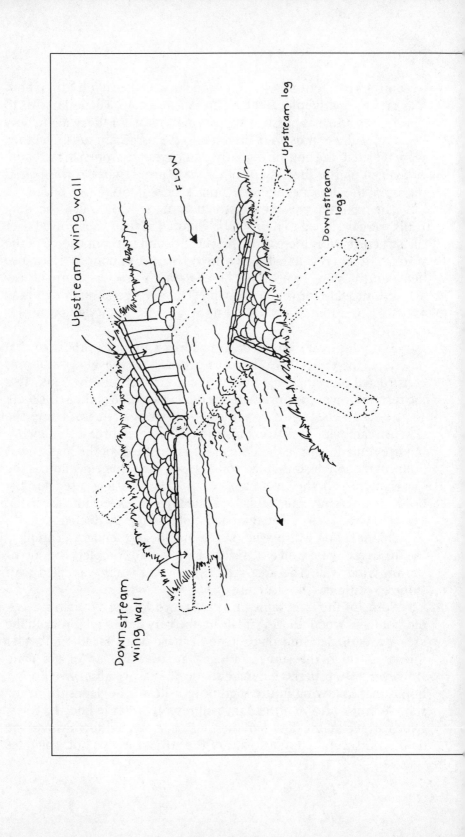

Upstream wing wall

FLOW

Upstream log

Downstream logs

Downstream wing wall

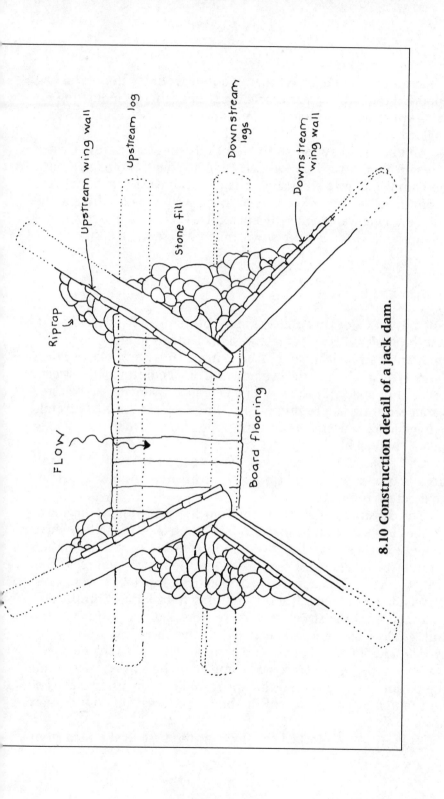

FLOW

Riprap

Upstream wing wall

Upstream log

Stone fill

Downstream logs

Downstream wing wall

Board flooring

8.10 Construction detail of a jack dam.

upstream. Rocks and gravel that, along with the bottom logs, had supported the flooring are eroded from beneath. If the flooring remains watertight, so that the dam doesn't fail, excellent cover is provided for trout.

An interesting variation on the jack dam, which Houser termed "a weird dam," was built on Left Branch Young Woman's Creek. This dam was angled across the stream. The downstream bottom log is both the base of the downstream wing wall on one bank and the upstream wing wall on the other bank. This dam creates a scour hole and directs flow toward the downstream wing wall/deflector.

Channel Block

Generally, PFC does not utilize channel blocks in its habitat enhancement programs. PFC realizes that side channels often provide very important rearing habitat for juvenile trout. However, at Left Branch Young Woman's Creek the combination of: (1) the threat the stream posed to the road; (2) the lack of adequate flow in any of the three channels during late summer; and (3) the conclusion that juvenile rearing habitat was not limiting the population led to the decision to build a channel block.

The channel block used on the Left Branch Young Woman's Creek was a large log and stone-crib structure. This block was approximately 100 feet long.

The construction of the channel block began with the digging of trenches in the bed and banks for the bottom logs. In this case three parallel trenches were backhoed and extended approximately ten feet into the banks. Logs were placed in the trench, and rebar was used to secure the logs to the streambed. Lap joints were used between logs, and rebar was driven through the joints. Construction continued until the structure was two logs high, or as high as the banks. Log cross braces, put between the three rows of logs to provide additional stability, were secured with rebar (figure 8.11).

When the log structure was completed, the crib was filled with stone. Riprap was placed at the upstream and downstream ends of the channel block to prevent the block from washing out at high flows.

This structure blocked the flows at the base of the road from going into the channel, which subsequently divided into three smaller ones. The flow is now directed into a new channel that was dug with a backhoe. This new channel re-enters the old channel about one-quarter of a mile downstream.

Monitoring

Monitoring of this project will consist of electrofishing studies by the area biologist. His principal concern will be that young-of-the-year production will be decreased at the expense of attempts to increase habitat for larger trout.

Summary of Findings

Construction was still underway during the site visit. Thus, the success of the project is unknown. Houser reports, however that after one year the channel block is still functioning well.

Still, one wonders why there is a shortage of larger trout and what is limiting their production. The choice of jack dams to create pools was not based upon a limiting-factor analysis of adult-trout habitat and may or may not be successful. Perhaps lateral scour pools, for example, would have been more appropriate than plunge pools. Only time will tell, but the incremental approach used by PFC may be helpful in determining the success of the jack dams. Because it will take several years for the population to respond to these changes, the monitoring must extend for several years following construction.

The loss of side-channel rearing habitat through the construction of the channel block was a conscious decision based on the conclusion that adequate rearing habitat was available.

This type of concern could be raised for any project where the pre-project inventory and limiting-factor analysis are done in a cursory manner or not at all. In lieu of the pre-project inventory and limiting-factor analysis, PFC has taken the approach of building a structure, evaluating its performance over several years, and directing future enhancement efforts on the basis of this evaluation and monitoring. This approach is more hit-and-miss than if the inventory and analysis are conducted. As a result it may prove to be more costly.

AERIAL VIEW

MAIN CHANNEL

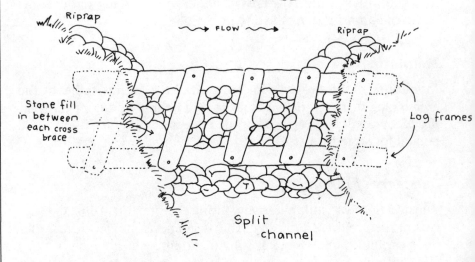

Riprap

→→ FLOW →→

Riprap

Stone fill
in between
each cross
brace

Log frames

Split
channel

SIDE VIEW

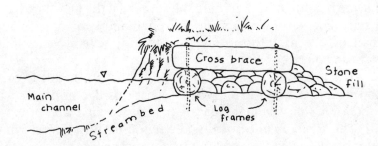

Cross brace

Stone
fill

Main
channel

Streambed

Log
frames

8.11 Three views of a channel block. *Aerial, end, and side views of a channel block.*

END VIEW

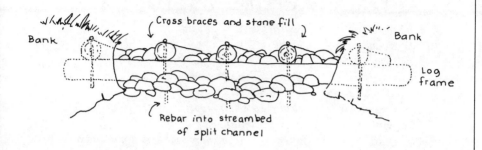

Bank

Cross braces and stone fill

Bank

Log
frame

Rebar into streambed
of split channel

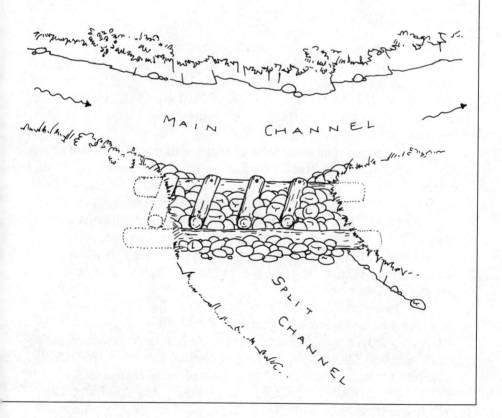

MAIN   CHANNEL

SPLIT
CHANNEL

CRANBERRY RIVER, WEST VIRGINIA

Location	*Southeastern West Virginia*
Project status	*Public*
Project leader	*Peter E. Zurbuch*
Landowner	*Monongahela National Forest*
Rehab. length	*25 miles*
Limiting factor	*Acidic water and cover areas for trout*
Problem	*Acid precipitation*
Prescription	*Stream neutralization with limestone sand and silt*
Begin date	*1987*
End date	*Ongoing*
Current status	*Work is in start-up phase as of November 1989*
Estimated cost	*$800,000 for construction and $80,000 per year operation costs*

Background

Many streams draining the northern extent of the Appalachian Mountains in eastern West Virginia are not especially inviting to trout because their waters can often reach lethal levels of acidity. The problem results in part from the shale geology of the range. This produces an acidic soil, which contributes little alkalinity to the streams.

Alkalinity is a measure of the stream's ability to buffer itself from high acidic inputs. A stream's alkaline or acidic condition is expressed in a pH scale. Values run from 0 to 14 with 7 representing neutrality. All pH values less than 7 represent increasing acidity; pH values greater than 7 represent increasing alkalinity. Streams with a high alkalinity—like some Pennsylvania limestone streams—can receive acidic inputs without large changes in water pH. However, because most of the land in eastern West Virginia is acidic, the streams are also acidic.

Compounding this problem is the fact that these mountains have been mined for many years, and acid mine drainage has severely affected many of the mountain-stream trout populations. As a result the West Virginia Department of Natural Resources (WVDNR) has been attempting to neutralize acidity of streams since 1959.

Mine reclamation and treatment of acid mine drainage have greatly improved water quality in the state, and good fisheries now exist where there had been none for 40 years or more. However, the control of acid production from coal mining is being offset by increased acid deposition in the form of acid rain and snow from burning high-sulfur coal to generate electricity. In the lightly buffered waters of the Appalachians, the advent of acid precipitation is reversing the gains made in water quality and trout populations.

The Cranberry River is a beautiful stream bordering wilderness lands in the Monongahela National Forest. The lush forest, which includes beautiful flowering rhododendrons, provides a lovely setting for what was once one of West Virginia's premier trout streams (figure 8.12).

Today, the 25-mile-long Cranberry River is a virtual biological desert. Trout populations have declined steadily over the past 25 years. Recent electrofishing surveys reveal total trout standing crops of three pounds per acre (i.e., one acre of stream contains three pounds of trout), but these are mostly trout left from the spring stocking program.

The demise of the Cranberry River appears to have been caused by acid precipitation. The pH of the Cranberry River at its mouth

8.12 Cranberry River, West Virginia. *The Cranberry River was once one of West Virginia's premier trout streams. Acid precipitation has virtually eliminated trout from this stream.*

averages 5.7 and drops below 5.0 during high flows. According to Peter Zurbuch, head of wildlife research and special projects for WVDNR at Elkins, brook and brown trout can survive at pH values as low as 5.5, but rainbow trout are much less tolerant of acidic conditions.

Zurbuch began to research stream acidity neutralization in the late 1950s when he placed bags of hydrated lime in small tributaries with the hope that the lime would slowly dissolve and neutralize the acidity. Those early efforts have evolved into the highly engineered self-feeding drums and limestone storage stations developed at WVDNR's Otter Creek research facility. The same kind of high-tech station is currently being used to treat the Cranberry River.

Inventory Methods

PHYSICAL

Much of WVDNR research work on acidity neutralization has been conducted at Otter Creek, which is located near Elkins, West Virginia, about 50 miles northeast of the Cranberry River drainage. Stream-flow and water-chemistry data (pH, alkalinity) were collected from Otter Creek from 1964 to 1968 and from 1984 to the present. Similar stream-flow and water-quality data have been collected biweekly at eight stations on the Cranberry River for eight years.

BIOLOGICAL

Electrofishing surveys have been conducted on both streams, and the data from Otter Creek have been used to document the effectiveness of the neutralization program. The Cranberry River data have documented the decline of the trout population over the past 25 years.

Limiting-factor Analysis

The average annual values for pH and acidity have not changed significantly over time. However, acidity during the winter months has more than doubled since the late 1960s. This is significant. Because much of the watershed is within a wilderness area, there have been no activities that could have created additional acid loads.

The only explanation is the impact of highly acidic rain and snow that is often below a pH of 4.0.

The acidity and pH are at their worst in the spring when acid snow is melting and coming into contact with thawing soil. This combination leads to pH levels that will kill trout, which has completely changed the trout-stocking strategy of WVDNR. Trout used to be planted from January through June. Now trout are not stocked until after the spring runoff has been completed and water quality improves. In 1988 trout were not planted in Cranberry River until late May.

Project Design and Implementation

The most cost-effective control of acid precipitation is at the electricity generating plant. Burning low-sulfur coal is one of many options to remove sulfur from the emissions before they leave the stack. Unfortunately, these options have not been exercised to a sufficient extent.

The Otter Creek research facility consists of three self-feeding rotary drums that were designed and constructed to mitigate acid precipitation. The Otter Creek facility, which was rebuilt with the current equipment in 1983, is located at the upper boundary of the Otter Creek Wilderness. Immediately upstream of the facility, the average annual flow is 10 cfs with a pH of 4.5. Immediately downstream of the facility, treatment increases the pH level to 8.4 to 8.7. Ten miles downstream, where Otter Creek leaves the wilderness, the average annual flow is 80 cfs and the pH ranges from 6.0 to 6.5.

Similar treatment facilities are being built on the two main tributaries of the Cranberry River. The installation on Dogway Fork was near completion during the site visit in July 1988. The North Fork Cranberry River facility is scheduled to be completed in 1990. It is anticipated that these two facilities can maintain the pH of the Cranberry River at 7.0 at a point 20 miles downstream where the current pH range is 4.5 to 6.0.

Each installation consists of: (1) a dam and sluiceway (figure 8.13); (2) a building that houses the self-feeding drums and stores the limestone rock; and (3) the self-feeding drums (figure 8.14).

The principle behind the installation is quite simple. A portion of

8.13 Dam and sluiceway at Dogway Creek, West Virginia. *The dam and sluiceway were constructed at the Dogway Creek facility in 1988.*

8.14 Water-powered drums at Dogway Creek, West Virginia. *Water from the sluiceway provides the power to turn the self-feeding drums at the Dogway Creek facility.*

the water released from the dam flows down the sluiceway and turns the drums. The limestone rock inside the turning drum breaks down as it bounces off baffles and other rock to produce a limestone slurry that effectively neutralizes the stream's acidity. In addition, a calcium carbonate silt also is carried out of the drum by the water flow.

The stream's greatly increased alkalinity is soon reduced downstream by the acidic water of its tributaries. A critical aspect of designing these stations is the ability to determine what pH and alkalinity the water must have as it leaves the station in order to have a pH of 6.0 or greater at the stream's mouth. The amount of alkalinity added to the stream in the form of dissolved limestone is controlled by the number of self-feeding rotary drums and the percent of stream flow used to operate them. For example, the Dogway Fork station will have three drums; the North Fork Cranberry River station will have six drums.

The self-feeding aspect of the rotary drums is a fairly recent design feature that not only has reduced manpower requirements but also increased efficiency. The original drums were hand loaded with 1,800 pounds of stone, which would last four days at high flow.

To improve the rotary-drum treatment, in 1981 WVDNR and the College of Engineering at West Virginia University collaborated to design and construct a self-feeding rotary drum and storage bin. The design goals were to: (1) develop a self-feeding drum powered by stream flow; (2) produce the proper output of limestone fines relative to stream flow; (3) maintain unattended operation with minimum maintenance; and (4) devise a bin storage system that would hold one week's supply of stone. The self-feeding drums devised from this cooperative research effort are now in operation at Otter Creek and Dogway Fork.

The self-feeding mechanism is powered by stream flow. The turning drum powers a flexible drive shaft, which controls the release of rock from a ten-ton storage bin into the drum. An important aspect of this system is that as stream flow increases, rock is delivered more quickly to the individual drum and more drums are activated. This is essential because increased flow requires more calcium carbonate slurry to adequately treat the water. The drums can turn over a range of flows from about 1 quart per second to 40 gallons per second.

A pool immediately downstream of the Otter Creek station

contains a large amount of limestone sand and silt sediment. During high flows the sand and silt are distributed throughout the stream. Zurbuch feels that having this material distributed throughout the system contributes to the treatment of the acid waters. He cites the fact that when Otter Creek floods, and when runoff is the most acidic, the drums become flooded. They will not turn, but the downstream water quality still remains good. Zurbuch believes that the quality remains high during these times because treatment is being provided by the limestone sand and silt that have accumulated on the streambed.

Winter conditions, too, require special design considerations. A four-month supply of limestone rock must be stored inside the building during winter. If the rock gets wet, it freezes and jams the self-feeding mechanism. The drums themselves have frozen on rare occasions when the temperature fell to minus 28 degrees Fahrenheit. As soon as it warmed, however, they broke free and began functioning again.

The only portion of the building that requires heat is the area where the self-feeding apparatus is located. This area is well insulated, and heat is provided by propane gas.

The total cost of constructing the two stations on Cranberry River tributaries is estimated at $800,000. The average annual operation costs—including limestone, salaries, propane, etc.—is estimated at $80,000.

The average value of an angler day (i.e., one person fishing for one day) varies from area to area, but generally seems to fall in the range of $20 to $40 per day. At $20 per day it would take an average of 40,000 angler days over the lifetime of the project to justify the construction costs. An additional 4,000 angler days per year would be necessary to offset the annual maintenance costs. WVDNR is anticipating an increase of 100,000 angler days per year on the Cranberry River. Clearly, the project is justified economically.

Monitoring

Monitoring consists largely of continuing the water-chemistry and trout-population survey work.

A study has been undertaken to determine the effect of limestone silt on the aquatic biota, particularly insects, in these streams.

Summary of Findings

The Otter Creek station has been effective at increasing the pH and alkalinity of the stream. Brook trout are now abundant in the stream and are even spawning successfully in the treatment reach.

In a preliminary manner Zurbuch has compared the cost and effectiveness of the rotary drums to the lime silos-slurry technology developed in Sweden and now being used in several locations in the United States. The lime silos release a limestone slurry to the stream to increase alkalinity and pH. Zurbuch found that although construction costs of the drum station are more expensive, the advantage of using limestone aggregate makes it less expensive in the long run.

The Otter Creek and Cranberry River stations are both fairly isolated. Each station is located at the end of a narrow dirt road bordering a wilderness area in mountainous country. It is unlikely that semi-truckloads of lime slurry could be delivered to these locations in the winter, as is necessary for operation of the silos. The rotary-drum stations are stocked with limestone in the fall when roads are in relatively good shape. Once a week during the winter, maintenance personnel use four-wheel drive trucks or snowmobiles to reach the stations and load the bins from the stockpiled rock in the comfort of the heated buildings.

Postscript

It is easy to be initially skeptical about this technology. It appears to be an expensive technological fix. However, given the lack of resolve of the federal government to deal with acid precipitation at the smokestack and the projected benefits to anglers, the self-feeding rotary drum may be very appropriate technology for dealing with this stream-acidity problem.

Zurbuch would like to try a very low-tech approach to the treatment of small tributaries whose headwaters are accessible by road. He plans to experiment with dumping quarry-produced limestone sand and silt into the streams. The spring freshet would distribute the sand, as it does the sediments produced by the rotary drums, to reduce the acidity of the tributary streams entering Cranberry River within the wilderness area.

Although the efficient use of limestone reduces the cost of treating acidified waters, the costs are still immense. Zurbuch believes only a few high-quality stream fisheries will qualify for treatment when the recreational benefits are compared to the costs. He believes that if acid rain and snow are not dramatically reduced, many watersheds will become totally depleted of their dwindling alkaline reserves. And if the alkaline reserves are depleted, it would result in the irreparable loss of many fisheries, not only in the mountains of West Virginia, but throughout the eastern United States and Canada.

CONFEDERATE GULCH, MONTANA

Location	*Broadwater County*
Project status	*Publicly funded*
Project leader	*Dr. Ray J. White*
Landowner	*Private*
Rehab. length	*1,200 feet*
Limiting factor	*Scarcity of gravel streambeds for trout spawning*
Problem	*Mining practices and flood that eliminated accumulation of woody debris to trap gravels*
Prescription	*Install log sills to simulate woody debris accumulations that trap gravel in naturally forested, undisturbed mountainous streams*
Begin date	*1986*
End date	*Ongoing*
Current status	*Being monitored*
Estimated cost	*$20,000*

Background

Confederate Gulch, rising in the forested Little Belt Mountains near Helena, Montana, acquired its name from the Southern Confederacy veterans that mined the channel for gold in the late 1860s. The Montana Bar deposit in Confederate Gulch was the richest gold discovery in the world during the period 1864 to 1866. The population of the town of Diamond City grew from essentially zero in 1864 to five thousand in 1865. Since the peak of gold-mining activity in the area, Confederate Gulch has been dredge-mined as well, particularly during the 1930s and 1940s.

During the gold-fever heydays, Confederate Gulch was a tributary to the Missouri River in southwestern Montana. Today the Missouri is dammed and Confederate Gulch is tributary to the Canyon Ferry reservoir. This reservoir supports a $3 million per year trout and yellow perch fishery. Until the late 1980s the trout planted were Arlee-strain rainbow trout, which did not reproduce in the wild. The Montana Department of Fish, Wildlife and Parks has stocked the reservoir with DeSmet rainbow in hopes of establishing a naturally reproducing rainbow-trout population that attains a larger size than the short-lived Arlee strain.

To experiment with and demonstrate methods of restoring trout spawning and rearing habitat in streams that had been disrupted by placer mining, Dr. Ray J. White of Montana State University obtained a research contract from the Montana Department of Natural Resources and Conservation in 1986. Confederate Gulch was selected as the study site.

Mining severely disrupted this stream's natural evolution. The hydraulic placer mining of the 1860s lowered the valley floor as much as 30 to 40 feet (figure 8.15). The stream was left in various unnatural channelized shapes. Prestudy reconnaissance indicated that the project area contained little in-channel gravel and few riffles suitable for trout spawning. This rather steep mountain stream had few features, such as accumulations of large woody debris, that might trap gravels.

Inventory Methods

A 2.4-mile section of Confederate Gulch was selected for study. This reach was chosen because:

1. It contained a representative mix of existing channel diversity and problems.
2. It was long enough to obtain significant trout-population data.
3. It was accessible.
4. The cost of the work would not exceed the budget.

A series of contiguous 110-yard-long stations was established within the study section. Later in the study, as data on channel

8.15 Effects of placer mining at Confederate Gulch, Montana. *Hydraulic placer mining during the 1860s lowered the valley floor of Confederate Gulch, Montana, as much as 30 to 40 feet. This photo was taken from the historic level of the valley floor.*

characteristics, trout populations, and other variables became available, data from stations with similar characteristics were combined and analyzed.

PHYSICAL

Low-elevation color aerial photographs were taken. Preliminary base maps of the channel were drawn from these photographs at a scale of 1 inch equals 20 feet. Details of channel features were added later as the project progressed.

Several aspects of physical habitat were measured including:

1. Bed profile—the elevation of the deepest point in the streambed cross section was measured at each 110-yard transect station marker. The difference in elevation at successive markers was also measured. A streambed profile was drawn from these data.

2. Water width—water width was measured at 30-foot intervals.
3. Thalweg length—the length of the thalweg throughout the study area was measured using a fiberglass or steel tape.
4. Submerged hiding cover—submerged hiding cover was evaluated by wading through the channel to identify and measure pockets of cover. (Submerged cover may be provided by fallen trees, undercut banks, debris, large rock, deep pools, and other features.) Within each 110-yard study station, that area of cover was measured and divided by the total wetted area to obtain cover density.
5. Pool dimensions—the dimensions of all pools having water depth greater than 16 inches were measured.
6. Length of eroding bank—the amount of eroding bank on both banks was measured. The eroding bank percentage was calculated by dividing the total length of eroding bank by the total length of the study section.

A continuous-recording water-level gauge was operated year-round and calibrated to obtain a discharge record. Observations, such as ice cover, were also made. Areas of wetted streambed having gravel up to three inches in diameter at the surface were measured. The feature creating the gravel deposit—log, streambed irregularity, or plunge pool—was noted.

Biological

Trout-population estimates were made for each 110-yard study section by mark-and-recapture and electrofishing techniques. Within each station the captured trout were anesthetized, and the species and body length recorded. After processing, trout were released alive.

Estimates of numbers of trout within length groups (i.e., zero to four inches, four to eight inches, eight to ten inches) were calculated for each species within each study section.

Limiting-factor Analysis

The pretreatment inventory confirmed the initial impression that the channel contained very little trout-spawning habitat. The station with the most gravel had only 4.8 percent of its bed composed of this material. In 60 percent of the stations less than 1 percent of the bed was gravel.

Most of the gravel deposits larger than one square yard were associated with woody debris. The average size of gravel deposits formed by woody debris was about two square yards, whereas the average size of gravel deposits created by other features, such as rocks or bed irregularities, was only 0.6 square yards. The study area had very few accumulations of woody debris or abrupt bends in the channel, but where these existed, there were almost always significant deposits of gravel.

Although gravel was rare in the streambed, it was abundant in the stream banks and floodplain. Dr. White surmised that although gravel was surely eroded into the stream during high flows, little was deposited in the study area because the gravel that was washed into the stream was quickly flushed through the system. This was because there was a scarcity of woody-debris accumulations and of channel bends available to trap it.

In addition to inadequate spawning habitat, the stream suffered from a dearth of submerged hiding cover. Most of the stations contained less than 10 percent hiding cover, and many contained only 1 percent. Cover plus pools composed only 5.5 percent of the streambed in the study area. Dr. White concluded that the shortage of pools and hiding cover was limiting the rearing capability of the stream.

The trout-population studies corroborated the conclusions drawn from the physical-habitat data analysis. The abundance of young trout was low in proportion to older trout. In all study sections the number of young-of-the-year trout (mostly brook trout with some rainbow/cutthroat hybrids) was less than yearling trout. (In trout populations having normal reproduction, the number of trout in one year class should be much greater than those in the next older one, especially in the young age classes.)

In addition to having poor age-class structure, most stations had very low populations. One station contained a standing crop of 18.5 pounds per 110 yards, which is moderate, relative to other trout streams in Montana. This was the same section that had the most pool area, most hiding cover, and most gravel bed. Over 50 percent of the stations contained a trout biomass of less than 4.4 pounds per 110 yards.

Winter observations of the stream revealed that major portions of the study reach remained free of ice cover even during the coldest periods, when temperatures dropped to minus 40 degrees Fahrenheit. This was attributed to stream-flow recharge by relatively warm groundwater. This favorable thermal regime bodes well for attempts to increase reproductive and juvenile rearing habitat for trout.

In summary, Dr. White concluded that the rarity of gravel and cover was limiting the reproductive and juvenile rearing capability of the stream. Both of these limiting factors are directly related to scarcity of large woody debris in the stream and to the relatively straight channel form—conditions that resulted from mining activities that occurred in the drainage.

Project Design and Implementation

DESIGN

The primary objective of the project's structural design was to develop a variety of structures to trap gravel and form spawning riffles. Secondarily, the structures would also create plunge pools, which would provide trout-rearing habitat.

The structures chosen were straight and V-shaped log-sill gravel traps. These structures were selected to mimic natural accumulations of large woody debris. The sills were placed in groups with varying distances between them (e.g., single, relatively isolated structures versus structures near enough to interact hydraulically for better trapping of gravel). The straight sills were placed obliquely across the channel to direct flow at cover on the bank.

Six sites were selected in which to build the log-sill gravel traps. Two to nine sills were scheduled for construction at each site. The primary criteria for selection of the sites were: (1) high, but relatively stable, banks into which the sills could be keyed; (2) construction-machinery access; and (3) proximity to the existing road. To preclude any change in the existing relationship between the stream and roads, no structures were placed in portions of the stream directly adjacent to the road.

The design of both the straight and downstream-pointing V sills incorporated an offset double-log feature. The upper log of the sill overhangs the downstream side of the bottom log. This feature allows the water to plunge vertically from the top log and backwash beneath the structure, providing cover associated with the plunge pool. The bottom log and a buried upstream apron of boards and wire mesh allow this undermining of the structure and prevent the structure's collapse (figure 8.16).

The overall objective of the design was to slow velocities upstream of the sill to allow the stream to drop its gravel load. Rearing cover for young trout may be provided in the plunge pool and particularly along the bank that receives current from the diagonal structure. A gravel bar will also form at the run out of the plunge pool as water velocity again decreases and as material picked up while scouring the pool is deposited. The water will then accelerate toward the next structure, and the process will begin anew (figure 8.17).

CONSTRUCTION

To begin construction, a one-foot-deep trench was backhoed in the streambed and extended into the banks where the bottom log (or logs, in the case of the V-shaped sill) of the sill would be placed. The

8.16 Log-sill construction details at Confederate Gulch, Montana.
The upstream apron of the log sills was constructed of boards and wire, and covered with cobble and gravel.

8.17 A completed V-shaped log sill. *The downstream pool will provide cover, and the gravel upstream of the sill will provide spawning habitat.*

trench extended into the banks six to eight feet (figure 8.18). The lodgepole-pine logs used for sill construction were 10 to 12 inches in diameter. The foot-deep trench allowed this bottom log of the straight sills to be placed in the stream so that the top of the log was even with the streambed surface.

For the V structure, the top of the bottom logs was level with the top of the streambed at the bank. At the apex of the V, much of the log was above the top of the streambed because the logs had to be level, even though the streambed elevation dropped over the length of the structure.

The next step in construction of the straight log sills was to place them in the trench with the backhoe. For the V-shaped sills the two logs making the V and the bracing log between them were assembled on shore. The two logs making the V were secured at the joint with a long bolt or with a rebar pin.

Figure 8.18 shows the backhoe placing the lower logs of a V-shaped sill in the bank key slots and trench. The operator held these logs in place with the bucket of the backhoe as ³/₄-inch holes were drilled down through the logs. An air hammer was used to

8.18 Placement of the bottom logs of the V-shaped sill structure in the stream. *The ends of the logs extend six to eight feet into the stream banks.*

drive five-foot-long pins of ³/₄-inch steel rebar through the holes and into the streambed to secure the bottom log.

The next step was to place the second log on top of the first. This log overshot the first log on the downstream side by approximately 45 degrees. As the backhoe operator held the second log in place, holes were drilled at a 45-degree angle through the top and bottom logs. The air hammer was again used to drive five-foot-long rebar pins through the logs and into the streambed.

After the structure was secured, the backhoe operator backfilled the key slots in the bank. Boulders were hand picked to armor the key slots. At the V-shaped sills, hand picked boulders and rubble were placed inside the V to bring the elevation of the streambed up to the top of bottom log (figure 8.16).

Rough-cut pine-slat two by fours were then nailed to the top of the bottom log and the bracing log of the V structure so that they extended upstream. An apron of hog-wire fencing was stapled on top of the slats (figure 8.16).

The backhoe operator next dug a plunge pool immediately

downstream of the structure. The excavated material, which contained significant amounts of gravel found beneath the armor layer, was placed on the upstream side of the structure. A completed V-shaped sill is shown in figure 8.17.

With the backhoe the three-person construction crew completed two to three structures per day. The V sills took more time and materials than did the straight sills.

Monitoring

Since construction of this project was completed in late summer 1988, a post-treatment monitoring program has not yet been initiated.

Summary of Findings

The hydraulic gold mining of the 1860s and later episodes not only severely altered the stream channel but also eliminated nearly all the riparian vegetation. Large cottonwood trees and alder bushes eventually regrew along the stream banks, and at times many of them must have toppled into the channel or been felled into it by beavers. However, in 1986 at the outset of the study, the channel contained few logs, beaver dams, or other woody debris that might have trapped gravel washed downstream during high flows. Although the stream banks and surrounding land contained large amounts of gravel, the only significant deposits of gravel at the surface of the wetted streambed were at the few locations of downed tree trunks or brush-debris accumulations. The scarcity of large woody debris in 1986 may have been the result of the devastating 1981 flood or channel clearances involved in rebuilding the road that shared the canyon floor with the stream. These had been washed out in various places by the flood. The 1981 flood also washed away all of the stream's beaver dams. However, by 1986 one dam had been rebuilt. In 1987 there were two more, and by the fall of 1988, ten beaver dams could be found in Confederate Gulch.

Overall, the goal of the project was to simulate natural woody-debris accumulations that not only trap gravel for spawning but create habitat for juvenile rearing as well.

LITTLE PLOVER RIVER AND
LUNCH CREEK, WISCONSIN

Location	*Portage County, Wisconsin*
Project status	*Public*
Project leader	*Robert L. Hunt*
Landowner	*Public*
Rehab. length	*0.45 miles*
Limiting factor	*Insufficient underbank hiding/resting cover for adult trout*
Problem	*Excessive stream-bank woody vegetation, slumping stream banks, sparsely rooted aquatic vegetation*
Prescription	*Remove stream-bank woody vegetation and replace with marsh meadow grasses*
Begin date	*April 1973*
End date	*May 1973*
Current status	*Excellent; recutting of stream-bank strips summer of 1989*
Estimated cost	*$1,365*

Background

Little Plover River and Lunch Creek, like the Wisconsin streams discussed in chapter 7, are low-gradient, predominately sand-bottomed streams that have very stable discharge regimes. The low-gradient, meandering channels of these small but potentially productive streams distinguish them from the other forested streams described in this chapter.

The Little Plover River, a seven-mile-long brook-trout stream, and Lunch Creek, a 10-mile-long brown-trout stream, were chosen by Robert Hunt to evaluate effects of streamside brush removal on trout habitat, trout populations, and the sport fishery. To a visiting biologist from the semi-arid West, the notion that one could improve trout habitat and trout populations by *removing* streamside brush defies conventional logic. But in Wisconsin dense stands of stream-side woody vegetation, especially speckled alder (*Alnus rugosa*), can indeed reduce available trout habitat and trout populations.

Speckled alder is a weak-limbed plant. The snow and ice that accumulate on branches cause them to droop and drape into the water. Since they do not always lift these drooping limbs in the spring, the limbs that trail in the stream reduce current velocities and cause silt to be deposited along the stream banks. Gradually, the thalweg moves away from the banks and any cover associated with them. During occasional floods chunks of such alder-lined banks tend to be dislodged, causing the channel to gradually widen and become shallower.

In addition to reducing bank cover by siltation or slumping, dense growths of alder and other channel-shading trees and shrubs may limit trout populations by shading out aquatic plants that are the basis of the food chain of these streams. Finally, dense growth of alder thatched across a stream makes it extremely difficult to fish. Once again quoting from Leopold's *Sand County Almanac*:

I wade waist deep to the head of navigation, poke my head insolently into the shaking alder, and look within. Jungle is right! A coal black hole above, so canopied in greenness you could not wave a fern, much less a rod, above its rushing depths. And there, almost rubbing his ribs against the dark bank, a great trout rolls lazily over as he sucks down a passing bug.

Obviously, in this case the alder was not yet forcing the thalweg away from the bank, but it did pose a problem for the angler.

White and Brynildson suggested that removal of dense brush from the banks of some Wisconsin streams could have several beneficial consequences for trout and the sport fishery. These benefits include:

1. Creation of more desirable habitat for trout as a result of greater growth of aquatic plants. These provide shelter for trout and constrict flow to increase scouring, deepen pools, and increase bank undercuts.
2. Firmer stream banks that consist of encroaching grassy turf less susceptible to erosion, plus a gradual narrowing and deepening of the stream channel.
3. Increased production of aquatic insects because of increased aquatic plants.
4. Increased growth of trout as a result of increased aquatic insects.

Also, slightly increased water temperatures could increase trout growth rates.
5. Easier season-long fishing conditions.

The streamside vegetation of Little Plover River in the treatment and reference (or control) zones was dominated by speckled alder with an overstory of scattered elm, ash, birch, maple, and occasional clumps of dogwood. The treatment zone of the Lunch Creek riparian forest was dominated by tamarack and a scattering of shrub clumps of speckled alder, dogwood, nine bark, poison sumac, and elderberry. The reference area was a natural sedge meadow.

Inventory Methods

PHYSICAL

The continuous stream-flow discharge characteristics of the Little Plover were obtained from U.S. Geological Survey (USGS) records. However, because there was not a USGS gage site on Lunch Creek, the limited stream-flow information for this site was obtained by taking occasional measurements with a Gurley stream-flow meter.

Stream length of both streams was measured along the thalweg. Average water depth, average water width, and water surface area were calculated from data obtained at transects established at 50-foot intervals throughout the reference and treatment zones. Water depth and substrate composition were determined at one-foot intervals along the transects. These measurements were made annually through the three-year (1971 through 1974) pretreatment period.

Stream temperatures were recorded continuously during the pretreatment period at two sites on Little Plover River. Maximum-minimum thermometers were used to collect year-round temperature information at two sites on Lunch Creek.

Net radiation—the difference between incoming and reflected sunlight—was measured in the Little Plover River treatment and reference zones in August 1972 before removal of the shade canopy. Similar measurements were made in both zones in 1974 and 1976 following treatment. No such measurements were made at Lunch Creek.

Water samples were collected in all treatment and reference areas prior to treatment. These samples were analyzed for pH, total alkalinity, and conductivity.

BIOLOGICAL

Quantitative estimates of rooted aquatic plants and trout populations were made during the pretreatment phase.

The estimates of the area of rooted aquatic plants were made only at Little Plover River and then only once prior to treatment. Field sketches of plant beds were made in early September when growth was expected to be at its maximum. Species comprising the beds were noted. The sketches were later drawn to smaller scale on graph paper, and the amount of streambed covered with aquatic plants was computed.

Trout-population samples were obtained by electrofishing techniques. Population estimates were made using mark-and-recapture techniques. Statistical tests were conducted on three types of pretreatment versus posttreatment trout-population data: (1) number of trout per mile in spring and fall; (2) biomass of trout per mile in spring and fall; and (3) number of legal-sized (6-inch) trout per mile in spring and fall. For Lunch Creek the number of quality-sized (ten inches and greater) brown trout per mile in spring and fall was also calculated.

Creel-census data were collected during two pretreatment years (1970 and 1972) at the Little Plover River. Creel-census work was not conducted at Lunch Creek.

Limiting-factor Analysis

The purpose of this evaluation was to determine whether dense growth of speckled alder was limiting trout populations and the sport fishery. The trout habitat and populations were monitored following brush removal to determine if trout habitat, the trout populations, and the fishery responded positively to this treatment.

Project Design and Implementation

At little Plover River two 0.23-mile reference zones were established immediately upstream and downstream of the 0.45-mile treatment zone. At Lunch Creek a 0.78-mile reference zone was established downstream of the 0.54-mile treatment zone. As noted above, the vegetation in the Little Plover River reference and treatment zones was similar, consisting of alder with an overstory of scattered hardwood-tree species. At Lunch Creek the treatment zone was dominated by tamarack and alder. However, the reference zone was established in a natural sedge meadow—the kind of habitat it was hoped would be created in the treatment zone.

Woody vegetation was cut at ground level and removed from strips approximately 30 feet wide parallel to the stream banks within the treatment zones. Trees and shrubs near the stream edge were carefully felled away from the stream to avoid disturbing the channel. This cut material was piled away from the stream along the edge of the cleared zone. The cutting was done in May 1973 on Little Plover River and November through December 1973 along Lunch Creek.

The cut stumps of shrubs and trees were sprayed with herbicides to discourage fast regrowth. A few days later the treatment zone of Little Plover River was seeded with a commercial mixture of three grasses: Kentucky blue grass (*Poa pratensis*), creeping red fescue (*Festuca rubra*), and bird's-foot trefoil (*Lotus corniculatus*). The Lunch Creek treatment zone deliberately was not seeded.

Figure 8.19 shows the Lunch Creek treatment zone in 1988. Hunt reports that the brushing must be done every seven to eight years to keep the woody vegetation from re-invading the stream corridor. Brushing was done for the third time in 1988 along Lunch Creek, and for a second time in 1989 along Little Plover River.

The cost of completing the brushing work has been calculated by Hunt at $5,000 to $6,000 per mile for each brushing.

Monitoring

Monitoring of these projects took place over two separate periods—1973 through 1977 and 1981 through 1983.

The monitoring techniques used were essentially the same as those used during the pretreatment inventory, with a few minor changes during the 1981 through 1983 monitoring period.

PHYSICAL

Physical habitat was measured during the period 1973 through 1977 as described under inventory methods. However, during the 1981 through 1983 monitoring effort, stream morphometry/habitat transects were established every 100, rather than every 50, feet.

8.19 Stream-bank brushing at Lunch Creek, Wisconsin. *The stream-bank brushing project of Lunch Creek as it looked in 1988. The dense forest in the background formerly grew to the stream bank, which is now lined by a sedge meadow.*

The abundance of rooted aquatic plants, which had not been measured at Lunch Creek previously, was determined in 1983, using the same techniques used at Little Plover River in 1970 and 1983.

Underbank hiding cover for trout was quantified along both streams by conducting continuous transect surveys along each bank. Banks that provided at least six inches of bank overhang with a minimum of six inches of water beneath were measured.

All water temperatures recorded during 1981 through 1983 were taken using maximum-minimum thermometers.

B I O L O G I C A L

Trout populations were monitored during both posttreatment phases as they had been during the pretreatment phase.

The 1981 through 1983 monitoring effort did not include a creel census.

Summary of Findings

The results of the physical-habitat measurements reveal that removal of woody stream-bank vegetation led to changes in stream-channel morphology that should have been beneficial to trout populations (table 8.1).

The first set of posttreatment data indicates that although both streams were narrower following brushing, they were no deeper. In fact, Little Plover River was shallower. This was attributed to the fact that following normal stream discharge in 1973, the period 1974 through 1977 was exceptionally dry and stream flows were very low. Thus, despite the fact that the stream channels narrowed following treatment, as hypothesized, depth did not increase. In fact the decrease in water width may have resulted, in part, from the reduced flows, which allowed exposed stream edges to become quickly revegetated with grasses and sedges.

Trends in trout-population statistics declined in treatment and reference zones in both Little Plover River and Lunch Creek during the first posttreatment period. The poorest trout stocks occurred in both streams during 1977, the last year of the first posttreatment evaluation and the study year of poorest stream flow.

On the basis of the channel morphology, stream-discharge data, and trout-population data collected during the first posttreatment monitoring, Hunt concluded that decreased stream flows were limiting the trout population during this time. Because flow was limiting the trout populations, no response to other beneficial habitat changes could take place.

The second posttreatment evaluation was undertaken when stream flows approached more normal values in 1981. At that time, the channel-morphometry data show the treatment zones on both streams becoming deeper and narrower than they were prior to treatment (table 8.1). The reference zones did not show this trend.

The square-foot coverage of aquatic macrophytes increased tremendously in the treatment zone of Little Plover River. There was also more streambed coverage of aquatic plants in the treatment zone of Lunch Creek than in the reference zone. Unfortunately, there is no pretreatment aquatic-plant data for Lunch Creek.

The Little Plover River trout population did not respond to the brushing treatment as did in-stream habitat. Abundance and total weight of brook trout in both zones of Little Plover River recovered

Table 8.1

Comparison of Little Plover River and Lunch Creek Channel Characteristics in Treatment and Reference Zones (Pre- and Post-Brushing Treatment)

Study Stream	Mid-Channel Length (Miles)	Surface Area (Acres)	Mean Depth (Ft.)	Mean Width (Ft.)	Channel Volume (Cubic ft.)	Aquatic Macrophytes (Cubic ft.)
Little Plover						
Treatment zone						
Pretreatment (1970)	0.45	0.77	0.57	14.2	18,983	0
Posttreatment (1973–1977)	0.45	0.56	0.53	10.3	12,805	—
Posttreatment (1983)	0.45	0.70	0.91	12.8	27,730	11,336
Reference zone						
Pretreatment (1970)	0.46	0.77	0.55	13.7	18,446	295
Posttreatment (1973–1977)	0.46	0.69	0.50	12.4	15,029	—
Posttreatment (1983)	0.46	0.83	0.65	14.8	23,434	1,948
Lunch Creek						
Treatment zone						
Pretreatment (1970)	0.54	0.88	0.98	13.5	37,560	—
Posttreatment (1973–1977)	0.54	0.86	0.98	13.2	36,712	—
Posttreatment (1983)	0.54	0.84	1.00	12.5	35,625	4,007
Reference zone						
Pretreatment (1970)	0.78	1.02	1.23	10.7	54,644	—
Posttreatment (1973–1977)	0.78	1.14	1.11	12.1	55,121	—
Posttreatment (1983)	0.80	1.13	1.04	11.0	48,698	3,057

during the 1981 through 1983 period from the declines experienced during 1974 through 1977. However, abundance and biomass in the treatment zone did not improve in comparison to parallel values from the reference zone. Hunt concluded that the trout-population recovery in both sections was primarily in response to improved stream flows. None of the recovery could be clearly attributed to the brushing work.

The abundance of legal-sized trout and quality-sized brown trout increased significantly in the Lunch Creek treatment zone during the 1981 through 1983 period in comparison to pretreatment values for this zone and posttreatment values in the reference zone. Thus, the trout population in this stream, in comparison to the standing stock of trout in the treatment zone, appeared to benefit from both increased stream flow during 1981 through 1983 and the induced improvements in trout habitat.

Postscript

This case history is very interesting from the standpoint of limiting factors. It is clear that from 1974 through 1977 the most crucial limiting factor was stream flow. During 1981 through 1983 stream discharges returned to normal, and the Lunch Creek trout population responded positively to in-stream habitat changes brought about by brushing of the stream banks. There was an increase in the number of larger brown trout in the treatment reach.

However, some unidentified factor continued to limit the population of brook trout in the Little Plover River. Although population rose in response to increased stream flows, it did not appear to respond to changes in habitat brought about by the brushing work. Hunt speculates that lack of natural reproduction within or near the treatment zone or reduced recruitment of age 0 trout may be the most likely limiting factors.

Two final notes to this story regard fishability and water temperature. The researchers were concerned that by reducing shade increased water temperatures might be detrimental, or lethal, to trout. This did not prove to be the case despite the extreme low flows. The researchers attribute this, in part, to the inputs of cool groundwater to the stream. As a general rule of thumb, Hunt suggests that if the maximum water temperature during the hottest part of the year is in the mid-60-degree range, and if the streams have stable groundwater inputs, it is safe to conduct a brushing project without fear of increasing water temperatures to levels lethal to trout.

The creel census revealed that during the first posttreatment monitoring (1976), angler use and harvest rates increased in all study zones on the Little Plover River, as compared to the two seasons of pretreatment creel census. Thus, at Little Plover River increased harvest of a previously lightly fished trout population was the only benefit for the sport fishery created by removing woody stream-bank vegetation.

SOURCES

Jones Creek, Georgia

Monte Seehorn, Jim Kidd, and Larry Neuhs of the U.S.D.A. Forest Service provided all of the information contained in this case history.
Written sources include:
Seehorn, Monte, 1982. Evaluating Fish Population Response to Installation of Instream Cover Devices in Five Appalachian Streams. U.S.D.A. Forest Service internal report.
————. 1982. *Trout Stream Improvements Commonly Used on Southeastern National Forests*. Jackson, WY: Rocky Mountain Stream Habitat Management Workshop.
————. 1985. *Fish Habitat Improvement Handbook*. U.S.D.A. Forest Service Southern Region Technical Publication no. R8-T-7.
————. 1985. Interim Report: Evaluating Fish Population Response to Installation of Instream Cover Devices in Five Appalachian Streams. U.S.D.A. Forest Service internal report.
White, R., and Brynildson, O. M. 1967. *Guidelines for Management of Trout Stream Habitat in Wisconsin*, Wisc. Dept. of Natural Resources, Techn. Bull. no. 39. Madison, WI.

Left Branch Young Woman's Creek, Pennsylvania

Dave Houser and Karl Lutz described a number of projects in the Bellafonte area of north-central Pennsylvania.
Written sources include:
Miller, T. G., and Tibbott, R. n.d. *Fish Habitat Improvement for Streams*. Pennsylvania Fish Commission.

Cranberry River, West Virginia

Peter Zurbuch and Ray Menendez provided all of the information presented here.
Written sources include:
Zurbuch, P. E. 1984. Neutralization of Acidified Streams in West Virginia. *Fisheries* 9(1):42–47.

Confederate Gulch, Montana

Dr. Ray J. White, Montana State University, Bozeman, Montana, provided all of the information contained in this case history.
Written sources include:
Binns, N. A. 1982. *Habitat Quality Index Procedures Manual.* Cheyenne, WY: Wyoming Game and Fish.
White, R. J.; McClure, W. V.; and Gerdes, S. J. 1987. Stream Restoration on Confederate Gulch, Deep Creek and Grasshopper Creek. Phase I Report: Pre-Planning Investigation. Prepared for Montana Department of Natural Resources and Conservation, Helena, MT.
_____. 1988. Stream Restoration on Confederate Gulch—Canyon Study Area. Phase II and III Report: Pre-Project Design. Prepared for Montana Dept. of Natural Resources and Conservation, Helena, MT.

Little Plover River, Wisconsin

Robert Hunt provided publications, insight, and a field review of Lunch Creek.
Written sources include:
Hunt, R. L. 1979. *Removal of Woody Streambank Vegetation to Improve Trout Habitat,* Dept. of Nat. Res., Tech. Bull. no. 115. Madison, WI.
_____. 1985. *A Follow-up Assessment of Removing Woody Stream Vegetation Along Two Wisconsin Trout Streams.* Dept. of Nat. Res. Research Rpt. no. 137. Madison, WI.
Leopold, A. 1949. *A Sand County Almanac.* New York: Oxford Press.
White, R. J., and Brynildson, O. M. 1967. *Guidelines from Management of Trout Stream Habitat in Wisconsin.* Dept. of Nat. Res. Tech. Bull. no. 39. Madison, WI.

Chapter **9**

URBAN STREAMS

RAPID CREEK, SOUTH DAKOTA

Location	*Rapid City*
Project status	*Public*
Project leader	*Ronald Glover*
Landowner	*City of Rapid City*
Rehab. length	*3.3 miles, plus an additional 2.1 miles*
Limiting factor	*Lack of pools, holding areas, and meanders*
Problem	*Channelized stream*
Prescription	*Wing deflectors, bank covers, riprap, boulder placements*
Begin date	*1977*
End date	*1988*
Current status	*Excellent brown-trout population, all structures are functioning*
Estimated cost	*$364,000*

Background

Rapid Creek, the largest stream emanating in the Black Hills of South Dakota, flows 60 miles from its origin to its confluence with the Cheyenne River. Midway along its course, Rapid Creek flows through Rapid City.

Over the past century, as Rapid City has grown, the creek has been extensively channelized. In the early 1900s Rapid Creek produced large catches of fat brown trout—an 18-pound 3-ounce brown trout was taken near Baken Park in 1928—but channelization gradually turned the meandering creek into little more than a relatively straight and wide drainage ditch. With much of the trout habitat wiped out, the fishery inevitably suffered, but the creek itself remained very productive from a water-quality and aquatic-insect perspective.

Channelization reduced the total length of Rapid Creek within the Rapid City area by almost 19 miles between the early 1900s and 1972. Rapid Creek was channelized to convey floodwaters quickly through Rapid City. The spin-off of these flood-control efforts was believed to be a more attractive area for commercial and residential developments.

In the interim between the turn of the century and 1972, Pactola Reservoir was built near the headwaters of Rapid Creek. The reservoir was constructed in 1956 to provide flood control, and also to store water for municipal and agricultural uses. Over the years Pactola Reservoir has managed to maintain the sometimes unruly Rapid Creek at a calm, average stream flow of 29 cfs.

That was not the case, however, in June 1972 when 12 to 16 inches of rain from a tremendous thunderstorm struck between the reservoir and the city. Flood torrents raged down Rapid Creek at a peak flow of over 50,000 cfs—1,725 times the average flow. More than 230 people were killed in the flood, and millions of dollars in damage occurred.

Several years after the terrible flood, Rapid City officials applied for and received Bureau of Outdoor Recreation funds to build and develop recreational opportunities in the floodplain.

A greenbelt was established along Rapid Creek, and in 1977 city officials contacted the South Dakota Department of Game, Fish and Parks (GFP). They presented the agency with an unusual request: Improve the trout-fishing opportunities of Rapid Creek within the Rapid City city limits. Before the year was out, the GFP completed a habitat restoration project at Sioux Park. Rapid Creek's problems, however, were not over.

In 1978 a half-mile section of Rapid Creek within the city limits was modified by the U.S. Army Corps of Engineers as part of yet another floodway project. As a result of the Army Corps project, Rapid Creek's stream width increased from about 30 feet to approximately 90 to 130 feet. Extensive habitat damage occurred and the brown-trout population drastically declined. Following negotiations with the Army Corps, GFP designed the Baken Park restoration project for this second reach of Rapid Creek.

Inventory Methods

PHYSICAL

The habitat was so thoroughly destroyed at both Sioux and Baken parks that there was not a perceived need to conduct pre-project habitat inventories. However, a survey of the stream sections was conducted to obtain channel widths, depths, distances, and elevations that would be used in designing the projects.

BIOLOGICAL

Trout populations were sampled using electrofishing techniques. Population estimates were derived using mark-and-recapture methods from 1978 through 1983. In 1984 and 1985 a different sampling technique was used to provide population estimates. Young-of-the-year trout were not included in the population estimate work.

Limiting-factor Analysis

Ron Glover, the GFP biologist responsible for these projects, did not conduct a limiting-factor analysis. The highly altered condition of Rapid Creek made it abundantly clear to Glover that the stream needed to be narrowed, deepened, and a meandering pattern restored. Glover was also concerned that the wide, shallow stream was marginally warm for trout survival during the summer. He hoped that narrowing the channel would help reduce water temperatures.

Project Design and Implementation

The intent of the construction was to lengthen the stream by restoring some of its original meander pattern. This would be difficult because the stream was constrained by the development along it.

In addition to lengthening the stream, Glover wanted to create a narrower, deeper channel, which would provide a diversity of habitat and lower water temperatures for trout in summer.

Because the channel had to be capable of transmitting extremely large flows, the creation of a floodplain within the existing channel was a major design criterion.

Finally, the structures used to create the meandering channel had to be able to function at 29 cfs and still withstand very high flood flows.

In 1969 Glover had made a trip to Wisconsin to look at Hunt's work on Lawrence Creek. The structures he would use in Rapid Creek—bank covers and wing deflectors—were similar to those designed by Hunt. However, to withstand the high flows Rapid Creek sometimes carries, the structures Glover eventually built were larger than those used by Hunt in Wisconsin.

Sioux Park

The project reach was 2.8 miles long. Nine wing deflectors, five bank covers, and eight riprap areas were built into the stream. Before restoration began in 1977, this reach of Rapid Creek was a wide, shallow stream with laid-back, dished-out banks (figure 9.1). The first step in constructing the bank covers at this site was to drive wooden pilings into the streambed. Construction took place in the late fall and early winter when the stream banks were frozen and not subject to erosion. After the pilings were driven, they were cut off so that the tops of pilings were even with water surface at this low-flow time of year. Five-by-eight-foot concrete slabs were placed on top and cabled to the pilings (figure 9.2). Large rock was distributed on top of the slab, and riprap was arranged on the bare bank behind the cover structure. Finally, sod was placed on top of the large rock. In this way approximately five feet of undercut bank was created along this 200-foot stretch of formerly unstable stream bank.

A large deflector was constructed on the opposite bank. To build the deflector, a trench five to six feet wide and one and one-half feet deep was backhoed from the streambed and filled with two- to four-foot round boulders. The area within the outline of the trench was filled with material dredged from the channel and sodded (figure 9.3). Figure 9.4 shows the *honey hole*, as it is now referred to, ten years after construction was completed.

9.1 Sioux Park reach of Rapid Creek, South Dakota. *Prior to restoration the creek was wide and shallow with unstable banks, which provided little cover for trout.*

PHOTO COURTESY OF RON GLOVER.

9.2 Cover-structure construction at Rapid Creek, South Dakota. *Construction of the bank cover structure at Sioux Park. This photo shows a five-by-eight-foot concrete slab being placed on top of wooden pilings.*

9.3 Completed cover structure at Rapid Creek, South Dakota. *This photo shows the completed cover structure on the right bank and the deflector on the left bank, which has just been sodded and seeded.*

9.4 Sioux Park project ten years after restoration (1988).

BAKEN PARK

The Baken Park project reach was one-half mile long. Thirteen wing deflectors and four riprap areas were built into the stream. For the Baken Park project a series of large deflectors was used to create a meandering pattern within a narrow, deep channel. This project also created a floodplain within the old channel to aid in passing flood flows. Figure 9.5 is a picture of the 130-foot-wide channel at Baken Park in 1978, following the Army Corps of Engineers' flood-control project.

Large deflectors, several hundred feet long, were constructed as described for the Sioux Park project. A backhoe was used to excavate the four- to five-foot-wide and one and one-half-foot-deep trench that forms the outline of the deflectors. Large two- to four-foot round boulders were placed in the trench to raise the deflector up to one and one-half feet above the low flow of the creek. The area within

PHOTO COURTESY OF RON GLOVER.

9.5 Baken Park, Rapid Creek, prior to restoration. *The Baken Park reach of Rapid Creek after completion of the flood-control project designed by the Army Corps of Engineers. The stream is wide, shallow, and has no floodplain.*

the trench was filled with material dredged from the channel, covered with topsoil, and seeded (figure 9.6).

The final product in 1987, nine years after construction, appears in figure 9.7. This photo illustrates how this construction method converted a wide, straight, shallow channel with no floodplain into a narrow, deep meandering channel with a floodplain that is capable of conveying the flood flows of Rapid Creek.

An important aspect of the construction was to keep these structures low in profile. They are only one to one and one-half feet higher than the water surface at low flows. When flood flows occur, they pass over these low-profile structures without tearing them out.

Large riprap was used on both projects to protect eroding stream banks. This large, angular material also provides breaks in the flow that create cover and lies for trout. Large rock was placed in the channel in three boulder groups to provide feeding stations and cover for trout.

PHOTO COURTESY OF RON GLOVER.

9.6 Construction of Baken Park deflectors. *Construction of high deflectors in the Baken Park reach created a narrow, deep, meandering channel with associated floodplain.*

PHOTO COURTESY OF RON GLOVER.

9.7 Baken Park project, 1987.

Monitoring

The monitoring program has consisted of conducting trout-population estimates with electrofishing techniques. Mark and re-capture was used from 1978 through 1983, and depletion sampling and removal was employed in 1984 and 1985. When using the mark-and-recapture technique, trout collected during the marking run were measured and a hole was made in their caudal fin with a paper punch. They were then released. The recapture run was con-ducted the following week. When using the technique of depletion sampling and removal, 100-yard sections were blocked with nets at each end to prevent trout from escaping. Captured trout were identi-fied, measured, and released below the downstream net.

Only naturally reproduced trout were included in the data anal-ysis. GFP stocks catchable brown trout in areas of Rapid Creek downstream of the project sites. Naturally reproduced and stocked trout are segregated on the basis of coloration and fin erosion. From spending so much time in concrete raceways, the fins of hatchery-reared trout show obvious signs of wear or erosion.

Summary of Findings

The brown-trout population at Sioux Park increased by 94 percent between 1978 and 1985, although it fluctuated during this time. For instance, from 1978 to 1979 there was a 36 percent increase in brown trout, but from 1979 through 1982 the population decreased. The decrease was attributed to heavy silt loads entering the stream from a 32-hectare housing-development construction site. A flood in 1982 scoured the silt from the pools, and the brown-trout population responded with a 121 percent increase in 1983. The winter of 1983 through 1984 was extremely cold, and it is believed to be the cause for a 60 percent decrease in the population in 1984. The population then showed a 90 percent increase the following year. The densities of brown trout larger than eight inches increased from 285 in 1980 to 345 in 1985. They did not fluctuate as widely during this period as the density of smaller trout. The mountain and white-sucker populations remained at low levels from 1978 through 1985.

Prior to the work at Baken Park, mountain and white suckers were the most numerous species. By 1985 densities of mountain suckers had dropped 89 percent and white suckers dropped 73 percent. During the same period brown-trout densities increased by 404 percent. The densities of all species declined from 1978 to 1979. This was probably in response to construction activities that lasted until spring 1979. Mountain and white suckers returned to 1978 levels in 1980 and 1981. They declined sharply in 1982 and continued to decline through 1984. There was a small increase in density of suckers in the 1985 samples.

The brown-trout population declined in 1979 but increased from 1980 to 1983. The population again decreased in 1984. This was thought to be due to the severity of the 1983 through 1984 winter. The population density increased again in 1985. Brown trout longer than eight inches increased from 139 in 1980 to 202 in 1983 and 277 in 1985.

These data indicate that the projects benefited the naturally reproducing brown trout but caused a decline in the sucker populations. Glover attributes this change to three factors. First, the narrowing of the channels increased velocity and replaced the wide, warm, shallow pools that were the favored habitat of the sucker populations with deep pools and associated cover preferred by brown trout.

Although accurate records of pre- and post-project water temperatures are not available, the second factor is believed to be the overall reduced water temperatures. Based upon the limited water temperatures available, Glover believes that the project stream reaches are five to ten degrees Fahrenheit cooler on the hottest summer days than they were prior to the restoration projects. Third, the adult brown-trout population is helping to control the sucker population through predation on small suckers.

This work did not include a creel census. Glover reports that anglers are frequently seen fishing throughout the year, and their success is said to be good. Glover estimates that the number of angler days has increased from 200 to 300 per mile per year to 900 to 1,000 per mile per year. The natural reproduction has been sufficient to sustain this increased fishing pressure.

As mentioned above, the average annual flow of Rapid Creek is 29 cfs. There has been some concern expressed over the ability of these structures to withstand a major flood. In 1982 the flood waters in Rapid Creek reached 1,800 cfs, and water depths over the Sioux and Baken Park projects were as great as five feet. The only damage incurred to the structures was the loss of some sod on the upstream edges of wing deflectors in Baken Park.

Some of these structures are actually increasing in size. Silt deposited in the lee of some of the deflectors has been invaded by plants, leading to further narrowing of the channel.

The cost of these projects averaged $67,000 per mile, which may appear quite expensive. Glover feels this expense is easily justified. The South Dakota GFP figures that each angler day generates $25 of income in the form of licenses, tackle, gas, and food. Given an increase of 3,500 angler days per year (700 per mile times 5 miles equals 3,500), at $25 per day that is an increase of $87,500 of local revenue per year. At that rate the projects paid for themselves in only four years. Glover fully expects these structures to be functioning in 40 years with only minor annual maintenance required.

This case history and the story of Little Crabby Creek, which concludes this chapter, demonstrate the use of large-scale structural approaches to stream habitat management. The intensive structural approach described for Rapid Creek is a reflection of the value placed on the urban developments in relation to the value placed on a naturally functioning stream system.

WEST VALLEY CREEK, PENNSYLVANIA

Location	*Chester County*
Project status	*Largely private with public cooperation and access*
Project leader	*Valley Forge Chapter, Trout Unlimited*
Landowner	*Private corporation*
Rehab. length	*2,600 feet*
Limiting factor	*Wide, shallow water that lacked holding and cover areas for trout*
Problem	*Quarry mining, industrial and suburban growth*
Prescription	*Re-introduce meanders and narrow total channel width*
Begin date	*1978*
End date	*Ongoing*
Current status	*Work continues on stream and in public and private-sector meetings*
Estimated cost	*$2,500, plus $5,000 in donated materials; all labor is volunteer.*

Background

West Valley Creek is a small, low-gradient (less than 1 percent) stream trying to meander through a predominantly limestone valley in Chester County, Pennsylvania. Because of its proximity to Philadelphia, Chester County is one of the fastest-growing counties in the United States. Development consists largely of the conversion of agricultural land to urban/suburban housing and light-industrial land uses. The various and myriad development proposals have kept the Valley Forge Chapter (VFC) of Trout Unlimited scrambling to restore and preserve the integrity of this stream.

The VFC began work on West Valley Creek in 1978 when its project application was accepted by the Pennsylvania Fish Commission. It provided technical assistance under the state's Adopt-a-Stream program. The project focused on the restoration of a half-mile stretch of stream that had been channelized to permit development of a limestone quarry. However, during the course of their work on this stream, VFC members became acutely aware of other development activities that had the potential to thwart their best trout-habitat restoration efforts.

Figure 9.8 is a rough diagram of the West Valley Creek drainage. Several small limestone springs, which are tributaries to West Valley Creek, are critical to the fishery. They provide clear, cold water that helps keep West Valley Creek water temperatures suitable for brown trout even during hot summer days. These small streams are also very important nursery areas for fry and juvenile trout. Cool water, cover provided by abundant watercress, and large numbers of fresh-water shrimp provide ideal rearing habitat. However, construction activities were eliminating riparian vegetation and exposing these clear, cold tributaries to the warming rays of the sun. In addition construction-related erosion was contributing silt to these tributaries and reducing their potential as spawning and rearing areas.

Farther upstream, residential and light-industrial development was slated for a 1,500-acre farm. VFC had serious concerns that the source of water to support this major development might be West Valley Creek, one of its tributaries, or the limestone aquifer that feeds them. They were also concerned about the fate of wastewater generated by the residential and industrial uses. Because of the silty nature of the soils in this area, there was, in addition, some concern about future construction-related stream sedimentation.

Two other major concerns of the VFC were: (1) a proposed four-lane highway, which could severely affect the stream, especially during construction; and (2) a sewage pumping plant located adjacent to the stream. Of primary concern was the possibility that, given the need to treat increasing volumes of wastewater, the pumping plant could be converted to a sewage treatment facility, which would discharge its treated waste into the stream.

Inventory Methods

PHYSICAL

A series of transects was established at 50-feet intervals along the half-mile stretch of channelized stream adjacent to the limestone quarry. The water width and maximum water depth were measured at each transect. Water temperatures were recorded. Photographs were taken at a number of points along the stream, although permanent photo points were not established.

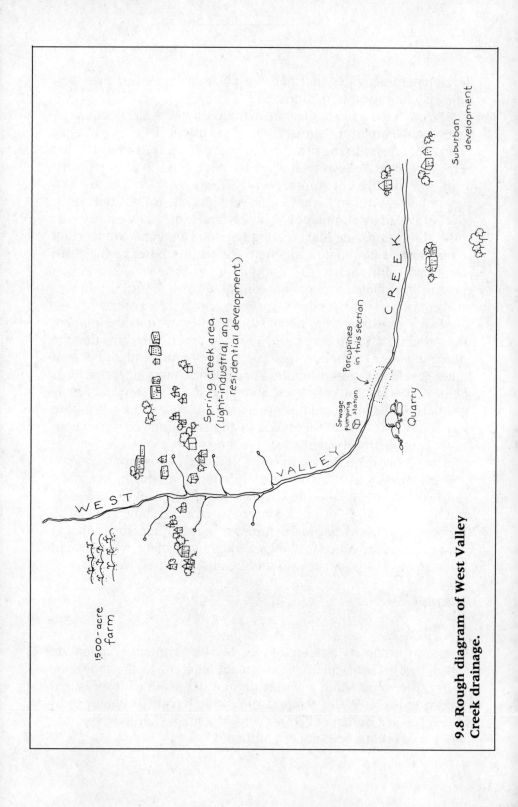

9.8 Rough diagram of West Valley Creek drainage.

The preparation of a drainage map that shows land use and proposed developments continues to be updated as VFC expands its work in the drainage.

BIOLOGICAL

Trout-population estimates were made using electrofishing techniques. This effort was carried out by the Pennsylvania Fish Commission with assistance of VFC.

Limiting-factor Analysis

The channelization in the vicinity of the quarry removed riparian vegetation and widened the stream, which transformed it into a large solar collector. Consequently, water temperature was considered an important potential limiting factor.

In addition to causing an increase in water temperature, the channelization had left the stream totally devoid of habitat diversity. In this channelized stretch the stream basically consisted of one long, wide, shallow riffle. The decrease in habitat diversity associated with the channelization was also considered to be limiting trout production.

VFC felt that wild-trout reproduction was being limited by siltation from construction activities. Although the stream was annually stocked with trout, VFC wanted to establish a naturally reproducing wild-trout population.

Project Design and Implementation

As the project design evolved from VFC's limiting-factor analysis, the membership decided to attempt to narrow and restore a meandering pattern to the stream's channelized reach, which would lead to reduced water temperatures, as well as to increased habitat diversity. An attempt to enhance natural brown-trout reproduction was also part of the project design. Finally, VFC wanted to educate the public about the fishery resource in a manner that would eventually influence public and private land-use decisions that could affect West Valley Creek.

The channel-restoration efforts were based on White and Brynildson's *Guidelines for Management of Trout Stream Habitat in Wisconsin*. The efforts began with the construction of several small triangular wing deflectors. The deflectors were constructed of hand-placed rock. No attempt was made to anchor these rocks into the bed or bank.

The deflectors created a meandering flow pattern. Silt and sand began to build up both on the deflectors and downstream in the lee of the structures. These deposits of silt and sand were quickly colonized by vegetation. At the apex of the deflector, the stream cut deep holes in the streambed.

The initial success with the deflectors led VFC to expand its construction activities in scope and concept. Annual fall monitoring of channel width, depth, and trout populations helped to guide additional structural projects.

Deflectors that had already been built were enlarged. One variation was the porcupine deflector. To create this deflector, steel pipes were driven into the stream in the shape of a triangular wing deflector (figure 9.9). Branches, limbs, and even Christmas trees were woven between the steel pipes. These structures were placed at the

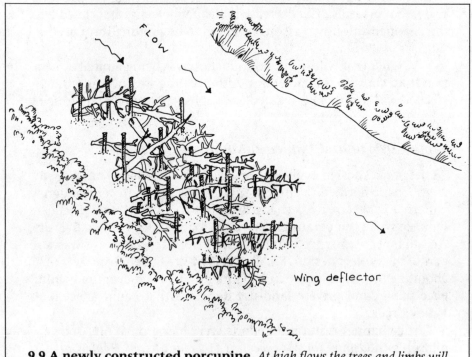

9.9 A newly constructed porcupine. *At high flows the trees and limbs will trap sediment, eventually building a mud bar that will be invaded by vegetation.*

head and along the length of riffles. They were built to narrow the stream by two-thirds. The porcupines were very effective at trapping silt and debris, and were soon overgrown with vegetation. The narrowing of the channel by the porcupine led to increased velocities and scoured pools.

Another variation on the deflector was the use of a sill log or rock berm in association with the deflector. This extension of the deflector angles upstream and across the flow. Then, the flow is directed toward the opposite bank, where it scours a hole. It is essential that this bank be stable. This structure is similar to the revetment/cover-log structure described in the Jones Creek case history.

VFC also used rock to build riffles. The construction of riffles utilized hand-placed small rubble. Boulders were placed with a backhoe to create cover and trout lies. The riffles have remained in place despite several large flow events.

ESTABLISHING A WILD BROWN-TROUT FISHERY

In an attempt to enhance the very small naturally reproducing populations of brown trout, brown-trout eggs were placed in Whitlock-Vibert boxes and buried in the gravel substrate of a tributary stream. Shortly thereafter, a heavy rain brought high flows and accompanying sediment loads that smothered the eggs.

The need to locate suitable planting sites sheltered from floods led VFC to the small spring-creek tributaries mentioned above. The following fall Whitlock-Vibert boxes with brown-trout eggs were placed in two of the spring creeks, and hatches were excellent. The nearly constant 50-degree Fahrenheit water allowed the fry to hatch in December and grow all winter. By March the fry were two to three inches long, and by June they were four to six inches long.

This brown-trout egg-hatching program has been in effect since 1981. In 1986 three-year classes of stream-born brown trout resided in West Valley Creek. At that time, however, no natural reproduction had been documented.

Monitoring

PHYSICAL

The transects at 50-feet intervals that were established prior to the project are visited annually and measurements of water temperature, width, and depth are taken. Photographs are taken on a regular, but sporadic, basis. The land-use map is continuously updated. VFC members walk various portions of the stream during all seasons to monitor not only the condition of the structures but also development activities.

BIOLOGICAL

Each fall electrofishing surveys are conducted. These surveys are just once-through-the-section passes, not multiple-pass mark-and-recapture efforts. The results are approximations of the trout population.

LAND USE

The most important aspect of the ongoing monitoring plan is to remain current on development proposals and to stay involved in the land-use planning and decision-making process.

Summary of Findings

The average width and depth measurements taken at the transects are presented in table 9.1. These data reveal that the project has been successful in narrowing the channel and deepening the flow.

The results of the annual electrofishing efforts in the quarry section of the stream are provided in table 9.2. These data are not truly quantitative, but it appears that there has been an increase in both the number of wild trout and total trout over the course of this project.

TABLE 9.1
AVERAGE STREAM WIDTH AND DEPTH, QUARRY SECTION,
WEST VALLEY CREEK, CHESTER COUNTY, PENNSYLVANIA

Year	Average Width (in feet)	Average Depth (in feet)
1981	31.6	10.6
1982	31.4	14.5
1983	23.5	13.4
1984	22.9	15.3
1985	18.7	12.5
1986	19.6	14.2
1987	19.9	14.9

TABLE 9.2
RESULTS OF ELECTROFISHING SURVEYS, QUARRY SECTION,
WEST VALLEY CREEK, CHESTER COUNTY, PENNSYLVANIA

Year	Wild Trout	Stocked Trout	12-Inch + Trout	Total Trout
1981	1	13	0	14
1982	18	13	2	31
1983	4	5	0	9
1984	10	15	7	25
1985	Missed	- -		
1986	33	17	1	50
1987	30	17	4	44

Postscript

The effort to stay abreast of an increasing number of development proposals and influence private and public land-use decisions has required much more work than the habitat restoration efforts. VFC has led tours of West Valley Creek and presented many slide shows to school children, service organizations, private developers, and township and state officials.

VFC has monitored development activities and has been quick to point out violations of construction-practice laws to township officials. Its involvement in township land-use planning has led to the defeat of a proposed zoning change for a shopping mall and more careful analysis of the proposed four-lane highway by Pennsylvania's Department of Transportation.

The negotiations of easements also have been an important aspect of VFC's work. The two miles of stream below the quarry and before the confluence with the Brandywine River are part of pastoral farms that have been protected from future development by conservation easements.

Public access to the half mile of stream bordering the quarry where reclamation efforts have taken place has been guaranteed for ten years through a Pennsylvania Fish Commission easement. The state requires such easements on all Adopt-a-Stream projects that are on private land.

VFC was instrumental in the negotiation of a public-access easement between a developer and the township. This easement includes a provision whereby the developer agrees not to disturb the native vegetation within 20 feet of either bank of the stream. This is especially important because the stream is one of the small spring creeks where brown trout are being hatched. This easement assures that the public will have access to the stream for recreation.

VFC also worked with a private developer to mitigate a commercial development by preserving a small spawning and rearing tributary. The Little Crabby Creek story follows this case history.

The social and political aspects of the project are judged by Joe Armstrong, former VFC president, to be the most important part of the work. The continued work of VFC membership—both in the stream and in state, township, and private meeting rooms—has given VFC increasing credibility, which, in turn, has led to greater influence and more success in preserving this stream.

LITTLE CRABBY CREEK, PENNSYLVANIA

Location	*Chester County*
Project status	*Private*
Project leader	*Weston*
Landowner	*Trammel Crow Corporation*
Rehab. length	*1,200 feet*
Limiting factor	*Not applicable*
Problem	*Proposed development threatened to eliminate trout habitat*
Prescription	*Reconstruct stream to allow development and provide trout habitat*
Begin date	*1985*
End date	*1986*
Current status	*Work completed*
Estimated cost	*$370 per foot*

Background

Little Crabby Creek is a small, low-gradient (less than 1 percent), spring-fed stream in Chester County, Pennsylvania. It rises on a forested ridge and flows for less than one mile through a rapidly growing suburban area before its confluence with Little Valley Creek. Little Valley Creek flows into Valley Creek, which meanders through Valley Forge National Park to its confluence with the Schuylkill River.

Despite its small size, Little Crabby Creek has yielded 12- to 15-inch brown trout. However, for Wayne Poppich and his fellow members of the Valley Forge Chapter (VFC) of Trout Unlimited, the importance of Little Crabby Creek goes far beyond those nice browns.

Little Crabby Creek is an important spawning and rearing stream, which pumps juvenile trout into Little Valley Creek and Valley Creek, where they grow big and feisty. The nearly perfect spring-fed water temperatures for raising young trout, combined with the abundant spawning gravels and very prolific freshwater shrimp, give this stream importance that belies its size. This tiny stream harbors a wild-trout population estimated at one trout per foot of stream.

When VFC learned of plans to develop an office-park complex along the banks of the creek, its members became understandably concerned. They became doubly concerned when it was discovered that the plans called for damming the creek to create a small lake environment within the complex. When it was ascertained that damming the stream would flood spawning areas, block upstream passage of trout migrating to spawn, and increase downstream water temperatures, VFC, as well as representatives of other conservation groups, approached the landowner to discuss the possibility of modifying the development plans.

Negotiations had been underway for some time when the landowner sold the property to Trammel Crow Company (TCC). TCC had similar plans to develop the site into an office-park complex, and negotiations continued with its representatives. TCC and its architectural consultant worked with various conservation groups, including VFC, Pennsylvania Fish Commission, U.S. Fish and Wildlife Service, and U.S. Army Corps of Engineers to create a development plan that would meet the concerns of the conservation groups and the permit requirements of the various agencies.

The final plan left the stream free flowing and disturbed only a 270-foot meander of the stream (figure 9.10A). This section of stream was destined to be filled in and covered by a roadway embankment. A man-made 180-foot section of stream would replace the filled meander. One hundred feet of this relocated channel would flow through twin-box culverts beneath an access road (figure 9.10B). Weston, a consulting firm, was retained by TCC to conduct pre-project ecological surveys, design the new stream channel, and monitor the response of stream life to the relocation.

Inventory Methods

PHYSICAL

A habitat inventory was undertaken on the 1,200-foot project section of stream to determine the relative abundance of pool, riffle, and glide habitats, substrate available for spawning, and general habitat condition. A qualitative inventory, it consisted of a walk through the area by the project biologist and design engineer. The length of each habitat attribute was determined by pacing the distance of that habitat type along the bank. (This stream is no more than 15 feet wide at any location.) Other qualitatively evaluated habitat attributes included shade cover, bank undercut, and water width and depth.

BIOLOGICAL

The stream's trout and aquatic invertebrates were also qualitatively evaluated. To assess the aquatic macroinvertebrate populations, the stream was divided into five contiguous sections. An equal amount of time was spent in each section collecting invertebrates with a kick screen. The intent was to determine the insect and other invertebrate species present and their relative abundance.

Weston also electrofished these sections to determine the trout species present and the relative abundance of trout between stations.

Limiting-factor Analysis

A limiting-factor analysis was not conducted. The intent of the pre-project inventory was to provide information on the current channel condition. This information was then used to aid in the design of the new man-made channel.

Project Design and Implementation

The project design called for the replacement of a 270-foot section of a natural meander bend with a shorter, man-made reach. This short-

9.10 Little Crabby Creek, pre- and post-construction.

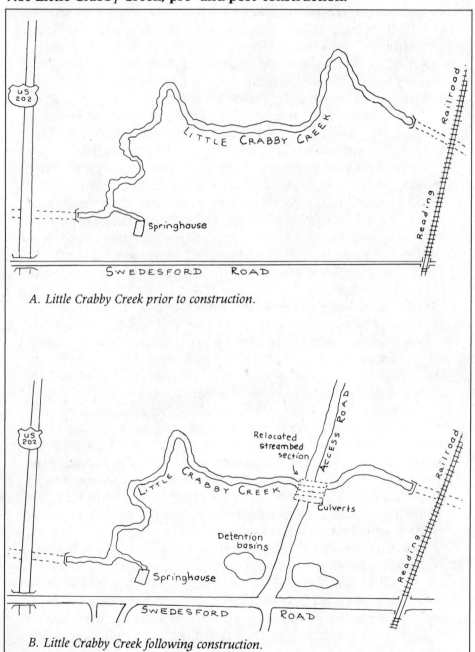

A. Little Crabby Creek prior to construction.

B. Little Crabby Creek following construction.

ening of the channel resulted in increased gradient and water velocity through this reach. The effort to deal with this increased velocity and gradient, and still maintain the same percentage of pool/riffle/glide habitats, was a major design consideration. Another important aspect of the design was the creation of a meandering low-flow channel within the newly created floodplain and stream to ensure that trout could move freely through the section even at low flows.

A boulder berm was created at the upstream end of the relocated channel. The step/pool below the berm would dissipate much of the increased energy of the shortened stream. Boulders situated in the pool would provide cover and also help to dissipate energy. The large boulders were river rock obtained from the Pocono Mountains. Weston wanted to use rounded river rock rather than the angular rock found on the construction site. The more aesthetically pleasing river rock would be less apt to have a sharp edge that might cut a trout attempting to navigate the turbulent flows over the berm.

The river rock was also used to riprap the outside banks of bends created in the stream.

The floodplain, channel, and low-flow channel were created from scratch. After the course of the new channel was staked out, heavy equipment was used to dig the new channel. Once the channel was formed, it was lined with a nonwoven geotextile material. This was done to ensure that flows would stay in the channel and not disappear into the newly created streambed.

Stream-washed gravel, rubble, and boulder substrate were then placed in the stream. The placement reflected the anticipated flow regime across the channel. For example, cross section A (figure 9.11) shows boulders placed at the outside of the meander to protect the newly created bank from erosion. Cobble and rubble were placed near this outside bank, where water velocities would be highest. The cobble and rubble gradually grade to gravels on the concave bank where gravel deposition would naturally take place.

River-washed gravel was placed in the straight reach beneath the bridge in hopes of creating spawning habitat. Two log sills were placed in this reach also. These logs serve: (1) as gravel traps to ensure that the gravel stays in place; (2) to form downstream plunge pools where some of the stream's increased energy is dissipated (figure 9.11, cross section B); and (3) to direct the flow in a meandering pattern.

During the construction of the new channel, Little Crabby Creek flowed through a temporary diversion channel. When construction was completed, the flow was diverted into the new channel. The remaining small pools were pumped to collect the trout, as the flow dropped in the diversion channel. Ninety-eight brown trout, most of them young-of-the-year, were collected and transferred to the newly created stream channel.

Monitoring

A biological monitoring program was initiated six months following construction of the channel. The monitoring program consisted of collecting quantitative aquatic macroinvertebrate samples every six weeks for one year and conducting electrofishing surveys of the trout populations.

Summary of Findings

The results of the first macroinvertebrate sampling conducted in November 1986 revealed that the stream section had been colonized by 29 different species of invertebrates. The electrofishing survey yielded 37 brown trout from this section of stream.

Continued monitoring of the trout population has revealed that population estimates can change substantially over relatively short periods of time. Gerry Dinkins, Weston's project biologist, reports that he, the Pennsylvania Fish Commission, and VFC believe this variation is in response, at least in part, to water temperatures in Little Valley Creek. They speculate that as water temperatures in Little Valley Creek become critically high, trout move into the cooler, spring-fed waters of Little Crabby Creek. Thus, this small spring creek is not only an important spawning and nursery area. It may also be a critical refuge for Little Valley Creek trout during hot weather. Dinkins has collected as many as 660 brown trout from a 660-foot section of this stream. These numbers, given the small size of the stream, provide an indication not only of the stream's productivity but also of its importance as a fishery resource in the midst of a rapidly urbanizing area. This importance is also reflected in the $370 per foot of relocated-stream price tag associated with this project.

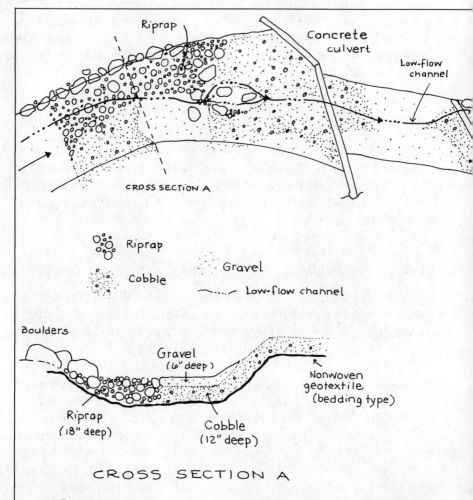

9.11 Three post-construction views of Little Crabby Creek. *Aerial and cross-sectional views of reconstructed Little Crabby Creek channel.*

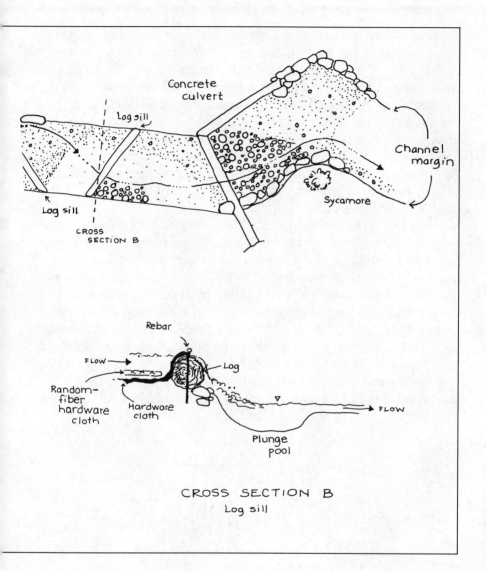

CROSS SECTION B
Log sill

Postscript

There are three interesting sidebars to the Little Crabby Creek story. Downstream of the project, the creek flows through two concrete culverts. These culverts provided no trout habitat. In an attempt to create rearing habitat in these culverts, VFC has drilled holes in the concrete floor of the culverts and bolted six- by six-inch lumber to the floor (figure 9.12). This has created a meandering pattern through the culvert, greater depth, areas of low velocity, and deposition of gravel. Electrofishing efforts inside the culverts yielded over 20 juvenile trout, where there had previously been none. Undoubtedly, a number of fry and juveniles were missed because of the darkness inside the culverts.

Following the work on this project, a high-density town-house community was proposed to be developed upstream. A major concern was a marshy, difficult-to-develop 17-acre parcel of land, where many of the springs that lend Little Crabby Creek its limestone, spring-creek character rise. Eventually, the developer agreed to deed this parcel to the township for use as a park. VFC played an integral role in the negotiations leading to this solution. As Joe Armstrong said, "Typically, one project leads to the next one as we get involved and learn what is going on."

Little Crabby Creek is a catch-and-release fishery. Given the increasing demand for trout fishing, coupled with the continual loss

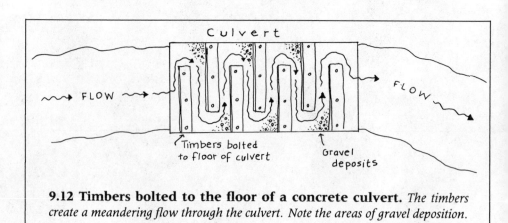

9.12 Timbers bolted to the floor of a concrete culvert. *The timbers create a meandering flow through the culvert. Note the areas of gravel deposition.*

of good trout habitat and the high costs of hatchery-stocked fisheries, catch-and-release fishing regulations will probably have to be more widely established. Unfortunately, Little Crabby Creek is managed as catch and release because of concerns that the trout may be tainted with PCBs and other toxic wastes. Catch and release will become an increasingly important management tool, but it should come about to increase fishing opportunities, and not because the trout are too toxic to eat.

SOURCES

Rapid Creek, South Dakota

Ron Glover, SDGFP, provided all of the information presented in this case history. Written sources include:

Glover, R., and Ford, R., 1983. *The Use of Instream Flow Incremental Methodology to Evaluate the Effects of Habitat Restoration on Trout Populations in Rapid Creek, South Dakota.* South Dakota Dept. of Game, Fish and Parks, Rpt. no. 83-6. Rapid City, SD.

Glover, R. 1986. *Trout Stream Rehabilitation in the Black Hills of South Dakota.* Fifth Trout Stream Habitat Improvement Workshop, Lock Haven, PA. Pennsylvania Fish Commission, Harrisburg, PA.

West Valley Creek, Pennsylvania

Joe Armstrong provided a wealth of information, and contributed valuable time to explain the complexities of the West Valley Creek project. Written sources include:

Owens, O. D. 1986. *Porcupines and Triangles: Restoration of Dredged Limestone Stream.* Fifth Trout Stream Habitat Improvement Workshop. Lock Haven, Pennsylvania. Pennsylvania Fish Commission, Harrisburg, PA.

White, R. J., and Brynildson, O.M. 1967. *Guidelines for Management of Trout Stream Habitat in Wisconsin.* Dept. of Nat. Res. Tech. Bull. no. 39. Madison, WI.

Little Crabby Creek, Pennsylvania

Joe Armstrong and Wayne Poppich of the Valley Forge Chapter of Trout Unlimited and Gerry Dinkins of Weston shared their insights regarding this project. Written sources include:

Bogardus, R.; Philipp, K.; and Dinkins, G. 1987. Trout and Community Development: The Story of Little Crabby Creek. *The Weston Way* 13(2):2–9.

Chapter 10

A MISSION TO SET THINGS RIGHT

As we approach the year 2000, trout anglers can take comfort in knowing that interest in trout-stream habitat restoration has never been greater. In 1990 at least 23 states and 6 Canadian provinces had trout-stream restoration programs. Before the decade ends an estimated $100 million will be spent in the United States and Canada on habitat restoration for anadromous salmonids alone.

There is reason to feel encouraged that there is such a strong commitment to restore the continent's trout-fishing opportunities, yet the science of habitat restoration is still not well understood. That should stimulate new investigations into the mechanics of trout-habitat restoration, but, to paraphrase Aldo Leopold, if we are going to intelligently tinker with trout habitat, then we must save all the pieces. The best way to accomplish that is to start with good watershed and riparian habitat management. Then look closer and more critically at restoration work that is intended to yield fast results.

In the 1990s the best trout-habitat restoration work will be done by fisheries biologists, hydrologists, stream geomorphologists, soils scientists, and botanists who will work together and rigorously follow a methodology that includes: (1) a pre-project inventory of the drainage; (2) an analysis of limiting factors; (3) a selection of restoration techniques—including land-management practices appropriate to the conditions in the watershed; and (4) an evaluation of the project's results.

Some of the very best trout-habitat restoration projects in North America could have been better if they had been guided by a more systematic approach. In the future, as the science and the industry matures, it will not be fiscally nor politically feasible to ignore thorough and systematic methods because the individuals footing the

290

bills will demand proof that the work, when evaluated, achieved the promised results.

Most projects today begin with some level of pre-project inventory work to identify limiting factors. In too many cases, however, the restoration plan is based on a loose notion that a stream may need deeper pools, more riffles, or more pronounced bank undercuts to produce more and bigger trout. When the end result is not the same as the one anticipated, it is usually because no one took the time to actually identify the factors that were limiting the trout population. Worst of all, there are many trout-habitat restoration projects where the end result remains unknown because the projects have never been evaluated.

It's time to change. Practitioners have a responsibility to their science, as well as to the public, to demand that adequate funding be provided for evaluation. Post-project evaluation is the only way to learn from both successes and failures and thus ensure that public and private restoration dollars will be continually put to better use.

SEEKING A BALANCE BETWEEN LAND-USE CHANGES AND IN-STREAM STRUCTURES

The future of trout-habitat rehabilitation lies in the development of restoration plans that contain an appropriate mix of land-management changes and in-stream structural-habitat work. It is futile and wasteful to place a number of habitat enhancement structures in a stream if the land-use practices that made those structures necessary are not changed. Similarly, land-use changes in themselves may not be adequate to meet short-term management goals. The previous case histories have been offered to demonstrate the range of options from strictly land-management changes (Camp Creek) to total dependence on in-stream structural work (Rapid Creek) that are available to a restoration team.

Unquestionably, the future's most successful trout-habitat restoration projects will possess plans dictated by land use, the characteristics of the stream, land ownership, and the environmental, political, and economic agenda of the individual, organization, or public agency doing the work. At Camp Creek, for instance, the livestock-grazing scheme was changed relatively easily because BLM managed the land and conducted the restoration work. At Rapid Creek it was apparent land-use changes were not going to be part of the restoration plan because the highly valued developments along the stream and on the floodplain were there to stay. The introduction of highly engineered in-stream structures was not only appropriate at Rapid Creek but required by activity in the drainage.

When seeking a balance between the wide range of projects that fall between the extremes of Camp and Rapid creeks, however, it must be understood that trout-habitat restoration is a long-term project. What took a month, a year, or a decade to destroy can take hundreds of years to restore through changes in land use. This point will likely cause agony to some private landowners and public agencies hoping to see much faster results, but it is a fact that every project leader must face—especially public agencies whose broad mission is to care for the land for future generations. Appropriately designed in-stream structures can benefit the fishery in the interim, but the long-term goal of self-sustaining health should not be ignored while attempting to provide trout-fishing opportunities today.

As Wayne Elmore and Robert Beschta cautioned: "Where improvement of a degraded channel is desired, the selection of a structural approach is seemingly driven by a desire for instantaneous gratification. We are currently using a fast-food approach to stream management."

WHY GO TO THIS EFFORT? FOR THE TROUT

A successful restoration project can lead to better fishing and a well-deserved sense of accomplishment. But the benefits go far beyond this and can even include aiding in the survival of a species.

Genetic diversity is critical for the long-term survival of all plant and animal species. A species must have enough different mixtures of genetic types to survive changing environmental conditions. These different genetic types of the same species may have no obvious value today, and probably aren't even recognized as different. However, their genetic makeup and the sometimes divergent life-history strategies they develop may have been crucial to past survival and may be just as crucial to their survival in the future.

A remarkable example of how little is known about the possible genetic ties to salmonid life-history strategies, and the profound implications that lack of understanding has for one pursuing trout-stream enhancement, was provided by Jennifer Nielsen at the 1989 meeting of the Western Division of the American Fisheries Society. Nielsen is trying to discover how water velocity at particular focal points influences the behavior and reproductive development of juvenile coho salmon.

Nielsen observed that juvenile coho in thalweg habitats display territorial behavior for feeding stations. She watched young coho hold feeding stations and compete aggressively for drifting and floating food items. She also observed apparently displaced juvenile coho in slower water-edge and backwater habitats and discovered that they patrol larger feeding areas, show less competition for feeding territories, and feed primarily on terrestrial insects floating on the water.

Nielsen found that the females in thalweg habitats have higher growth rates during the summer-rearing period than the females rearing in the slower-water habitats. These data are not particularly surprising and could lead some of the best trout-habitat rehabilitators to assume that a conversion of slow-water habitats to faster-water habitats would result in increased production of coho juveniles.

Nielsen, however, did not make that assumption. When she took females from both the slow- and fast-water habitats to examine their ovaries, she found that the smaller, slow-water cohos had significantly more developing eggs in their ovaries than the fast-water cohos. No significant difference in male reproductive development was observed between the two populations.

Are these two populations genetically different? Do they represent different paths the species has taken to better ensure reproductive success? In either case it gives one pause, because an attempt to increase production of coho juveniles by converting slow-water habitats to faster-water habitats may deprive the species of a genetic mix and an alternative life-history strategy.

THE VALUE OF TROUT-HABITAT REHABILITATION

As stated at the outset, stream rehabilitation is but one way of increasing fishing opportunities. It is not a panacea. However, well-conceived stream rehabilitation projects not only create wild-trout fishing opportunities. They can also help to maintain the genetic diversity of the species, which could help to ensure the future existence of the fishery and the trout. These kinds of projects will, in addition, allow for the restoration of some of the natural beauty and productivity of a stream that have been destroyed through man's activity.

When considered in this light, there is good reason to approach every project with the understanding that trout are the end product of the relationship between the stream and its valley. Close attention must be paid to land use in the drainage and how it may affect the stream. Structural solutions to in-stream habitat deficiencies by themselves will not provide long-term dividends. Only the wise stewardship and management of the lands within the drainage will allow the long-term self-sustaining health of our streams and their trout populations.

Finally, and most importantly, it is vital to recognize the value of protecting and preserving streams and drainages that remain in good health. It is critically important to protect these streams—whether the stream is located in a rapidly urbanizing area, like Little Crabby Creek, Pennsylvania, or is a wilderness river that is being destroyed by the burning of fossil fuels hundreds of miles away, like the Cranberry River in West Virginia.

The relatively few remaining healthy and undisturbed streams must be preserved because they are the last best hope for the continued survival of our native trout species. In addition, they provide us with the opportunity to study the naturally occurring relationships between the stream, its valley, and the trout. The knowledge we obtain from these undisturbed streams can be used to better direct future restoration and enhancement efforts. The emphasis of all land management and fish and game agencies, private clubs, and individuals interested in trout and trout fishing should be the preservation of our healthy streams.

In 1949 Leopold wrote: "A thing is right when it tends to preserve the integrity, stability, and beauty of the biotic community. It is wrong when it tends otherwise." Trout-habitat restorationists on a mission to set things right will do well to listen to that advice.

SOURCES

Elmore, Wayne, and Beschta, Robert L. 1988. The Fallacy of Structures and the Fortitude of Vegetation. Paper presented at California Riparian Systems Conference, Sept. 22–24, 1988, at Univ. of California at Davis, CA.

Leopold, A. 1949. *A Sand County Almanac.* New York: Oxford Press.

Nielsen, Jennifer. 1989. Western Division of the American Fisheries Society.

GLOSSARY

Adfluvial: Adfluvial fish hatch in streams, migrate to a lake or reservoir to mature, and return to their natal stream to spawn.

Age class: Animals of a certain age in years, usually designated by Roman numerals. For instance, young-of-the-year—animals that have not yet reached their first birthday—are in age class O, yearlings are in age class I, two-year-olds in age class II, and so on.

Aggradation: The geologic process by which streambeds, floodplains, and the bottoms of other water bodies are raised in elevation by the deposition of material eroded and transported from other areas. It is the opposite of **degradation.**

Alluvium: A general term for all deposits resulting directly or indirectly from the sediment transport of streams, including the sediments collected in riverbeds, floodplains, lakes, fans, and estuaries.

Anadromous: Hatching in fresh water, anadromous fish migrate to the ocean, mature there, and return to fresh water to spawn.

Anchor ice: Ice formed below the surface of a stream, on the streambed, or upon a submerged body or structure.

Aquifer: An underground zone or layer that is a good source of water. An aquifer may be an underground zone of gravel or sand, a zone of highly shattered or cracked rock, a layer of sandstone, or a layer of cavernous limestone.

Armoring: (a) The formation of an erosion-resistant layer of relatively large particles on the surface of the streambed that resists degradation by water currents. (b) The application of various materials to protect stream banks from erosion.

Backwater: (a) A pool type formed by an eddy along channel margins downstream from obstructions, such as bars, root wads, or boulders, or as a result of back flooding upstream from an obstructional blockage. Sometimes separated from the channel by sand/gravel bar. (b) A body of water, the stage of which is controlled by some feature of the channel downstream from the backwater, or in coves or covering low-lying areas and having access to the main body of water.

Bank revetment: A layer of large, durable materials, usually rock but sometimes car bodies, broken concrete, etc., used to protect a stream bank from erosion. May also refer to the materials themselves.

Base flow: The portion of the stream discharge that is derived from natural storage (i.e., groundwater outflow and the draining of large lakes and swamps or other sources outside the net rainfall that create surface runoff); discharge sustained in a stream channel, not a result of direct runoff, and without the effects of regulation, diversion, or other works of man. Also called sustaining, normal, ordinary, or groundwater flow.

Base level: The level or elevation to which a stream-channel profile has developed.

Bioenergetics: The flow of energy through a living organism, population, or ecosystem.

Channelization: Straightening of a stream or the dredging of a new channel to which the stream is diverted.

Cover structure: Any structure that provides hiding places for trout. Common cover structures are bank covers, half logs, root wads, and boulders.

Creel census: A study to determine type of fishing, time of fishing, time spent, species and sizes of individuals caught, catch per unit time of fishing effort, and waters fished.

Deflector: An artificial, erosion-resistant point bar. The purpose of deflectors is to keep the current moving swiftly in a sinuous course. When properly located and constructed, they can keep a stream channel moderately deep and allow the current to scour pools at stream bends.

Degradation: The geologic process by which streambeds and floodplains are lowered in elevation by the removal of material. It is the opposite of **aggradation**.

Discharge: Volume of water flowing in a given stream at a given place and within a given period of time, usually expressed as cubic meters or cubic feet per second (cfs).

Dished out: Refers to stream banks that have bank angles greater than 90 degrees. Synonym: laid back.

Dynamic equilibrium: A condition of a system in which there is a balanced inflow and outflow of material.

Eddy: A circular current of water, sometimes quite strong, diverging from and initially flowing contrary to the main current. It is usually formed at a point at which the flow passes some obstruction or on the inside of river bends. Often forms backwater pools or pocket water in riffles.

Embeddedness: The degree that larger particles, such as boulders, rubble, or gravel, are surrounded or covered by fine sediment. Usually measured in classes according to percentage of coverage of larger particles by fine sediments. (See figure 4.7.)

Energy efficiency: Effective operation as measured by a comparison of energy accrued with energy expended.

Floodplain: Any flat, or nearly flat, lowland that borders a stream and is covered by its waters at flood stage.

Focal point: The location, and the conditions at that location, occupied by an organism. Microhabitat measurements are thus focal-point measurements.

Freshet: A rapid, temporary rise in stream discharge and level caused by heavy rains or rapid melting of snow and ice.

Fry: Fish up to the time when the yolk sac has been absorbed.

Geomorphology: The branch of geology that deals with the origin and nature of landforms. The active forces that shape landforms are water, ice, wind, and gravity.

Glide: A slow-moving, relatively shallow type of run. Calm water flowing smoothly and gently, with moderately low velocities (10 to 20 cm./ sec.), and little or no surface turbulence.

Gradient: (a) The general slope or rate of change in vertical elevation per unit of horizontal distance of the water surface of a flowing stream. (b) The rate of change of any characteristic per unit of length.

Habitat attributes: A single element, such as velocity, depth, cover, etc., of the habitat or environment in which a fish or other aquatic species or population may live or occur. Synonym: component.

Habitat suitability curve: A graph constructed by evaluating information on the effect of a habitat variable on the growth, survival, or biomass of a fish species. The curve is built on the assumption that increments of growth, survival, or biomass plotted on the y-axis of the graph can be directly converted into an index of suitability from 0.0 to 1.0 for the species; 0.0 indicates unsuitable conditions and 1.0 indicates optimum conditions.

Hydraulics: Refers to water, or other liquids, in motion and their action.

Incised channel: A stream that through degradation has cut its channel into the bed of the valley.

Large woody debris: Any large piece of relatively stable woody material having a diameter greater than ten centimeters and a length greater than one meter that intrudes into the stream channel. Synonym: LOD, large organic debris, log. Specific types of large organic debris include:

Affixed logs: Single logs or groups of logs that are firmly embedded, lodged, or rooted in a stream channel.

Bole: Term referring to the stem or trunk of the tree.

Large bole: Ten meters or more in length; often embedded, remains in the stream for extended periods.

Small bole: Less than ten meters, usually sections of bole; seldom stable, usually moves downstream on high flows.

Deadheads: Logs that are not embedded, lodged, or rooted in the stream channel but are submerged and close to the surface.

Digger log: Log anchored to the stream banks and/or channel bottom in such a way that a scour pool is formed.

Free logs: Logs or groups of logs that are not embedded, lodged, or rooted in the stream channel.

Root wad: The root mass of the tree. Synonym: butt ends.

Snag: (a) A standing dead tree. (b) Sometimes a submerged fallen tree in large streams. The top of the tree is exposed or only slightly submerged.

Sweeper log: Fallen tree whose bole or branches form an obstruction to floating subjects.

Types of large organic-debris accumulation:

Clumps: Accumulations of debris at irregularly spaced intervals along the channel margin, not forming major impediments to flow.

Jams: Large accumulations of debris partially or completely blocking the stream channel, creating major obstructions to flow.

Scattered: Single pieces of debris at irregularly spaced intervals along the channel.

Limiting factor: The total crop of any organism will be determined by the abundance of the substance that, in relation to the needs of the organism, is least abundant in the environment. This substance is the limiting factor.

Longitudinal profile: A graphical presentation of elevation versus distance, as in channel cross sections and longitudinal sections. In open-channel hydraulics, it is a plot of water-surface elevation against channel distance.

Meandering: Characterized by a clearly repeated pattern of curvature as seen from above.

Microhabitat: That specific combination of habitat elements in the locations selected by organisms for specific purposes and/or events. Expresses the more specific and functional aspects of habitat and cover. Separated from adjoining microhabitats by distinctive physical characteristics, such as velocity, depth, cover, etc.

Nick point: The point at which a stream is actively eroding the streambed downward to a new base level.

Oxbow: A looping river bend cut off from the main flow by a new channel broken through the neck of its enclosed peninsula.

Pool: (a) A portion of a stream with reduced current velocity, often with water deeper than the surrounding areas, and which is frequently usable by fish for resting and cover. (b) A small body of standing water (e.g., in a marsh or on the floodplain).
Backwater: *see* **Backwater.**
Corner: A lateral scour pool resulting from a shift in channel direction.
Dammed: Water impounded upstream from a complete or nearly complete channel blockage, typically caused by a logjam, beaver dam, rock slide, or stream-habitat-improvement device, such as a boulder berm, gabion, or log sill.
Eddy: *see* **Eddy.**
Flat: A wide, shallow pool of low turbulence. Sometimes used synonymously with glide.
Lateral scour: Formed by the scouring action of the flow as it is directed laterally or obliquely to one side of the stream by a partial channel obstruction, such as a gravel bar or wing deflector.
Plunge: (Also falls pool, plunge basin.) A pool created by water passing over or through a complete or nearly complete channel obstruction, and dropping vertically, scouring out a basin in which the flow radiates from the point of water entry.
Pocket water: A series of small pools surrounded by swiftly flowing water, usually caused by eddies behind boulders, rubble, or logs, or by potholes in the streambed.
Secondary channel (*see* **Side channel**): Relatively small, sometimes isolated pools in a smaller braid of the main stem and usually associated with gravel bars.
Slack water: Pool-like depressions along the stream margin and on the floodplain that contain water only during high flow or after floodwaters recede. More transient in nature than secondary-channel pools, they may contain water for only a few days or weeks.
Trench: A pool characterized by a relatively long, slotlike depression in the streambed, often found in bedrock-dominated channels.

Under scour: Formed by scouring under a stream obstruction, such as a log. Sometimes called upsurge pool.

Population density: The number of individuals per unit area of a species inhabiting a particular area.

Redd: An area of streambed dug out by a female trout before spawning and in which she buries her eggs after spawning.

Riffle: A shallow rapids where the water flows swiftly over completely or partially submerged obstructions to produce surface agitation, but standing waves are absent.

Riparian: Pertaining to anything connected with or immediately adjacent to the banks of a stream or other body of water.

Root wad: The root mass of the tree. Synonym: butt ends.

Roughness: A measure of the irregularity of streambed materials as they contribute to resistance to flow. Commonly measured in terms of Manning's roughness coefficient.

Side channel: Lateral channel with an axis of flow roughly parallel to the main stem, which is fed by water from the main stem; a braid of a river with flow appreciably lower than the main channel. Side-channel habitat may exist either in well-defined secondary (overflow) channels or in poorly defined watercourses flowing through partially submerged gravel bars and islands along the margins of the main stem.

Sinuous: Slight curvature as seen from above within a belt of less than approximately two channel widths.

Size class: Animals of a certain size. The size classes are usually determined by the distribution of sizes of animals in the population. Size classes often relate directly to age classes. For instance, fish in the size class two to four inches could be mostly age class I in a particular population.

Slough: (a) Low, swampy ground or overflow channels where water flows sluggishly for considerable distances. (b) Side-channel slough formed by channelization. (c) A sluggish channel of water, such as a side channel of a stream, in which water flows slowly through low, swampy ground, or a section of an abandoned stream channel containing water most or all of the year, but with flow only at high water, and occurring in a floodplain or delta. (d) A marsh tract lying in a shallow, undrained depression on a piece of dry ground. (e) A term used for a creek or sluggish body of water in a bottomland.

Stream: A natural watercourse containing flowing water at least part of the year, supporting a community of plants and animals within the stream channel and the riparian vegetation zone. Streams in natural channels may be classified as follows:

a. Relative to time

Ephemeral: One that flows briefly only in direct response to precipitation in the immediate locality and whose channel is at all times above the water table.

Intermittent or seasonal: One in contact with the ground water table that flows only at certain times of the year as when the water table is high and/or when it receives water from springs or from some surface source, such as melting snow in mountainous areas. It ceases to flow above the streambed when losses from evaporation or seepage exceed the available stream flow.

Perennial: One that flows continuously through the year. Synonym: permanent stream.

b. Relative to space

Continuous: One that does not have interruptions in space.

Interrupted: One that contains alternating reaches that are perennial, intermittent, or ephemeral.

c. Relative to groundwater

Gaining: A stream or reach of stream that receives water from the zone of saturation.

Insulated: A stream or reach of stream that neither contributes to nor receives water from the zone of saturation. It is separated from the zones of saturation by an impermeable bed.

Losing: A stream or reach of stream that contributes water to the zone of saturation.

Perched: Either a losing stream or an insulated stream that is separated from the underlying groundwater by a zone of aeration.

d. Other

Incised: A stream that through degradation has cut its channel into the bed of the valley.

Stream bank: The portion of the channel cross section that restricts lateral movement of water at normal water levels. The bank often has a gradient steeper than 45 degrees and exhibits a distinct break in slope from the stream bottom. An obvious change in substrate may be a reliable delineation of the bank.

Lower bank: The periodically submerged portion of the channel cross section from the normal high waterline to the water's edge during the summer low-flow period.

Upper bank: That portion of the topographic cross section from the break in the general slope of the surrounding land to the normal high waterline.

Streambed: The substrate plane, bounded by the stream banks, over which the water column moves. Synonym: stream bottom.

Substrate: The mineral and/or organic material that forms the bed of the stream. (See table 4.1.)

Tailspill: The area of a redd where substrate excavated upstream by the female is deposited.

Territoriality: A persistent attachment to a specific territory; the pattern of behavior associated with the defense of an animal's territory.

Thalweg: The line connecting the lowest or deepest points along a streambed.

Turbulence: The motion of water where local velocities fluctuate and the direction of flow changes abruptly and frequently at any particular location, resulting in disruption of laminar (smooth) flow. It causes surface disturbance and uneven surface level, and often masks subsurface areas because air bubbles are entrained in the water.

Velocity: The time rate of motion; the distance traveled divided by the time required to travel that distance.

Fish velocity or focal-point velocity: Represents the velocity at the location occupied by a fish, measured at the fish's snout. Synonyms: snout velocity, facing velocity.

Mean column velocity: The average velocity of the water measured on an imaginary vertical line at any point in a stream. A measurement at 60 percent of the depth, measured from the surface, closely approximates the average velocity for the water column. In water greater than 76 centimeters in depth, the average of measurements made at 20 percent and 80 percent of the depth approximates the mean column velocity.

Mean cross-sectional velocity: Represents the mean velocity of water flowing in a channel at a given cross section. It is equal to the discharge divided by the cross-section area of the cross section.

Thalweg velocity: The mean column velocity at the thalweg.

Visual isolation: Set apart by not being seen. Visual isolation of fish from other fish is caused by breaks in the topography of the streambed, debris, aquatic plants, turbulence, and other objects in the stream.

SPONSORS

MONTANA DEPARTMENT OF FISH, WILDLIFE AND PARKS

Montana Department of Fish, Wildlife and Parks is the state agency assigned to manage the fish, wildlife, and certain natural resources for the recreational benefit of the Montana public and their guests. Along with other programs the department maintains a strong commitment to protection and enhancement of fish and wildlife habitat. This commitment has helped to maintain quality fish and wildlife resources for public enjoyment.

NATIONAL FISH AND WILDLIFE FOUNDATION

The National Fish and Wildlife Foundation is a private, nonprofit conservation organization dedicated to encouraging, accepting, and administering private gifts and property for the benefit of, or in connection with, the activities and services of the U.S. Fish and Wildlife Service, as well as other activities that will further the conservation and management of fish, wildlife, and plant resources of the United States.

The foundation was established to provide a vehicle for infusing fresh and creative approaches into the management of the nation's wildlife resources. The foundation maintains a particular emphasis on developing cooperative efforts between the public and private sectors. It seeks to harness the cooperation of the business community, government agencies, and private individuals to develop solutions for priority wildlife fish and plants conservation programs.

PATAGONIA, INC.

Since Patagonia makes clothing for fly-fishermen, it has an interest in river protection and restoration. But the concern goes deeper. Since 1984 Patagonia has supported environmental causes, including the donation of at least 10 percent of the company's pretax profits for the last four years. Patagonia gives because it cares about the earth and believes that the degradation of our planet is at a critical stage.

THE TIDES FOUNDATION

The Tides Foundation is a public charity that promotes creative nonprofit and philanthropic activity through its grant making, projects, and management contracts programs. The six general areas in which organizations can find assistance are: land use, preservation, and stewardship; economic public policy and enterprise development; environment and natural resources; international affairs; community affairs; and social justice.

WILLIAM S. TOWNE

William S. Towne is a philanthropic individual who has consistently provided support to Montana Land Reliance. He was the recipient of the 1988 Montana Land Reliance Conservation Award.

TROUT UNLIMITED

Trout Unlimited is a not-for-profit North American fisheries conservation organization, whose mission is to conserve, protect, restore, and enhance trout, salmon, and steelhead fisheries in their watersheds. With 60,000 members nationwide and over 30,000 international members, volunteer hours are first directed to protecting those salmonid watersheds in good condition. For those less fortunate watersheds where degradation has occurred, numerous local projects using the methods discussed in this handbook are undertaken by Trout Unlimited volunteers in partnership with local, state, and federal agencies.

U.S. FISH AND WILDLIFE SERVICE

Businesses associated with the manufacture or sale of fishing rods, reels, lines, and terminal tackle; electric outboard motors; certain sonar devices; certain imported watercraft and fishing tackle; gasoline used in boats; and other items that contribute excise taxes and import duties help fund the Federal Aid in Sport Fish Restoration Program administered by the U.S. Fish and Wildlife Service. This book was supported in part with Sport Fish Restoration Funds under U.S. Fish and Wildlife Service Grant Agreement no. 14-16-0009-89-1219.

U.S.D.A. FOREST SERVICE

The Forest Service's fisheries program Rise to the Future was established to increase the emphasis of fisheries management on national forests. It was designed to protect and improve fisheries habitats and provide the public with increased opportunities for quality fishing experience in the national forests.

The program has been very successful in achieving its original objectives. The fisheries budget has increased more than threefold since 1986, and the number of fisheries biologists has increased from 113 in 1986 to more than 220 in 1989. The Forest Service has established numerous partnerships with states, federal and tribal agencies, and user groups. It has worked cooperatively in funding and developing projects to improve our fisheries. Emphasis of fisheries management in our forests has increased substantially, resulting in more productive fish habitat and better fishing opportunities for the public.

ABOUT THE AUTHOR

Christopher J. Hunter is an aquatic ecologist living in Helena, Montana. Following completion of his master's degree program at the University of Montana, he served as a Peace Corps volunteer in Iran. Mr. Hunter was program chairman of the Riparian Resource Management Workshop held in Billings, Montana, in May 1990. He is currently president of the Montana chapter of the American Fisheries Society.

ABOUT THE EDITOR

Tom Palmer is a writer, editor, and angler living in Helena, Montana. He has been a staff writer and editor for newspapers in Montana and Colorado. He is currently employed by the Montana Department of Fish, Wildlife and Parks, where he works in a variety of editorial capacities.

ABOUT THE ILLUSTRATOR

Writer-artist Ellen Meloy has illustrated two children's books and several wildland conservation publications for Yellowstone National Park. Her writing has appeared in *Outside, Harper's*, and other magazines, and in *Montana Spaces*, an anthology of essays published in 1989. She lives in Montana and Utah.

INDEX

ALSO AVAILABLE
FROM ISLAND PRESS

Ancient Forests of the Pacific Northwest
By Elliott A. Norse

The Challenge of Global Warming
Edited by Dean Edwin Abrahamson

Coastal Alert: Ecosystems, Energy, and Offshore Oil Drilling
By Dwight Holing

The Complete Guide to Environmental Careers
The CEIP Fund

Creating Successful Communities: A Guidebook for Growth Management Strategies
By Michael A. Mantell, Stephen F. Harper, and Luther Propst

Crossroads: Environmental Priorities for the Future
Edited by Peter Borrelli

Economics of Protected Areas
By John A. Dixon and Paul B. Sherman

Environmental Disputes: Community Involvement in Conflict Resolution
By James E. Crowfoot and Julia M. Wondolleck

Environmental Restoration: Science and Strategies for Restoring the Earth
Edited by John J. Berger

Forests and Forestry in China: Changing Patterns of Resource Development
By S. D. Richardson

From *The Land*
Edited and compiled by Nancy P. Pittman

Fighting Toxics: A Manual for Protecting Your Family, Community, and Workplace
By Gary Cohen and John O'Connor

Hazardous Waste from Small Quantity Generators
By Seymour I. Schwartz and Wendy B. Pratt

Holistic Resource Management Workbook
By Alan Savory

In Praise of Nature
Edited and with essays by Stephanie Mills

Overtapped Oasis: Reform or Revolution for Western Water
By Marc Reisner and Sarah Bates

Permaculture: A Practical Guide for a Sustainable Future
By Bill Mollison

The Poisoned Well: New Strategies for Groundwater Protection
Edited by Eric Jorgensen

Race to Save the Tropics: Ecology and Economics for a Sustainable Future
Edited by Robert Goodland

Recycling and Incineration: Evaluating the Choices
By Richard A. Denison and John Ruston

Reopening the Western Frontier
From *High Country News*

Resource Guide for Creating Successful Communities
By Michael A. Mantell, Stephen F. Harper, and Luther Propst

Rivers at Risk: The Concerned Citizen's Guide to Hydropower
By John D. Echeverria, Pope Barrow, and Richard Roos-Collins

Saving the Tropical Forests
By Judith Gradwohl and Russell Greenberg

Shading Our Cities: A Resource Guide for Urban and Community Forests
Edited by Gary Moll and Sara Ebenreck

Wetland Creation and Restoration: The Status of the Science
Edited by Mary E. Kentula and Jon A. Kusler

Wildlife and Habitats in Managed Landscapes
Edited by Jon E. Rodiek and Eric G. Bolen

Wildlife of the Florida Keys: A Natural History
By James D. Lazell, Jr.

For a complete catalog of Island Press publications, please write:
Island Press
Box 7
Covelo, CA 95428

or call: 1-800-828-1302